THE
ICARUS
PARADOX

NEW LESSONS IN THE DYNAMICS OF
CORPORATE SUCCESS, DECLINE, AND RENEWAL

THE
ICARUS
PARADOX

*How Exceptional Companies
Bring About
Their Own Downfall*

Danny Miller

HarperBusiness
A Division of HarperCollins*Publishers*

International Standard Book Number: 0-88730-453-2

Library of Congress Catalog Card Number: 90-5039

Printed in the United States of America

Designed by Joan Greenfield

Library of Congress Cataloging-in-Publication Data

Miller, Danny.
  The Icarus paradox : how exceptional companies bring about their
own downfall : new lessons in the dynamics of corporate success,
decline, and renewal / Danny Miller.
      p. cm.
  Includes bibliographical references (p.) and index.
  ISBN 0-88730-453-2
  1. Business failures—United States—Case studies. I. Title.
HD2785.M54 1990   90-5039
338.7′4′0973—dc20   CIP

90 91 92 93 CC/HC 9 8 7 6 5 4 3 2 1

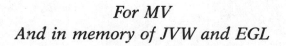

For MV
And in memory of JVW and EGL

CONTENTS

LIST OF TABLES AND FIGURES

Tables

Figures

================ ACKNOWLEDGMENTS ================

This book is the product of so many people. It is a pleasure to thank them heartily, and to absolve them forthwith of any inadequacies that remain here despite their best efforts.

I owe first of all a great debt to two past teachers, the late Henry Tutsch and the late Thomas Kubicek, both of whom believed in me when no one else did and helped a lost young man find his way so many years ago.

Much of this book was written while I was AGT Visiting Professor at the University of Alberta. Jean-Louis Malouin, my friend and the dean of the U of A's Faculty of Business, commented with much wisdom on each chapter. He also helped in the selection and classification of cases, and gave me encouragement and advice at the most critical junctures. Jean-Louis even sacrificed the occasional game of pool to boost my morale. His wife Heléne served up some wonderful meals during my stay in Edmonton, and gave me a sumptuous Christmas cake to take back to Montreal to keep me going during the final stretch of writing.

Lloyd Steier's sense of what this book was and should be about usually exceeded my own. I had to scurry for pen and pad every time we met to be sure not to lose too many of Lloyd's indispensable insights. I am so grateful to him for his advice and friendship—and for the writing equipment in his van.

Thanks also to the energetic, boisterous soccer-enthusiast-cum-department-chairman Royston Greenwood. Royston's incisive criticism penetrated to the heart of the inadequacies of my early drafts and guided my attempts to improve them. Readers owe him much. Also at the U of A, Bob Hinings, Mansour Javidan, and Joy Gilsdorf made excellent suggestions, and Dale Cunningham was marvelously prompt in gathering much of the case material for Chapter 8.

Jean-Marie Toulouse, Marcel Cote, and Taieb Hafsi at Montreal's Ecole des Hautes Etudes Commerciales have given me so much support for many years. Jean-Marie, and indeed HEC as an institution, came to my rescue in 1980, granting this non-teaching Anglophone the help he needed when it was available nowhere else. I am forever in their debt.

Though he never would have suspected it, Henry Mintzberg's example gave me the courage and inspiration to embark on this project. The "Berg" 's enthusiasm, encouragement, mentorship, and above all his friendship have meant so much to me through the years. Henry got me going in this racket, and "his monster" still hasn't quite forgiven him.

Peter Friesen's ideas and criticism have propped up my work now for over a decade. He has been my most cherished research collaborator, and if there is anyone who is more responsible for this work than the author, it is he.

Bill Starbuck is the man to whom this work owes its single greatest intellectual debt. Many of the central issues to emerge here are a product of Bill's seminal articles. Throughout, I tried to hold myself up to Bill's impossible standards of clarity, novelty, and precision; and when entangled in the pivotal Chapter 6, I kept asking, Hasn't Bill already said much of this far more articulately? Of course he has. I thank Bill for his gifts to the field and for his unfailing friendship.

I am also grateful to Joseph Lampel—friend, cycling partner, hosteler to the itinerant academic, and wonderful critic—whose genius at organization and nomenclature will no doubt help to sell this book. Joe's comments on the early drafts of the trajectory chapters forced me to shoot for a far tighter and more cohesive manuscript. Friends and doctoral students Jamal Shamsie and Anil Miglani also made extremely valuable comments, as did Camille Morin Tutsch, Ming-Jer Chen, and Jay Conger. Bob Payette was so very generous with his ideas and computer help. And I have benefited from my collaboration and many conversations with Manfred Kets de Vries.

Thanks, too, to my infinitely tolerant doctoral students at the University of Alberta for putting up with my obsession with the thesis of this book—even when it had nothing whatever to do with their class. And to the dauntingly competent librarian Jody Hebert at McGill, and my able secretaries Mary Di Stefano and Merle Lobo, who helped in countless ways.

My parents, and my friends Bob Feinstein, Allan and Bill Rodman,

Barbara Chazonoff, Chen Wei-Cheng, Saranya Khumjan, Wang Ping, R. Ambarish, Chris Gilmore, and Nancy Siew helped get me through some of the rough patches in the writing, and in everyday life.

Executive Editor Virginia A. Smith of HarperBusiness has been a godsend with her enthusiasm, insight, and hospitality; as has Publisher Mark Greenberg with his good advice and hours of discourse about Quine, Heidegger, Whitehead, Kant, Hume, Hegel, MacTaggart, and Marx, all of whom have also helped me, in a less conspicuous way. My diligent and creative copy editor, Ann Adelman, made my manuscript ever so much more readable, and for this I am indeed very grateful.

Now I hope you will forgive my cloying use of the royal "we" throughout the book. It is to keep reminding the reader of this large and talented team of supporters.

Danny Miller
MONTREAL, CANADA
MARCH 12, 1990

Introduction

THE STORY, UNFORTUNATELY, IS AN OLD ONE. AMERICA'S INTERNA-
tional competitiveness has been declining now for over two decades.
Rivals in Japan, Taiwan, Korea, and many European countries have
been putting our managers to shame. Too many once great American
firms have become complacent, careless, and out of touch. They pursue short-term, bottom-line targets and bury themselves in technical
or financial intricacies, while they neglect the substance—the products and the customers—of their business. They stop making the right
stuff for the right markets and pay the price: earnings plummet, stock
prices collapse, and managers are dismissed. But there is also much
broader social damage, seen in such factors as costly protective tariffs,
massive layoffs, stressful working environments, and shoddy or even
hazardous products and processes. When our corporate stars fall,
many of us are the victims.

The problem has been recognized by some best-selling authors. Bill
Ouchi and others have advocated that American managers learn from
their Japanese counterparts by becoming more sensitive to their markets, more consensual in their decision making, more oriented toward the long term. Tom Peters and Robert Waterman, in their classic
In Search of Excellence, have argued for organizational flexibility, for
sticking to the knitting, and for getting closer to the customer. These
authors have attracted a lot of attention with their useful suggestions.
But they have addressed the solution without really identifying the
source of the problem; and unless we know *why* so many outstanding
American firms have fallen into decline, it will be hard to come up
with suitable remedies. We stand in danger of trying to graft sensible
techniques onto rotten corporate infrastructures that simply cannot
support them.[1]

It seemed high time for some preliminary research into how the mighty have fallen—into the decline of once great enterprises. This book examines the all too common problem of our proudest, most accomplished companies losing their competitive edge and falling victim to wasting trajectories of deterioration. The companies in our study include such giants as GM, P&G, IBM, Polaroid, and Walt Disney. Although some of these firms were able to recover, their declines were serious and enduring.

We identified four distinct yet very common trajectories that converted strong companies into declining ones. The *focusing* trajectory turned Craftsmen into Tinkerers, the *venturing* trajectory transformed Builders into Imperialists, the *inventing* trajectory converted Pioneers into Escapists, and the *decoupling* trajectory turned Salesmen into Drifters. In every case, firms moved toward excesses and deficiencies that were very much related to their starting states. Although the four trajectories do not exhaust the many ways in which firms can decline, they appear to be very common and immensely seductive. Indeed, as we go to press, they are being played out anew by the likes of Donald Trump, Drexel Burnham Inc., and Campeau Corp.

The roots of decline are extremely complicated and insidious, and they run very deep into the fabric of outstanding organizations. Indeed, it is the central paradox of this book that success itself and the things that cause it seem very much to contribute to decline. In order for firms to remain competitive, they must learn to master these "perils of excellence."[2] Our primary tasks here are to help managers recognize these dangers and to suggest ways of combating them.

Chapter 1 introduces our conceptual framework. It provides an overview of the successful strategies and the trajectories of failure to which they are susceptible. Chapters 2 through 5 discuss in detail each of the four trajectories: the strategies, leadership styles, cultures, and structures of a healthy starting configuration, and the changes that occur as the trajectory winds its destructive course.[3] Chapter 6 summarizes our findings about the causes of decline. Chapter 7 then suggests ways of avoiding decline and undertaking turnarounds. It also provides a detailed *Self-Assessment Questionnaire* to help managers discover the trajectories that might be threatening their own organizations. Finally, Chapter 8 makes more specific recommendations for coping with each of the four trajectories.

CHAPTER 1

The Icarus Paradox

THE FABLED ICARUS OF GREEK MYTHOLOGY IS SAID TO HAVE FLOWN SO high, so close to the sun, that his artificial wax wings melted and he plunged to his death in the Aegean Sea. The power of Icarus' wings gave rise to the abandon that so doomed him. The paradox, of course, is that his greatest asset led to his demise. And that same paradox applies to many outstanding companies today: their victories and their strengths often seduce them into the excesses that cause their downfall. Success leads to specialization and exaggeration, to confidence and complacency, to dogma and ritual. This general tendency, its causes, and how to control it, are what this book is all about.

It is ironic that many of the most dramatically successful organizations are so prone to failure. The histories of outstanding companies demonstrate this time and time again. In fact, it appears that when taken to excess the very factors that drive success—focused tried-and-true strategies, confident leadership, galvanized corporate cultures, and especially the interplay among all these things—can also cause decline. Robust, superior organizations evolve into flawed purebreds; they move from rich character to exaggerated caricature as all subtlety, all nuance, is gradually lost. That, in a nutshell, is the book's thesis.

Many outstanding organizations have followed such paths of deadly momentum—time-bomb trajectories of attitudes, policies, and events that lead to falling sales, plummeting profits, even bankruptcy. These companies extend and amplify the strategies to which they credit their success. Productive attention to detail, for instance, turns into an obsession with minutia; rewarding innovation escalates into gratuitous invention; and measured growth becomes unbridled expansion. In contrast, activities that were merely deemphasized—that were not viewed as integral to the recipe for success—are virtually extinguished. Modest marketing deteriorates into lackluster promotion and inadequate distribution; tolerable engineering becomes shoddy design. The result: strategies become less balanced. They center more and more upon a single, core strength that is amplified unduly, while other aspects are forgotten almost entirely.

Such changes are not limited to strategy. The heroes who shaped the winning formula of a company gain adulation and absolute authority, while others drop to third-class citizenship. An increasingly monolithic culture impels firms to focus on an ever smaller set of considerations and to rally around a narrowing path to victory. Roles, programs, decision-making processes—even target markets—come to reflect the central strategy and nothing else. And avidly embraced ideologies convert company policies into rigid laws and rituals. By then, organizational learning has ceased, tunnel vision rules, and flexibility is lost.

This riches-to-rags scenario seduces some of our most acclaimed corporations: our research on over one hundred such outstanding companies has turned up four variations on the theme, four very common "trajectories" of decline (see Table 1).[1]

- The *focusing* trajectory takes punctilious, quality-driven *Craftsmen*, organizations with masterful engineers and airtight operations, and turns them into rigidly controlled, detail-obsessed *Tinkerers*, firms whose insular, technocratic cultures alienate customers with perfect but irrelevant offerings.
- The *venturing* trajectory converts growth-driven, entrepreneurial *Builders*, companies managed by imaginative leaders and creative planning and financial staffs, into impulsive, greedy *Imperialists*, who severely overtax their resources by expanding helter-skelter into businesses they know nothing about.
- The *inventing* trajectory takes *Pioneers* with unexcelled R&D departments, flexible think-tank operations, and state-of-the-art products, and transforms them into utopian *Escapists*, run by cults of chaos-loving scientists who squander resources in the pursuit of hopelessly grandiose and futuristic inventions.
- Finally, the *decoupling* trajectory transforms *Salesmen*, organizations with unparalleled marketing skills, prominent brand names, and broad markets, into aimless, bureaucratic *Drifters*, whose sales

TABLE 1. The Four Trajectories

FOCUSING

	Craftsman ⟶	*Tinkerer*
Strategy	Quality leadership	Technical tinkering
Goals	Quality	Perfection
Culture	Engineering	Technocratic
Structure	Orderly	Rigid

VENTURING

	Builder ⟶	*Imperialist*
Strategy	Building	Overexpansion
Goals	Growth	Grandeur
Culture	Entrepreneurial	Gamesman
Structure	Divisionalized	Fractured

INVENTING

	Pioneer ⟶	*Escapist*
Strategy	Innovation	High-tech escapism
Goals	Science-for-society	Technical utopia
Culture	R&D	Think-tank
Structure	Organic	Chaotic

DECOUPLING

	Salesman ⟶	*Drifter*
Strategy	Brilliant marketing	Bland proliferation
Goals	Market share	Quarterly numbers
Culture	Organization man	Insipid and political
Structure	Decentralized-bureaucratic	Oppressively bureaucratic

fetish obscures design issues, and who produce a stale and disjointed line of "me-too" offerings.

These four trajectories have trapped many firms. The names include IBM, Polaroid, Procter & Gamble, Texas Instruments, ITT, Chrysler, Dome Petroleum, Apple Computer, A&P, General Motors, Sears, Digital Equipment, Caterpillar Tractor, Montgomery Ward, Eastern Air Lines, Litton Industries, and Walt Disney Productions.

A Case History

The glorious and ultimately tragic history of ITT well demonstrates the course of the second, so-called venturing trajectory.

Harold S. Geneen was a manager's manager, a universally acclaimed financial wizard of unsurpassed energy, and the CEO and grand inquisitor of the diversified megaconglomerate ITT. It was Geneen, the entrepreneurial accountant, who took a ragtag set of stale, mostly European telecommunications operations and forged them into a cohesive corporate entity. With his accountant's scalpel, he cut out weak operations, and with his entrepreneur's wand, he revived the most promising ones. He installed state-of-the-art management information systems to monitor the burgeoning businesses. And he built a head-office corps of young turks to help him control his growing empire and identify opportunities for creative diversification.[2]

At first, this diversification paid off handsomely, as it so aptly exploited the financial, organizational, and turnaround talents of Geneen and his crack staff. Many acquisitions were purchased at bargain prices and most beautifully complemented ITT's existing operations. Also, a divisional structure in which managers were responsible for their units' profits provided a good deal of incentive for local initiative. And Geneen's legendary control and information systems—with frequent appraisal meetings and divisional accountants reporting directly to the head office—ensured that most problems could be detected early and corrected.

Unfortunately, ITT's success at diversification and controlled decentralization led to too much more of the same. Their skills at acquisition and control made Geneen and his staff ever more confident that they could master complexity. So, diversification went from a selective tactic to an engrained strategy to a fanatical religion; decentralization and head-office control were transformed from managerial tools into an all-consuming, lockstep way of life. The corporate culture worshipped growth, and it celebrated, lavishly paid, and quickly promoted only those who could attain it. The venturing trajectory had gotten under way, and the momentum behind it was awesome.

In order to achieve rapid growth, Geneen went after ever more ambitious acquisitions that were further afield from his existing operations. From 1967 to 1970, just six of ITT's larger acquisitions—Sheraton, Levitt, Rayonier, Continental Baking, Grinnell, and Canteen—brought in combined sales of $1.8 billion; and a seventh, Hartford Fire, one of the largest property and casualty insurers in the United States, was about to be added. Loads of debt had to be issued to fund these acquisitions. In less than ten years Geneen the imperialist bought a staggering one hundred companies, a proliferation so vast that it exceeded the complexity of many nation-states; 250 profit centers in all were set up. Geneen, quite simply, had created the biggest conglomerate on earth, encompassing, by 1977, 375,000 employees in eighty countries.

Even Geneen and his sophisticated staff troops, for all their mastery of detail and their status as information-system gurus, could not manage, control, or even understand so vast an empire. But they tried, meddling in the details of their divisions, and pressing home the need to meet abstract, often irrelevant, financial standards. Political games took place in which head-office controllers would try to impress Geneen by making the divisions look bad; and divisional executives would, in turn, try to fool the controllers.

This obsession with acquisitions and financial control detracted from the substance of divisional strategy. The product lines of many units were neglected and became outmoded. Return on capital fell, and by the late 1970s many of the divisions were experiencing major operating problems. A subsequent CEO, Rand Araskog, had to sell off over a hundred units in an attempt to revive the company, in the process shrinking the workforce by over 60 percent. The great ITT had become a flabby agglomeration of gangrenous parts.

The general pattern is clear. Over time, ITT's success—or, more specifically, its managers' reactions to that success—caused it to amplify its winning strategy, and to forget about everything else. It moved from sensible, measured expansion to prolific, groundless diversification; from sound accounting and financial control to oppressive dominance by head-office hit men; and from an invigorating use of divisionalization to a destructive factionalism. The substance of basic businesses—their product lines and markets—was lost in a welter of financial abstractions. By concentrating exclusively upon what it did best, ITT pushed its strategies, cultures, and structures to dangerous extremes, while failing to develop in other areas. Greatness had paved the way for excess and decline as ITT the Builder became ITT the Imperialist.

Configuration and Momentum

The example of ITT reveals two notions that surfaced again and again when we looked at outstanding companies: we call these configuration and momentum.

Outstanding organizations are a little like beautiful poems or sonatas—their parts or elements fit together harmoniously to express a theme. They are perhaps even more akin to living systems whose organs are intimately linked and tightly coordinated. Although organizations are less unified than organisms, they too constitute *configurations*: complex, evolving systems of mutually supportive elements organized around stable central themes. We found that once a theme emerges—a core mission or a central strategy, for example—a whole slew of routines, policies, tasks, and structures develops to implement and reinforce it. It is like seeding a crystal in a supersaturated solution—once a thematic particle is dropped into solution, the crystal begins to form naturally around it. Themes may derive from leaders' visions, the values and concerns of powerful departments, even from common industry practices.

ITT's configuration, like all others, had a central theme and a "cast of players" (human, ideological, strategic, and structural) that completed the scenario. The theme was "rapid growth through expansion"; the cast included an entrepreneurial, ambitious CEO with his strategy of diversification and acquisition, a powerful financial staff who dominated because they could best implement this strategy, elaborate information systems and sophisticated controls, even decentralized profit centers that infused expertise into the far-flung divisions amassed by diversification. All these "players" complemented one another and were essential to the enactment of the play. And as with every configuration, the parts only make sense with reference to the entire constellation.[3]

Our research uncovered four exceptionally common but quite different configurations associated with stellar performance. We termed these Builders, Craftsmen, Pioneers, and Salesmen, and found that each was subject to its own evolutionary trajectory.

Our second finding was that organizations keep extending their themes and configurations until something earthshaking stops them, a process we call *momentum.* Firms perpetuate and amplify one particular motif above all others as they suppress its variants. They choose one set of goals, values, and champions, and focus on these more and more tightly. The powerful get more powerful; others become disenfranchised as firms move first toward consistency, then toward obsession and excess. Organizations turn into their "evil twins"—extreme versions or caricatures of their former selves.

Once ITT began to diversify, for example, it accelerated this policy because it seemed successful, because it was very much in line with the visions of what leaders and their powerful financial staffs wanted, and because it was undergirded by a vast set of policies and programs. Similarly, having implemented its financial control systems, ITT continued to hone and develop them. After all, these systems were demanded by the expanding scope of the firm; they were favored by the growing staff of accountants; and they were the only way top managers could exert control over existing operations and still have time to scout out new acquisitions.

But momentum itself is contagious and leads to a vicious cycle of escalation. At ITT, as diversification increased, so, in order to cope, did the size of the head-office staff and the time spent on divisional meetings. The staff's role was to generate still more attractive candidates for diversification, and that's what they did. Diversification increased still further, requiring even larger legions of accountants and financial staff. And so the spiral continued. In short, momentum, by extending the Builder configuration, led to the dangerous excesses of imperialism.

Such findings led us to expect that *outstanding firms will extend their orientations until they reach dangerous extremes; their momentum will result in common trajectories of decline.* And since successful types differ so much from one another, so will their trajectories.

THE TRAJECTORIES

The four trajectories emerged in a study we conducted of outstanding companies. Our earlier research suggested four very common, wonderfully coherent configurations, with powerful strategic advantages. To study the long-term evolution of these types for this project, we searched for successful companies that conformed to each type and had enough written about them to be analyzed in detail. We then tracked the companies for many years to discover what in fact happened to them. (Our research method and how we arrived at our types is summarized in the Appendix; the types themselves are described and compared in Tables 1 and 2.)

Many of the organizations will be well known to the reader. This was inevitable since we studied legendary performers that had been the subject of numerous articles and books. Also, many of our examples go back some years as we had to observe some rather protracted declines and revivals. Despite the familiarity of some of their subjects,

TABLE 2. The Configurations Compared

	CRAFTSMAN	BUILDER	PIONEER	SALESMAN
Strategies:	Quality Leadership	Expansion Diversification Acquisition	Differentiation via Innovation	Marketing Differentiation
Product-market scope:	Focused	Broad	Focused	Broad
Strategic change:	Stable	Dynamic	Dynamic	Stable
Key Goals:	Quality	Growth	Technical Progress	Market Share
Dominant Depts.:	Operations, Production, & Engineering	Planning & Control; Finance	R&D	Marketing
Structure:	Bureaucracy Many Controls	Divisional Profit Centers	Organic Flexible	Divisional Bureaucracy
Trajectory:	*FOCUSING*	*VENTURING*	*INVENTING*	*DECOUPLING*
Destination:	TINKERER	IMPERIALIST	ESCAPIST	DRIFTER

however, our narratives have a rather unusual twist. Instead of looking at how marvelous the good performers were, we will persistently be eliciting the seeds of decline from the flowers—and the fruits—of greatness.

Craftsmen, Builders, Pioneers, and Salesmen were each susceptible to their own unique trajectories. And firms of a given type followed remarkably parallel paths, albeit at differing speeds. For purposes of simple comparison, the four strategies are classified, in Figure 1, along two dimensions: *scope* refers to the range of products and target markets; *change* to the variability of methods and offerings. Excellent businesses are driven toward extremes along both of these dimensions (among others). Take scope. Firms that excel by focusing on one product or on a precisely targeted market come ultimately to rely on too narrow a set of customers, products, and issues. Conversely, firms that thrive by aggressively diversifying often become too complex, fragmented, and thinly spread to be effective. The same tendencies apply to strategic change as dynamic firms become hyperactive while conservative ones inch toward stagnation.

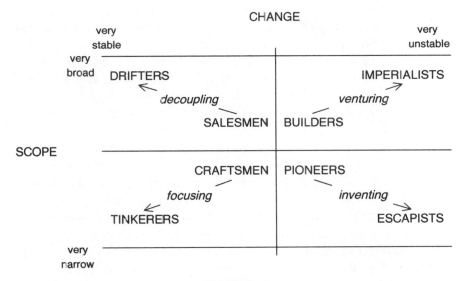

FIGURE 1
The Configurations and Trajectories Arrayed

The characteristics of each of our four trajectories are summarized below.

From Craftsmen to Tinkerers: The Focusing Trajectory

Digital Equipment Corporation made the highest quality computers in the world. Founder Ken Olsen and his brilliant team of design engineers invented the minicomputer, a cheaper, more flexible alternative to its mainframe cousins. Olsen and his staff honed their minis until they absolutely could not be beat for quality and durability. Their VAX series gave birth to an industry legend in reliability, and the profits poured in.

But Digital turned into an engineering monoculture. Its engineers became idols; its marketers and accountants were barely tolerated. Component specs and design standards were all that managers understood. In fact, technological fine-tuning became such an all-consuming obsession that customers' needs for smaller machines, more economical products, and more user-friendly systems were ignored. The Digital personal computer, for example, bombed because it was so out of sync with the budgets, preferences, and shopping habits of potential users. Performance began to slip.

Craftsmen are passionate about doing one thing incredibly well. Their leaders insist on producing the best products on the market, their engineers lose sleep over micrometers, and their quality-control staff rule with an iron, unforgiving hand. Details count. And quality is the primary source of corporate pride; it gets rewarded, and is the paramount competitive advantage. Indeed, it is what the whole corporate culture is about. Shoddiness is a capital offense. (There is also a cost-leader variant of the Craftsman that we will be discussing in Chapter 2.)

But in becoming Tinkerers, many Craftsmen become parodies of themselves. They get so wrapped up in tiny technical details that they forget that the purpose of quality is to attract and satisfy buyers. Products become overengineered but also overpriced; durable but stale. Yesterday's excellent designs turn into today's sacrosanct anachronisms. And an ascendant engineering culture so engrosses itself in the minutia of design and manufacture that it loses sight of the customer. Before long, marketing and R&D become the dull stepchildren, departments to be seen but not heard. And unfortunately, the bureaucratic strictures that grew up to enforce quality end up suppressing initiative and perpetuating the past.

From Builders to Imperialists: The Venturing Trajectory

Charles "Tex" Thornton was a young Texas entrepreneur when he expanded a tiny microwave company into Litton Industries, one of the most successful high-technology conglomerates of the 1960s. By making selective, related acquisitions, Litton achieved an explosive rate of growth. And its excellent track record helped the company to amass the resources needed to accelerate expansion still further. Sales mushroomed from $3 million to $1.8 billion in just twelve years.

But Litton began to stray too far from familiar areas, buying larger and more troubled firms in industries that it barely understood. Control systems were overtaxed, the burden of debt became unwieldy, and a wide range of problems sprang up in the proliferating divisions. The downward spiral at Litton was no less dramatic than its ascent.

Builders are growth-driven entrepreneurial companies, with a zeal for expansion, merger, and acquisition. They are dominated by aggressive managers with ambitious goals, immense energy, and an uncanny knack for spotting lucrative niches of the market. These leaders have the promotional skills to raise capital, the imagination and initiative to exploit magnificent growth opportunities, and the courage to take substantial risks. They are also master controllers who craft acute, sensitive information and incentive systems to rein in their burgeoning operations.

But many Builders develop into Imperialists, addicted to careless expansion and greedy acquisition. In the headlong rush for growth, they assume hair-raising risks, decimate their resources, and incur scads of debt. They bite off more than they can swallow, acquiring sick companies in businesses they don't understand. Structures and control systems become hopelessly overburdened. And a dominant culture of financial, legal, and accounting specialists further rivets managerial attention on expansion and diversification, while stealing time away from the production, marketing, and R&D matters that so desperately need to be addressed.

From Pioneers to Escapists: The Inventing Trajectory

By the mid-1960s, Control Data Corporation of Minneapolis had become the paramount designer of supercomputers. Chief engineer Seymour Cray, the preeminent genius in a field of masters, had several times fulfilled his ambition to build the world's most powerful computer. He secluded himself in his lab in Chippewa Falls, working closely with a small and trusted band of brilliant designers. Cray's state-of-the-art 6600 supercomputer was so advanced that it caused wholesale firing at IBM, whose engineers had been caught completely off guard by their diminutive competitor.

CDC's early successes emboldened it to undertake new computer development projects that were increasingly futuristic, complex, and expensive. These entailed substantial lead times, major investments, and high risks. Indeed, many bugs had to be purged from the systems, long delays in delivery occurred, and costs mushroomed. Science and invention had triumphed over a proper understanding of the competition, the customers, and production and capital requirements.

Pioneers are R&D stars. Their chief goal is to be the first out with new products and new technology. Consistently at the vanguard of their industry, Pioneers are, above all, inventors. Their major strengths lie in the scientific and technological capacities of their brilliant R&D departments. Typically, Pioneers are run by missionary leaders-in-lab-coats; PhDs with a desire to change the world. These executives assemble and empower superb research and design teams, and create for them a fertile, flexible structure that promotes intensive collaboration and the free play of ideas.

Unfortunately, many Pioneers get carried away by their coups of invention and turn into Escapists—firms in hot pursuit of a technological nirvana. They introduce impractical, futuristic products that are too far ahead of their time, too expensive to develop, and too costly to buy. They also become their own toughest competitors, antiquating prematurely many of their offerings. What is worse, marketing and production come to be viewed as necessary evils; clients as unsophisticated nuisances. Escapists, it seems, become the victims of a utopian culture forged by their domineering R&D wunderkinder. Their goals, which soar to hopelessly lofty heights, are expressed in technological rather than in market or economic terms. And their loose, "organic" structures might suffice to organize a few engineers working in a basement, but make for chaos in complex organizations.

From Salesmen to Drifters: The Decoupling Trajectory

Lynn Townsend ascended to the presidency of Chrysler at the youthful age of forty-two. He was known to be a financial wizard and a master

14

marketer. "Sales just aren't made; sales are pushed," Townsend would say. In his first five years as president, he doubled Chrysler's U.S. market share and tripled its international one. He also conceived the five-year, 50,000-mile warranty. But Townsend made very few radical changes in Chrysler's products. Mostly he just marketed aggressively with forceful selling and promotion, and sporty styling.

Chrysler's success with its image-over-substance strategy resulted in an increasing neglect of engineering and production. Also it prompted a proliferation of new models that could capitalize on the marketing program. But this made operations very complex and uneconomical. It also contributed to remote management-by-numbers, bureaucracy, and turf battles. Soon Chrysler's strategies lost focus and direction and its profits began to plummet.

Salesmen are marketers par excellence. That is their core strength. Using intensive advertising, attractive styling and packaging, and penetrating distribution channels, they create and nurture high-profile brand names that make them major players in their industries. And to place managers in especially close contact with their broad markets, Salesmen often are partitioned into manageable profit centers, each responsible for a major product line.

Unfortunately, Salesmen too are subject to a dangerous momentum that can transform them into unresponsive Drifters. They begin to substitute packaging, advertising, and aggressive distribution for good design and competent manufacture. Managers come to believe that they can sell anything as they concoct a mushrooming proliferation of bland, "me-too" offerings. This growing diversity of product lines and divisions makes it tough for top managers to master the substance of all their businesses. So they rely increasingly on abstract financial controls and an elaborate bureaucracy to replace the hands-on management of products and manufacturing. Gradually Drifters become unwieldy, sluggish behemoths whose turf battles and factionalism impede adaptation. In scenarios that come straight from Kafka, the simplest problems take months, even years to address. Ultimately, the leader is decoupled from his company, the company from its markets, and the product lines and divisions from each other.

These four trajectories show how outstanding companies—firms with character and a terrific strategic edge—can become specialized and even monomaniacal. Strengths are amplified to the point where one goal, one strategic vision, one department, and one skill overwhelms all others. All subtlety is lost. Design-whiz Craftsmen become hyper-focused Tinkerers, entrepreneurial Builders turn into impulsive Imperialists, inventive Pioneers become utopian Escapists, and responsive Salesmen become fragmented Drifters. Nuances vanish; only the bold, exaggerated features, the core obsessions, remain.

FORCES TO WATCH FOR

In reading about these four trajectories, you might want to keep in mind some of the "subtexts"—the hidden causes at work behind the scenes that drive every one of them. (These will be dealt with at length in Chapter 6.)

Sources of Momentum

LEADERSHIP TRAPS Failure teaches leaders valuable lessons, but good results only reinforce their preconceptions and tether them more firmly to their "tried-and-true" recipes. Success also makes managers overconfident, more prone to excess and neglect, and more given to shaping strategies to reflect their own preferences rather than those of their customers. Some leaders may even be spoiled by success—taking too much to heart their litany of conquests and the praise of their idolizing subordinates. They become conceited and obstinate, resenting challenges and, ultimately, isolating themselves from reality.

MONOLITHIC CULTURES AND SKILLS The culture of the exceptional organization often becomes dominated by a few star departments and their ideologies. For example, because Craftsmen see quality as the source of success, the engineering departments that create it and are its guarantors acquire ever more influence—as do their goals and values. This erodes the status of other departments and concerns, rendering the corporate culture more monolithic, more intolerant, and more avid in its pursuit of a single goal.

To make matters worse, attractive rewards pull talented managers toward rich, dominant departments, and bleed them away from less august units. The organization's skill set soon becomes more spotty and unbalanced, compromising versatility and the capacity for reorientation.

POWER AND POLITICS Dominant managers and departments resist redirecting the strategies and policies that have given them so much power. Change, they reason, would erode their status, their resources, and their influence over rival executives and departments. The powerful, then, are more likely to reinforce and amplify prevailing strategies than to change them.

STRUCTURAL MEMORIES Organizations, like people, have memories—they implement successful strategies by using systems, routines, and programs. The more established and successful the strategy, the more deeply embedded it will be in such programs, and the more it will be implemented routinely, automatically, and unquestioningly. Managers will rely on ingrained habits and reflex actions rather than deliberating and reflecting on new problems. Indeed, even the premises for decision making—the cues that elicit attention and the standards used to evaluate events and actions—will be controlled by routines. Yesterday's programs will shape today's perceptions and give rise to tomorrow's actions. Again, continuity triumphs.

Configuration and Momentum

The elements of leadership, culture, power, and structural memory are by no means independent. Indeed, they interact and configure to play out a central theme. Over time, organizations become more and more consistent with that theme. So much so that an adaptable, intelligent company can turn into a specialized, monolithic machine.

Take the Pioneer. Successful innovations reward and empower their creators, who will tend to recruit and promote in their own image. The resulting horde of "R&D types" then set up the flexible structures and design projects they find so invigorating. This further encourages innovation and the search for clients who value it. Meanwhile, other departments begin to lose influence and resources, and their skills diminish. So, cultures become monolithic, strategies more narrowly focused, skills more uneven and specialized, and blind spots more common. The firm has embarked on the inventing trajectory.

"Chain reactions" such as this make an organization more focused and cohesive. At first, the firm benefits greatly. But ultimately, concentration turns into obsession. All the prominent features become exaggerated, while everything else—auxiliary skills, supplementary values, essential substrategies, and constructive debate—vanishes.

The Paradox of Icarus

And this brings us to the Icarus paradox that traps so many outstanding firms: overconfident, complacent executives extend the very factors that contributed to success to the point where they cause decline. There are really two aspects to the paradox. The first is that *success can lead to failure.* By engendering overconfidence, carelessness, and other bad habits, success can produce excesses in strategies, leadership, culture, and structures. Icarus flew so well that he got cocky and overambitious.

The second aspect of the paradox is that many of the preceding causes of decline—galvanized cultures, efficient routines and programs, and orchestrated configurations—were initially the causes of success. Or, conversely, that *the very causes of success, when extended, may become the causes of failure.* It is simply a case of "too much of a good thing." For example, a focused strategy can produce wonderful competitive advantages as it mobilizes resources so efficiently; but when taken too far it becomes narrow obsession. Favoring certain departments and skills creates distinctive competences and galvanizes effort; but it can also produce intolerant corporate cultures. Similarly, routines promote efficiency and simplify coordination, but they can blind managers and mire the organization in its past. And, above all, cohesive, orchestrated configurations are indispensable for companies to operate effectively, but they can also create myopia. Icarus' wings and his courage were strengths; but when pushed to the limit, they became deadly.

Unfortunately, it is very hard sometimes to distinguish between the focus, harmony, and passionate dedication so necessary for outstanding performance, and the excesses and extremes that lead to decline.

CHAPTER 2

From Craftsmen to Tinkerers:
The Focusing Trajectory

No ONE COULD RACE DOWN THE COST CURVE FASTER THAN TEXAS Instruments. The Dallas-based semiconductor maker had an abiding ability to manufacture its chips at the lowest possible cost and to grab the largest chunk of the market. TI set the industry standard for 8K RAM chips and introduced a constant flow of popular, ever cheaper calculators for its consumer business. Its small market-based teams helped it stay close to customers and kept bureaucracy at bay. And its crack staff of production engineers achieved magnificent cost reductions that for many years allowed TI to dominate a major segment of the industrial microchips market.

Unfortunately, TI's attention to cost became a fetish. Eventually, nothing else mattered. Its "chip mentality" induced the company to chase suicidal economies by offering consumers a motley array of outdated, shoddy products—the $9.95 digital watches, for example, that had ugly plastic bands and outmoded LED displays. TI was also slow to move into the sophisticated CMOS microchips that were proving such a bonanza for its rivals, in large part because its tightfisted production engineers worried about the prospect of lower production yields. The firm had begun to sell on the basis of price alone, ignoring the need to update its products, to service its customers, and to customize its offerings for larger industrial clients.

Many of these problems were attributable to the "engineering" culture that had taken over. Two autocratic leaders, President J. Fred Bucy and CEO Mark Shepherd, Jr., turned TI's low-cost policy into a fanatical religion. They developed a notorious obsession with budgetary controls and created a massive bureaucracy to institutionalize their fixation on costs. Also, too few smart initiatives ever got past the scrimping, all-powerful manufacturing departments. TI was transformed into one of the most insular Tinkerers in the business.[1]

We found two common types of Craftsmen. *Quality leaders* perfect their products in quest of the ultimate in durability, reliability, and performance, devising superb, long-lived designs that require only occasional fine-tuning. *Cost leaders,* like TI, on the other hand, strive to make their no-frills products ever more efficiently, so that they are able to earn handsome profits at prices the competition would find intolerable. They rely on standardized, superefficient operations that prohibit many design changes. Craftsmen endlessly scrutinize their designs, pore over processes to save fractions of a penny per unit, and refuse to release a product until it has passed the toughest hurdles. Perfection is a way of life; and managers not patient enough to put up with the resulting delays had better leave. As one CEO told me: "We want it good, not Tuesday; in fact, we don't want it good, we want it perfect; and we're willing to wait until we get it exactly right."

Strong leaders run Craftsmen—leaders who inject their values and engineering philosophies deep into the fabric of their firms. They do this by their own frequent pronouncements and examples, and perhaps more important, through the enthusiastic engineering cultures that they create to enforce rigorous design and manufacturing standards. Such standards are institutionalized by acute quality and cost controls, and by small project teams that avidly pursue design improvements. Indeed, the Craftsman, like all of our types, is a cohesive configuration whose strategic, leadership, cultural, and structural aspects are complementary and mutually supportive.

Unfortunately, these detail-loving Craftsmen harbor the seeds of their own demise. Their excessive focusing can turn them into Tinkerers. Success creates a momentum that converts relevant, stable strategies into narrow, stagnant ones. A concerned parsimony, for example, develops into the miserliness that erodes quality and stifles innovation. An informed concern with quality turns into an obsession with technical standards irrelevant to most clients. And what had been understated, selective marketing and modest innovation now disappear almost entirely. Firms turn inward, away from their customers, as they fixate upon the few tactics credited with past success.

These strategic developments are very much undergirded by changes in leadership style and corporate culture. Success tends to make managers arrogant and overconfident. So, leaders freeze things by invoking doctrinaire cultures, by hoarding power, and by imposing bureaucratic strictures. Soon, cumbersome protocols come to damp out any fresh points of view, and prevailing obsessions are permanently etched in Kafkaesque rules and lockstep programs.

THE CRAFTSMAN*

CRAFTSMAN STRATEGIES

Quality Leadership

Quality leadership is achieved when one's products or services are clearly superior to the offerings of rivals, so superior that they are perceived as unique by customers and as very tough to imitate by competitors. There are, of course, different types of quality that Craftsmen pursue in manufacturing, including durability, reliability, and capacity. Craftsmen rendering services, on the other hand, strive for professionalism, friendliness, custom-tailoring, and diligence. Our quality leaders include Digital Equipment Corporation, Caterpillar Tractor, and Walt Disney Productions, all, ironically, lauded in 1982 by Tom Peters and Robert Waterman for their excellence.

Digital Equipment Corp. (DEC) was started by Ken Olsen in 1957 with $70,000 in seed money. He and a team of MIT-trained engineers developed the minicomputer, a refrigerator-sized alternative to the much larger and more costly mainframes. DEC's machines were so brilliantly engineered, and so eminently suited to their prospective industrial users, that they were in tremendous demand. These beautifully designed, supremely high-quality products ultimately made DEC the second largest computer company in the world, after "Big Blue" IBM.[2]

Indeed, DEC-made minicomputers were legendary for their quality and the loyalty they inspired in the experts who bought them. DEC thrived by selling minis to a highly select group of engineers, scientists, and companies that buy computers in large quantities and modify them for resale. "DEC has many loyal customers—so loyal," said one analyst, "that most would rather drop dead than switch from DEC."[3]

DEC's corporate philosophy affirmed that "growth is not our princi-

*In the narratives that follow, some phrases and passages appear in quotation marks. Even though authorship is not always divulged in the text, the sources for all such quotations are given in the Notes.

pal goal. Our goal is to be a quality organization and do a quality job, which means that we will be proud of our work and our products for years to come. As we achieve quality, growth comes as a result."[4] And excellent service accompanied DEC's reliable products. According to its annual report, "Digital believes that the highest degree of interaction in any of its activities needs to be in the area of company service and support."[5] The firm tried to stay close to its customers to promote trouble-free operation of their equipment. Perhaps even more important, DEC salesmen were seen as problem solvers. They avoided purchasing agents and worked directly with customers' engineers and operators. This allowed them to discover the most suitable products for their clients, and it helped customers learn more about their equipment. Better still, intense discussion between knowledgeable users and informed salesmen—"warm-armpit marketing," as it is known in the business—generated precious ideas for product-line improvements.[6]

DEC has traditionally allowed its customers to pull it into new product areas. The needs of its clients, discerned and conveyed by alert salesmen, induced the firm to come up with a host of overlapping products. In fact, DEC's intense awareness of customers motivated it to tailor new products to their needs very precisely, without much concern for the discreteness of the products themselves. As a result, many of the ten thousand items on its product list overlapped. And although this increased costs, it did enable DEC to create fierce buyer loyalty.[7]

Caterpillar Tractor, the heavy earth-moving equipment manufacturer based in Peoria, Illinois, was equally obsessed with the caliber of its products. Its main objectives were excellent quality, reliable performance, and loyalty in dealer relationships. Caterpillar had devoted itself long and single-mindedly to building a better, more efficient crawler tractor than anybody else in the world.[8] It was known for its superior materials, exacting tolerances, and crack machinists. According to *Business Week*, "Product quality is something Cat people hold as close as a catechism." The firm was rewarded with price-earnings multiples that far exceeded those of its competitors, and a forty-eight-year profit streak that ended only in 1982.[9]

Peters and Waterman write of their experiences in ordering equipment for the Navy: "We would go to almost any ends, stretching the procurement regulations to the limit, to specify the always more expensive Cat equipment. We had to, for we knew our field commanders would string us up if we didn't find a way to get them Cat."[10] Even back in 1938, Cat got the cream of the richest and most lucrative domestic business for heavy industrial tractors. It had a highly developed, broadly extensive distribution system, and its dealers made enormous margins. Cat soon became the number-one merchandiser of diesel power in the United States. Its high quality allowed it to maintain steady prices in time of recession. And, very typically, it met the depression of the 1930s with quality improvements rather than price reductions. President B. C. Heacock was famous for "publishing my prices, and letting competitors do what they want about it."[11]

Caterpillar offered its customers forty-eight-hour guaranteed parts-delivery service anywhere in the world, from a construction site in Nebraska to a village in Zaire. If it couldn't fulfill that promise, the customer got the part free. That is how confident Cat was. According to Peters and Waterman, "Once again, we are looking at a degree of overachievement that in narrow economic terms would be viewed as a mild form of lunacy; lunacy, that is, until you look at Caterpillar's financial results."[12]

Of course, quality leadership is not the exclusive province of manufacturers. It is also a favored strategy of some service firms. Walt Disney Productions, for example, was fanatic in its service obsession. Many observers rated Disney as one of the two best mass-service providers in America (after McDonald's). According to long-time Disney observer Red Pope: "I have come to observe closely and with reverence the theory and practice of selling satisfaction and serving millions of people on a daily basis successfully. It is what [Disneyland] does best. . . ."[13] Pope lauded the impeccably trained, infallibly polite, and enthusiastically helpful Disney staff. He talked of the hundreds of telephones scattered throughout the park to connect visitors to an almost omniscient question-answering service. Even the daily clean-up, he claimed, was carried out with exhausting dedication. In these and many other ways, overkill was said to mark every facet of Disney's operations, as it served its customers with consistent distinction and quality. Disney also produced some of the most wonderful cartoons and family films ever. Indeed, most of us grew up with *Bambi, Snow White,* and Mickey Mouse cartoons, and remember them as an integral part of our childhood.

Cost Leadership

The alternative major strategy found in Craftsmen is that of cost leadership. Cost leaders produce goods or render services at costs below the competition. This allows them to earn handsome returns at prices that would severely tax their rivals. But cost leadership is a process, not a state. It is not simply a matter of keeping costs down for one period. Rather, it involves staying ahead of the competition by devising ever more economical means of service or manufacture—continuing to lead the race down the cost curve by constantly learning cheaper ways of doing things. According to Harvard strategy professor Michael E. Porter, this continual learning and adjusting is the only way to obtain an *enduring* competitive advantage.[14] Our cost leaders include Eastern Air Lines, Montgomery Ward, and Texas Instruments. Typically, cost considerations prevent cost leaders from being quality leaders, or vice versa.

Although cost leaders use a very different strategy from quality leaders, they are every bit as zealous in pursuing their objectives. Texas Instruments, the diversified producer of electronic equipment, was a paragon of cost leadership in several of its divisions. TI rode the production learning curve in order to pare costs to the bone. It endured slim profit margins to achieve fat market shares, pricing very close to initial cost so as to generate volume and build up experience. This ultimately allowed TI to drive costs well below prices—prices that competitors found tough to match.[15]

Cost leadership enabled TI to set industry standards in 8K RAM computer memory chips. Also, the price for its highly popular SR-51 calculator plummeted from $225 in 1975 to $40 in 1979. In accomplishing this, TI reduced the number of its electronic components from 128 to 12.[16]

Eventually, TI became the lowest cost producer in the business. A relentless pursuit of efficient technology coupled with brute manufacturing power had assured it handsome market shares and enviable profit margins. In fact, for the twenty years ending in 1982, TI enjoyed a brilliant financial record, with sales quadrupling between 1977 and 1981 alone.

Cost leadership can be as relevant to service firms as to manufacturers. The success of Eastern Air Lines from the mid-1930s until the late 1950s was also due in large part to the parsimony of its domineering chief executive, Captain Eddie Rickenbacker. Despite his "dashing war record and flamboyant exterior," he had "the cautious soul of a greengrocer" when it came to spending money. Rickenbacker's frugality became an industry legend. A *Fortune* reporter heard him lecturing to his underlings, back in 1948: "I'm not talking about pennies, damn it, I want you to watch the mills." Rickenbacker succeeded in reducing per-mile maintenance costs by very tight scheduling, getting the most out of his aircraft. While it had a monopoly on many of its routes, this frugality made Eastern extremely profitable. From 1949 to 1960, it was the most consistent moneymaker in the highly volatile airline industry. In fact, during the early postwar years, while the industry was going through a drastic deficit-ridden shakeout, Eastern continued to pile up earnings. In 1959, it boasted twenty-five uninterrupted years of profits.[17]

One of the most useful occasions for cost leadership is during a turnaround. This was certainly true of the venerable Montgomery Ward under Sewell Lee Avery in the early thirties. Avery was still young when he took control of the faltering giant. Wards, at the time, had a large mail-order business and its 610 department stores were scattered in small towns throughout the country. More than 450 of the stores were losing money; in 1931, the firm lost $9 million. In three years, Avery turned this loss into a profit in part by introducing higher-priced lines of merchandise for the mail-order chain. As Avery said, "We no longer depend on hicks and yokels. We [now] sell more than overalls and manure proof shoes."[18]

However, most of the benefits came from Avery's aggressive cost cutting. In order to revitalize Wards, Avery proceeded with a series of major write-offs, scraping the company to the bone. He shut down losing units, trimmed overheads, and slashed unnecessary expenditures. He also coordinated the catalogue and retailing aspects of the business, building up complementary divisions in order to eradicate duplication. And Avery was compulsively thorough in his hunt for economies. As one analyst reported long ago: "He turned the place inside out, even to the fixtures and decorations." Before long, Avery was canonized as "the greatest businessman of his generation." He ran a tight and efficient ship, and his excellence as a cost cutter was widely heralded as an example for other retailers.[19]

Incremental Innovation

Craftsmen who are *quality leaders* cannot compete along all dimensions. There is a cost to their obsession with quality that usually prevents them from being leading innovators. For example, at DEC, quality was more important than either timeliness or novelty. As one company spokesman put it: "We must provide reliability. We purposefully lag the state-of-the-art by two to three years. We let our lead users—for example, government research labs—push us. Then we develop a reliable product for our OEM [original equipment manufacturer] customers and other end users."[20] In other words, the maxim of Craftsmen is "Don't be first—be best." It takes time to design and perfect the best products on the market. So, innovations tend to be modest and incremental. Also, quality is expensive. There simply aren't enough resources available for constant product-line renewal.

Caterpillar, too, was reluctant to be the first to come up with anything new in its markets. Cat let its rivals go through the hit-and-miss process of introducing new offerings and then moved in later with the best, most reliable product around. Rather than take risks on new products, it relied on matchless quality and reliable service to attract and keep its customers.[21]

Craftsmen who are *cost leaders* are also not known for their major product or service innovations. Too many expensive changes in methods of manufacture would eliminate their cost advantages. In fact, Texas Instruments' concern with cost caused it to fall behind in microprocessor technology, so that it was forced to become a second sourcer for the more progressive Intel and Mostek. However, although TI was too slow to take the initiative, it ultimately responded to the challenge with cheaply produced items of its own.[22]

Even though Craftsmen shun dramatic innovations, they often introduce incremental improvements to extend the range and usefulness of their lines. For example, TI worked out a number of new applications and product variations to keep its markets growing and its engineers motivated. According to Morris Chang, group vice-president of consumer products, "Every year you'll see one or two innovative products based on semi-conductors that perform new functions at low cost." One of these products was "Speak & Spell," a talking/spelling tutor for children that vastly exceeded the projected demand.[23]

Selective Marketing

Craftsmen who are quality leaders are generally unable to compete on the basis of either low prices or mass marketing. DEC, for example, spent lots of money in its quest for superb quality and excellent service. Its products were time-consuming and costly to design; its large and overlapping lines were expensive to produce and market; and its copious services boosted costs still further. DEC could not therefore sell its products very cheaply. High costs and extensive lines also prevented an expensive mass-marketing effort, which in any event would have been inappropriate for the proliferation of specialized market niches. Fortunately, DEC's dedication to quality and service produced clients who were satisfied, loyal—and insensitive to price.

DEC's marketing strategy was extraordinarily simple. It crafted machines in the belief that they would sell on their merits to a sophisticated audience—and they did. This strategy of "pumping iron," as it is known in the computer business, worked brilliantly for over two decades.[24]

In fact, according to *Fortune* magazine's Bro Uttal, DEC tends to "rely on customers to find uses for minicomputers, rather than burdening the company with huge costs of developing and marketing applications on its own. Digital salesmen, engineers selling to other engineers, nurture strong lasting relationships with customers. . . . It's surprising how little they've caused their own growth. For years they've been dragged along by interesting applications their customers came up with."[25]

Very much the same attitude prevailed at Caterpillar. For decades its stellar reputation engendered effortless sales. Indeed, Cat dealers often were pegged as order takers rather than salesmen. Sometimes this alienated the smaller contractors. According to one, "Cat always had an attitude that they were the very best and if you didn't own their equipment, you were second-rate." And Caterpillar's prices were usually well above those of the competition. But so was the durability of its products. In other words, superb quality and service accounted for Cat's success, not novelty, smooth salesmanship, or low price.[26]

PERFECTIONIST LEADERS AND CULTURES

Most Craftsmen are run by very strong leaders. Craftsmanship requires tremendous dedication and attention to detail, but this cannot occur without a forceful CEO who continually and emphatically insists that things be done just right. These leaders have no tolerance for deviations from the basic values. Employees who stray from the Craft philosophy, or even take it too lightly, are spoken to or pushed out. And craftsmanship is forever reinforced by the leader's visits to plants and offices, by his many personal encounters with all levels of employees, and by his pronouncements in public speeches, policy manuals, annual reports, and even in the press. The corporate philosophy is articulated loudly and often. And the boss both recruits and rewards those who best embody his philosophy. As Susan Fraker of *Fortune* tells us, Digital Equipment's Ken Olsen "is a technical virtuoso, and DEC grew in his image to become an engineer's Eden."[27]

The main contribution of the leader, however, is not his personal motivational effort. It is the corporate culture that he creates: the way he infuses day-to-day behavior with long-run meaning and purpose. Effective leaders carefully shape an organization's values, highlighting what is distinctive and vital about its aims and methods. They ensure that their company's culture will motivate and guide employees by providing inspired indoctrination in the corporate values; by engendering team spirit through invigorating rituals; and by giving everyone responsibility and an active role to play. Strong cultures permeate all levels of an organization and endure long after the founding leader has departed. Patrick Haggerty at TI, Ken Olsen at DEC, and Walt Disney at Disney were all masters at shaping corporate culture—at institutionalizing their personal values so that they became a way of life for employees throughout their organizations.

Training and Indoctrination

The culture at Disney became a business legend, perhaps in part because of the writings of Red Pope. According to Pope, "How Disney looks upon people, internally and externally, handles them, communicates with them, rewards them, is in my view the basic foundation upon which its five decades of success stand."[28]

In order to excel at service delivery, Disney trained its employees with an exacting thoroughness, instilling in them a sense of team spirit and responsibility. Indoctrination in the ways of the firm was mandatory for all levels of employees. This was highlighted by an annual week-long program called "cross utilization," in which Disney executives donned a theme costume and headed for the action. Again according to Pope, for a full week, the boss "sells tickets or popcorn," drives the monorail, parks cars, or whatever, in the theme parks. There is a special "language"—the employees out front are "cast members" and the personnel department is "casting." Whenever you are working for the public, you are "on stage." Trainees learned about upper-case "G" Guests. It took four days to learn how to take tickets, to be able to handle all the contingencies: "What happens when someone wants to know where the restrooms are, when the parade starts, what bus to take to get back to the campgrounds." Everyone had to attend Disney University and pass "Traditions I" before going on to specialized training. All new employees were immersed in the Disney philosophy and operating methods. No one was exempt.[29]

As Pope put it, "Disney expects the new CM [cast member] to know something about the company, its history and success, its management style before he actually goes to work. Every person is shown how each division relates to the other divisions . . . and how each 'relates to the show.' In other words, 'Here's how all of us work together to make things happen. Here's your part in the big picture.' "[30]

Indoctrination may also be achieved by making managers familiar with a wide array of functions. For example, at Caterpillar, to embue employees in the Cat way of doing business, the firm always started its potential managers near the bottom, usually right on the production floor. There were few instant stars.[31]

Team Spirit

Many Craftsmen work diligently to ensure that their employees feel they are an integral part of a supportive, special, even unique team—a select "can-do" group that always goes the extra mile. TI's culture, for instance, stressed hard work, corporate loyalty, and team spirit. The company made sure that managers were there for the long haul by recruiting them straight out of school while they were young and impressionable. In fact, TI hired 80 percent of its professional workers directly from college, and indoctrinated them early and systematically in the merits of effort, resourcefulness, and initiative—in short, in "the Protestant ethic, Texas style." Loyalty was so much prized at TI that years of service, rather than pay or position, became the most highly valued sign of status.[32]

Caterpillar employed rituals to enhance team spirit. Every year, Cat put on a "Machine Day." All employees and their families went to the equipment proving grounds for free beer and sandwiches. The machines were dressed up in costumes and given names. Hill-devouring and earth-moving contests then took place—"Everybody lapped it up."[33]

Even though Caterpillar became very much a multinational firm, its culture was extremely insular. Cat remained ethnocentric, even

"Illinois-centric," always spurning suggestions that it should transfer its international headquarters to New York City. Two thirds of the top executives were born in Illinois or states bordering it. They formed a cohesive, inbred group that worked, lived, and even socialized together. And they were so dedicated to their work that they are sometimes described as having "yellow paint in their veins." As one top executive said rather haughtily: "At Caterpillar we make capital goods that change the face of the earth. We don't make consumer products that are here today and gone tomorrow."[34]

And the clubbiness of Caterpillar's corps of managers was preserved even in its international operations. When Cat's executives went overseas, they remained just as tightly knit as they were at home. For example, all its managers in Tokyo lived in "Caterpillar Village," a single apartment building. They went to work together on the same bus and socialized almost exclusively with each other.[35] You can well imagine the type of esprit de corps this created—but it also would pave the way for a less salutary inbreeding and insularity.

Initiative, Responsibility, and Involvement

The Craftsman culture motivates employees by giving them important roles to play—by making everybody feel that he or she counts and has influence.

To promote commitment, involvement, and craftsmanship, managers at Texas Instruments were organized into small teams where young members could learn from their seniors and where everyone's contribution was visible and counted. It was Patrick Haggerty who created TI's People Involvement Program (PIP). For three to six months of the year, everyone had to join a team of eight to ten members in order to perform a specific project, improve productivity, or introduce a new product. Each team had a limited, concrete goal which it set itself, and its members included shop-floor people and an engineer. This spread initiative and responsibility. Haggerty's aim was to create a group of product champions and entrepreneurs throughout the company on the premise that people, not programs or systems, produce innovation. Team achievements were celebrated and broadcast, and teams were given recognition for their accomplishments even at the board level. At one point, there were about nine thousand such teams at TI.[36]

DEC also made much use of task forces—but in a novel way that encouraged action and accomplishment. Busy senior people were put onto each task force, people with many other responsibilities and therefore little time for red tape or formal meetings. These managers were accorded enough power to move things along briskly. To prevent excessive bureaucracy, no permanent staff people were assigned, written reports were discouraged, and action was preferred to analysis.[37]

ORDERLY STRUCTURES

"Structure" refers to an organization's distribution of power, its rules and regulations, its hierarchy, and its allocation of responsibilities. It also includes information, control, and coordinative systems. For Craftsmen, the central problem of structuring is to ensure that their craft is pursued effectively and with diligence, but in a way that does not destroy initiative. In other words, control must never extinguish motivation.

At TI, Haggerty introduced strict financial controls and strategic planning to manage TI's rapid growth and its increasingly complex business mix. Such controls also guaranteed that expenses would be held down and cost leadership achieved. But Haggerty made sure, too, that TI was biased toward action and improvement. Recall his extensive use of small, very temporary task forces that had explicitly narrow objectives. These made it easy for senior management to follow up on performance. They also put the pressure for timely achievement on team members. The emphasis on action was reinforced by minimizing the number of staff positions and curbing report writing. Paper shufflers were simply not welcome.[38]

TI's OST (Objectives, Strategies, Tactics) System of having only one or two key objectives per manager kept things simple. It also got everyone thinking strategically. Top management set broad objectives; other managers and engineers mapped out the precise strategies for achieving those objectives. Even the lowliest operating managers were charged with one of the few hundred tactical action programs. In other words, there were systems and controls, but no suffocation. And everyone got involved in decision making. Such participation was not only a cornerstone of motivation, it also brought to bear diverse viewpoints that prevented one-sided policies and costly errors.[39]

31

DEC, too, adopted a structure that combined tight controls with the creation of manageable, responsive units. The firm was organized into small, energized product groups that were quite independent and allowed managers to cater very closely to the needs of their clients.[40] To further discourage inertia, staff managers were frequently rotated into line positions. In fact, Digital staff members almost always came from the line—and before too long, they returned to it once again.[41]

Although Craftsmen employ exacting cost or quality controls, formal rules and rigid protocols for interacting are avoided. Caterpillar's top executives held informal daily "no agenda-no minutes" meetings. In this way managers were able quickly to spot and address significant problems and opportunities.

The decision-making style of Craftsmen tends to be somewhat informal, in part because of the emphasis on getting things done and the bias against staff and red tape, and in part because of the division of firms into small teams with a strong cultural identification. Core values are so deeply embedded in the minds of employees that some formal, bureaucratic controls can be dispensed with. However, because they try so diligently to safeguard quality or manufacturing economy, Craftsmen tend to be more bureaucratic than either Pioneers or Builders—a distinction that grows during their transition to Tinkerers.

THE TRANSITION TO TINKERER

Our Craftsmen performed spectacularly—many for a long while. But they began to stagnate as they developed tunnel vision and an authoritarian, monolithic culture. Eventually, many Craftsmen became Tinkerers. And one of the reasons for this transformation was their earlier success. Success does two things. First, it reinforces and amplifies current strategic tendencies, often taking them to extremes. Second, it contributes to changes in leadership and culture in a way that supports and aggravates these excesses.

For example, during the focusing trajectory that converts Craftsmen into Tinkerers, strategies come to revolve too narrowly around one or two central concerns, in this case, either low cost or a specialized kind of quality. The cost leadership of Craftsmen becomes the obsessive miserliness of Tinkerers. Quality leadership degenerates into the worship of irrelevant engineering standards. And the de-emphasis of marketing and innovation by Craftsmen becomes, in Tinkerers, total neglect. The strategic narrowing that takes place is almost palpable.

In part these changes are due to the momentum imparted to previous strategies by their past success. But they are also attributable to the changes in leadership, culture, and structure. Leaders become overconfident, arrogant, intolerant. They accord too much power to the engineering and production departments that shaped the central strategy And they create an attitude of conservatism—of trying to preserve the past recipes for success with monolithic standards, controls, and bureaucracy. In other words, during the transition from Craftsmen to Tinkerers, strong leaders become tyrants, cohesive cultures become conformist cabals, and tight controls are converted into bureaucratic shackles.

Collectively, these changes form a cohesive pathology that we call the focusing trajectory. (Figure 2 summarizes the focusing trajectory.)

TINKERER STRATEGIES

As firms come to favor an ever narrower path to success, they become increasingly intolerant of deviations from the recipe. Quality leaders embrace a technician's version of quality, ignoring both the customers' needs and emerging technologies. Cost leaders economize until they have nothing attractive left to sell. And both types of firms dwell exclusively on the minutia of designs or budgets. These obsessions monopolize managers' attention, causing them to ignore marketing, product-line renewal, and the external environment.

Quality Without Desirability

As quality-leader Craftsmen change into Tinkerers, quality, which had been a means of satisfying customers, becomes an end in itself. Quality alone is credited with past success; everything else is ignored. So Tinkerers start to devise indestructible products or pristine services that no one really wants. Sometimes their emphasis on quality makes costs and prices too high; at other times it causes an exclusive preoccupation with peripheral engineering details that allows the basic designs to become obsolete.

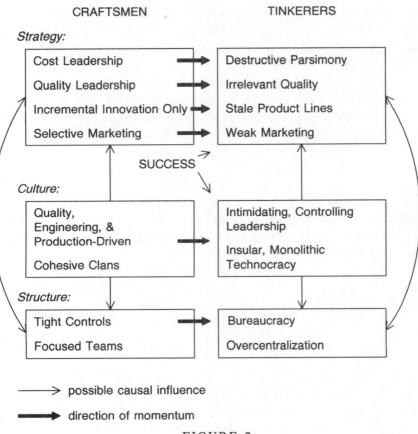

FIGURE 2
The Focusing Trajectory

DEC, for example, continued to create high-quality products, but began to neglect what its customers actually wanted. Its ill-fated microcomputer venture may be a case in point. DEC set out to capture the high-quality segment of the market, one that IBM supposedly could not address with its personal computer—the PC. It came up with a computer that was far more solidly built than IBM's—perhaps, given its cost, too much so. But it was late to enter the market, its designs were unpopular and expensive, and DEC introduced a confusing proliferation of lines that diluted demand. The specifics are informative.

First, DEC's Ken Olsen was slow to realize that newer, smaller computers were infringing on his minicomputer market. In 1982, the sales of microcomputers such as the IBM PC expanded by 77 percent, as compared to only 17 percent (down from 31 percent in 1981) for the market for minicomputers. In spite of such tremendous differences in potential, DEC was slow to enter the micro field, coming in a full year after IBM. And its machines sold sluggishly.[42]

Second, DEC's micros were built to very exacting standards. However, they were too expensive and suited only a very limited market. These products might have conflicted with DEC's own lines but were no threat to IBM. As Olsen explained, "DEC is not in the consumer business, our strategy is to serve industrial users. Our product is more solidly built and of higher quality [than IBM's]—it's like military hardware."[43] An engineer who helped develop one of DEC's personal computers said that DEC's machines were "the most over-engineered and undermarketed in the field."[44]

Third, DEC designed and marketed three micros when one would have sufficed. It couldn't decide between its Pro, Rainbow, and DEC-mate models. This made it confusing for customers. Also, for its Pro model, DEC created a unique operating system—the program that serves as the computer's central nervous system. Obviously, this made software firms reluctant to develop programs for it. DEC, it seems, was designing to please its engineers, not its customers.[45]

The upshot: the DEC Pro's sales were only 1 percent of those of the IBM PC. In 1982, after twelve years of uninterrupted growth, net earnings at DEC dropped 32 percent; in April, the stock price fell from $132 to $70.[46]

Caterpillar Tractor also extended its quality strategy too far. Its desire for state-of-the-art facilities to create excellent products clouded the need to adapt and cut back on capacity in the face of a declining demand. Cat was confident that its energy-related business—mainly the demand for pipelayers—would continue to grow. So it blithely added plant after plant, spending $836 million on capital projects in 1981 alone. Its rivals, who were very much feeling the pinch of declining oil prices, were shocked at this persistence. Soon Cat had 75 percent more plant space, with 25 percent lower production. This saddled Caterpillar with extremely high costs. And these were especially devastating in view of excess capacity in the industry, a maturing U.S. market, soft oil and gas prices, and a weak yen that amplified competition from Japan's efficient Komatsu.[47]

The financial results of the period were clear testimony to the severity of these challenges: from 1982 to 1984, Cat was mired in losses and was headed for its third straight unprofitable year, with a $92 million loss in the third quarter of 1984 alone.[48]

Some Tinkerers attempt to achieve what had been quality in the past, but is now irrelevant or even boring. Walt Disney's culture was so closed that it blinded managers to the obsolescence of their products. Disney continued to produce inoffensive "quality" entertainment that preserved the moral standards of a bygone age. But it offered quality that no one wanted, especially in its film division, where the failure to keep up with new trends proved almost fatal.

Disney's conservatism restricted it to making only wholesome, if rather stale, family movies. "If audiences are looking for something with redder blood, they will have to look elsewhere," President E. Cardon Walker used regularly to insist. Disney's bland *Condorman,* which was at first promoted using a poster of actress Barbara Carrera in a slit skirt, was too much for Walker. He immediately had the slit painted over.[49]

According to Myron Magnet of *Fortune* magazine, "The studio's resident producers ground out a thin stream of formulaic pictures fewer and fewer people would pay to see. A similar low-horsepower approach to television production led to CBS's cancellation of the hour-long *Wonderful World of Disney*, leaving the company without a regular network show for the first time in 29 years."[50]

When the film business fared poorly, Walker attributed it to "public taste" rather than questioning Disney's practices. He blamed his box-office routs on a shrinking market for wholesome family entertainment, even though contemporary films such as *E.T.* and *Star Wars* were breaking all records. As Walker rationalized at the time: "today's young adults want a more sophisticated point of view, with more sex and violence. We don't ever want to go that far."[51]

By 1982, Disney's biggest hit was still *Mary Poppins,* released in 1964. In fact, this was the last live action hit the company produced. The film division was saved only by the reissue of *Snow White, Fantasia, Bambi, Pinocchio,* and other Disney classics. Between 1977 and 1981, 50 percent of film revenues came from such reissues at a time when other studios were forging ahead with new products.[52]

One critic of the day remarked: "Until recently, it appeared that new ventures were undertaken only if Walt had conceived them or if they seemed like projects he would have approved." Walker did not disagree: "We have never been part of the Hollywood scene. Disney has been kind of isolated." The Wonderful World of Disney was the world of yesteryear.[53]

All of this took its toll on Disney's bottom line. As a result of too many bombs at the box office and a leveling off of earnings at the theme parks, profits fell from $135 million in 1980 to $93 million in 1983.

Destructive Parsimony

Just as an obsession with quality or standards can get out of hand, so can a blind crusade to economize. In both cases, an impoverished and inferior product or service results. Parsimonious Craftsmen become miserly Tinkerers.

At Eastern Air Lines, cost-consciousness increased profits during the monopoly years, but it became a problem when the airline had to compete. Eddie Rickenbacker's fervent parsimony sharply degraded Eastern's services. Overworked ticket sellers and gate attendants became famous for a rude offhandedness that drove away clients; the tacit attitude was that the customer was lucky to be allowed to fly with Eastern. Reservation errors and overselling were the rule.[54]

An excessive attention to costs also caused Eastern to trail the industry in buying new aircraft, so that its competitors almost always beat it in introducing a newer and more popular plane. Per-mile maintenance costs were reduced by tight scheduling, but this caused inconvenient flight times and spartan services. Some customers became so alienated that they formed an organization called WHEALS—We Hate Eastern Air Lines. Eastern had economized itself into the doghouse.[55]

Performance deteriorated precipitously. For Eastern, 1963 was its fourth successive worst year ever—it had lost $3.6 million, $9.6 million, $13.4 million, and $37.8 million in 1960, 1961, 1962, and 1963, respectively. Its share of trunk-line traffic fell from 18 percent in the late fifties to 12.8 percent in 1963.[56]

Disney, too, economized until it crippled its product lines. Cardon Walker was so frugal that he could no longer recruit proper talent for film making. In fact, one frustrated producer who quit the firm says he became increasingly disenchanted with the studio's practice of skimping on production values to save money—leaving out of Disney's celebrated cartoons such details as reflected images, the sparkle of water, whiffs of smoke from a fire. "Disney was also producing namby pamby stories, protecting youthful audiences from the grim realities of traditional fairy tales."[57]

If services such as those of Eastern and Disney can deteriorate as a result of cost cutting, then so can manufactured goods. Texas Instruments, which had for so long pursued efficiency in manufacture, began to combine the mistakes of focusing too narrowly on costs *and* submerging itself in irrelevant technical details. Its abiding obsession with cost and market share caused it to miss out on new generations of semiconductor leadership, doomed its home computer venture, and sabotaged its endeavors in consumer electronics.

TI employed the brute-force method of selling semiconductors. It spent a lot of money on large, inflexible new plants and labored furiously to make them the most efficient in the business. But it didn't notice that its microprocessors were falling far behind in power and features. Such lapses put TI at a real disadvantage vis-à-vis its more sophisticated and innovative rivals. The firm was, in effect, being forced to compete on price alone. By the early 1980s, TI found itself lagging behind in the very successful CMOS chip technology. It was beaten in high-speed, high-capacity chips by all of its rivals—Intel, Motorola, even tiny Zilog.[58]

This self-defeating obsession with cost even carried over into TI's consumer products, which were approached as though they were chips. The company assumed it could conquer markets by offering the most performance at the lowest price. It completely ignored fashion and styling. Take the abortive digital watch effort. As one former member of the watch group recalled: "Fred [Bucy] and Mark [Shepherd; TI's two top executives] kept pushing to slash the price to $9.95. That meant having a plastic band. We kept telling them consumers didn't want that, but they wouldn't listen."[59] Engineering specifications and cost figures mattered. Appearance and attractiveness did not.

Similar problems arose when TI tried to produce its own line of microcomputers. Again, the narrow focus on cost and engineering compromised the saleability of products. TI's "Professional" computer was a good machine, but it required different customized software and a separate inventory. So computer stores were reluctant to carry it, sales fell off, and the product failed.

The upshot of all this was that by 1983, TI was in big trouble. It folded its home computer business with a $660 million operating loss and write-down. Its annual loss in 1983 was $145 million. And in 1985,

TI was forced to derive 80 percent of its profits from the volatile semiconductor market because it had failed so thoroughly in consumer electronics.[60]

For Craftsmen, the attention to cost or quality drives them to de-emphasize product or service novelty and to avoid aggressive marketing. In Tinkerers, such deemphasis becomes a total void. Because only high quality or low cost are credited with importance, everything else is deemed a waste of time and money. So product lines turn stale, the customer is ignored, and firms lose sight of their environments.

Dated Product Lines and Service

Whereas Craftsmen were very selective in introducing new products, many Tinkerers are reluctant to bring out *anything* new. For example, by 1984, Walt Disney Productions had not made a Mickey Mouse cartoon for thirty years. It passed up the opportunity to appeal anew to an entire generation of children. Nor had it updated or advertised theme parks such as California's Disneyland. Disney even failed to develop its precious real estate. And no new characters or ideas were generated to keep people watching the TV shows or get them coming to the parks.[61]

Sewell Lee Avery's obsession with cutting costs badly eroded the retailing services of Montgomery Ward during the 1940s. The rigid controls and frugality that were responsible for the dramatic turnaround of Wards caused its subsequent downfall. At a time when competitor Sears, Roebuck was expanding into more promising areas and increasing its profits and revenues, Avery's major concern was boosting Wards's liquidity. He had become obsessed with the notion that another Great Depression was imminent. So he began to hoard cash, turning Wards into "a bank with a store front." By 1949, Wards had not opened a single store in eight years. On the thriving West Coast where the population had grown by 50 percent in ten years, Avery actually closed down some stores and imposed penurious economies on others. He wouldn't even paint many of his establishments, let alone install modern conveniences such as escalators or air conditioning. Wards's stores were becoming dowdy outlets located in all the wrong areas. In effect, Avery was liquidating his vast merchandising empire at a time when his competitors were expanding. The result was a surfeit of liquidity and a precipitous shrinkage in sales and profits in the early 1950s, at a time when the rest of the industry was performing beautifully.[62]

The venerable Caterpillar Tractor was renowned for its conservatism; it was only too happy to let its competitors be the pacesetters. In the increasingly turbulent and competitive market of the 1980s, however, this hesitancy proved a great liability. Cat was left with too many kinds of equipment that no one wanted, and too few types that were in demand.[63]

A Poor Understanding of Markets

Tinkerers are dominated by engineers—and by an engineering mentality. Technical considerations rule as designs are viewed solely in terms of their cost, efficiency, and capacity. And usually, competitors, customers, even the economy are all lost sight of.

This was especially true at Texas Instruments. TI's engineers, accustomed to industrial customers, lacked expertise in consumer markets. Recall the relentless cost cutting that made the digital watches so unappealing. TI also slashed prices to create demand for its foundering home computer. But the tactic, borrowed from industrial chip markets, failed to generate any lasting demand. In both instances, the firm had no idea of what its customers wanted.[64]

According to one analyst, TI "believed it could dictate to its customers rather than listen to them." Indeed, the home computer sprang mainly from management's desire to find a mass market for its newest microprocessor. Even when it became clear that the microprocessor was inappropriate for the market, TI refused to budge.[65]

TI also had a poor understanding of industry trends. In 1979, it decided to focus on chips for calculators and watches rather than developing metal-oxide semiconductor (MOS) computer memories and advanced microprocessors. Other semiconductor companies took the opposite tack. As it happened, the areas TI cut back on became the two hottest segments of the industrial semiconductor market.[66] Similarly, Caterpillar Tractor failed to foresee the coming decline in its highway business and the growth of urban construction, and this doomed it to a shrinking market.[67]

Poor Marketing

Craftsmen were not very avid marketers; but Tinkerers carry this passivity to an extreme and appear not to market at all. Cost and engineering details are all that seem to matter. Some Tinkerers, in fact, very purposely ignore the marketing function.

Olsen at DEC was by no means a fan of marketing. "I tell my marketing people that the main reason they like to advertise is so their mother-in-laws in Idaho will know they're doing their jobs," he said, only half jokingly. And Olsen was indeed very reluctant to advertise, protesting: "One minute of advertising in that [1983 Super Bowl] game would pay for 600,000 handbooks." Several marketers quit the company in frustration.[68]

When DEC finally realized the impact personal computers would have on the exploding office-automation market, it hurried into the business. Unfortunately, it failed to adapt its marketing and sales strategies to the new, less computer-friendly customers it encountered. DEC's products and manuals alike required an unrealistic amount of computer literacy.[69]

The puzzling proliferation of products only made matters worse. DEC's chaotic retail strategy sold each of its three kinds of personal computers through different types of outlets. Customers became thoroughly confused as no one knew where to find the various products. In fact, "DEC's ads never made it clear which friendly DEC dealer customers should go to for which product."[70]

Caterpillar experienced marketing problems as well. It was too slow to trim prices and attack costs in the face of Japanese competition. And it delayed giving its sales managers and dealers discounting authority, perhaps because in the past Cat never had to bother about prices. As a result, rivals began stealing market share. These problems were compounded since Caterpillar dealers failed to give adequate service to their smaller customers, wanting instead to continue to concentrate on selling their big machines to larger industrial and government projects. But now there was a shortage of such projects. And the precious alternative market of emerging customers was being brushed off.[71]

TI's marketing efforts were equally disastrous, since its managers seemed sublimely convinced that technologically sound products would sell themselves, and that retailers, dealers, and distributors—even customers, at times—were necessary evils. Intel and Motorola trounced TI in advanced microprocessors, in part because they promised delivery times and gave out cost and future price details that made it easy for buyers to engineer their systems around their chips. TI did not give out that information, treating the customer more "like an antagonist instead of a partner."[72]

As the president of a large business products company put it, "Coming from an engineering background, TI knows only about selling on the basis of price. But I have to give prompt service to my consumers—and I just can't get it from the manufacturer." In 1979, dealers were up in arms because they lost the whole back-to-school business for some TI calculators—the product just was not being delivered. Tinkerers' efforts stop, it seems, after their products have been manufactured.[73]

CONTROLLING LEADERS

We have seen how the success of past strategies causes them to focus on just a few qualities. Costs and design details, which had been the means to serve customers, become ends in themselves. This obsession creates resistance to change, an ignorance of the markets, and a wayward marketing strategy. Soon, desirable products develop into anachronisms that no one wants.

It is fascinating that the same narrowing of focus can be found in the leadership and culture of Tinkerers. In fact, many strategic problems can be traced back to the human side of the business. These troubles often begin with the leadership, then seep down into the corporate culture and ultimately into the structure of the company.

Past success breeds overconfidence. It creates an aura of invulnerability and infallibility around leaders and gives them a good deal of power. Leaders, in turn, are anxious to keep the firm on track by endlessly invoking the old recipes, which they codify through organizational myths, rituals, and formal policies. And just to be sure things don't go astray, the leaders themselves make all the important decisions—and some very trivial ones as well. Unfortunately, they can be brutal when questioned or challenged.

Three characteristics describe the leaders of Tinkerers. First, they are intolerant of dissent and manage by intimidation. Second, they hoard authority and insist on total control. Third, they immerse themselves in details, especially technical details, and as a result fail to see the big picture.

Management by Intimidation

The Haggerty years at TI were followed by the ascension of the domineering chairman, Mark Shepherd, Jr., and his equally forceful president, J. Fred Bucy. Both were intolerant and intimidating bosses. TI's past success, and their role in achieving it, made Bucy and Shepherd superconfident in the power of engineering and the magic of cost control. They *knew* these approaches worked. In fact, they had proved it. And this gave them immense influence, which they wielded all too vigorously.

Meetings were punctuated by table-pounding, table-kicking, and flying objects. Management by fear took over, especially if a subordinate presented disappointing forecasts. Bro Uttal relates one manager's recollections:

> "If Bucy or Shepherd didn't like something, they'd interrupt the presentation by saying 'That's bullshit! If that's all you have to say, we don't want to hear it.' Another senior guy walked out on my presentation because I had bad news." . . . Sometimes meetings became surreal. "We spent more time saying what we thought Fred and Mark wanted to hear than saying what we thought."[74]

Shepherd at TI erupted into rages that paralyzed subordinates. According to a former executive, "Shepherd once got so angry that he threw a loose leaf binder against the boardroom wall. Everything fell apart. We had orders to find new binders that could survive hitting a wall. I remember seeing people throwing binders at a wall until we found one that wouldn't come apart."[75]

The results were predictable. Product managers told Bucy and Shepherd only what they wanted to hear rather than what was really going on. Neither leader, for example, learned of the problems in their home computer division until the company was drowning in inventory.[76]

The same autocratic style prevailed earlier under a similarly enshrined Lee Avery at Montgomery Ward. Avery once said, "If anyone ventures to differ with me, I throw them out the window." And he very often did almost that, orchestrating massive purges of his executive corps. As he remarked after one of these campaigns, "I have never lost anyone I wanted to keep." His style was referred to in a well-known case from the Harvard Business School as one of "oppressive paternalism."[77]

At Eastern Air Lines, Captain Eddie Rickenbacker was "brash, opinionated, a hard man to argue with." To young managers he showed a benign paternal side; he liked to be called "Captain Eddie," and beamed when a subordinate hung his picture on the wall. However, even when he had over 17,500 employees, he ran a one-man show.[78]

During his semiannual gatherings with the company's hundreds of managers, every executive had to stand up and give an exhaustive account of his stewardship. Manning his own microphone, Rickenbacker could be brutally sarcastic: "For God's sake, don't go giving away things we haven't got to give. Anybody can give away $1. The thing is to give away $1 and get back $1.10. Don't forget that. Your whole future is in this company. If it isn't, get out of here."[79]

Amazingly, we find a similar leadership style at the cloyingly wholesome Disney. E. Cardon Walker, Disney's CEO from 1976 to 1983, was a stern, conservative, Idaho-born Mormon who joined the studio as a messenger boy in 1938. According to *Fortune* magazine's Myron Magnet: "Subordinates feared Walker as a tyrant, quick to ridicule underlings in public and impervious to any point of view but his own. He made decisions according to what he thought Walt would have done. As a result, the company steadily lost touch with modern taste, growing as hermetic as a religious sect or a Communist cell. Executives clinched arguments by quoting Walt like Scripture or Marx, and the company eventually supplied a little book of founder's sayings."[80]

In short, past victories have brought out the worst-excesses in managerial intolerance. And, as a result, executives are not getting the information that could alert them to the need for product-line renewal.

Excessive Control

In order to preserve their successful recipe, the leaders of Tinkerers try to control everything themselves. They do not trust others for fear that the "golden goose" will be killed.

At Texas Instruments, for example, Bucy and Shepherd were very reluctant to delegate authority. So, all power rested with them—at the top of the firm. "Both . . . are very autocratic, very powerful, very intent on controlling things," said a veteran of TI. Bucy, infamous for his prodigious shower of memos, always kept a computer ranking of the performance of each of his operating managers at hand. His obsession with control led some managers to call him "TI's Al Haig."[81]

Avery, too, wanted to command everyone directly, even those at the bottom of the organization. At Montgomery Ward, he encouraged employees way down in the hierarchy to end-run their bosses: "When I ask you for a report . . . you make it direct to me and don't take up the matter with any other official who may be involved."[82]

Avery's assertion of control was both covert and overt. At times he would manipulate his executives into telling him what he wanted to hear. Many felt they had been "trapped into saying yes to contradictory propositions slyly put forth by Avery on consecutive days." But Avery could also be less subtle. He was known to stalk through the company's offices loudly proclaiming, "I'll show them who runs Wards." The amount of useful advice the sporadically rampaging Avery would receive was clearly destined to wane.[83]

Details, Details

Even without overt intimidation, the leaders of Tinkerers are adept at damping the initiative of subordinates as they immerse themselves in the minutia of operations. Shepherd and Bucy at TI were engineers first and foremost. They loved to pore over the details of designs but gave little thought to broader issues or market trends. One former employee claimed that Bucy carted home so many memos that he needed a dolly to carry his briefcases, and that the TI jet whisked memos to him daily while he was vacationing in South Texas.[84]

Obviously, this concern with detail obscures a broader perspective. And it triggers the sort of meddling that demotivates other managers. According to one former employee, "We were working on a computer project, and Fred took some materials home one weekend. When he came back, he wanted to change the name of the project. It was silly. He couldn't see the big picture."[85]

The result of this exclusive focus on minutia is that no strategic reevaluation takes place. Product lines become stale and irrelevant as leaders confine their attention to tinkering at the margins.

TECHNOCRACY CULTURES

Craftsmen, we will recall, had strong, overarching values that guided their strategy. In Tinkerers, however, such values are replaced by a formulaic adherence to a rigid recipe for success. Leaders codify strategies into a sacrosanct policy document—in effect, a corporate bible. An insular, monolithic culture is the stifling result as all beliefs and approaches are frozen in the past. Sometimes, in fact, it is the ghosts of *departed* leaders who through their bible serve as absentee strategists.

Insular Technocracy

Overconfident leaders do not feel the need to look outside the organization—or outside of engineering—for good ideas. They are closed to their environments and are not motivated to interact much with customers. So Tinkerers act upon, instead of reacting to, their settings.

The TI culture under Bucy and Shepherd was insular, presumptuous, and at times arrogant. TI insisted on driving the market by pouring on sheer technology. A retired vice-president said: "If you're a company dominated by engineers, it's hard to give somebody what he wants when you know what he should have." Eighty percent of TI's seventy top officers had degrees in engineering or science; and they all had "a stubborn faith" in their own ideas.[86]

All too often, closed cultures make firms entirely ritualistic. TI's meetings to review operations and plans reminded a former marketing manager of "high school pep rallies." The object, said another veteran, wasn't to examine where TI was or should be heading, but to generate a blind "we'll-make-it-happen" attitude. This all occurred at a time when the firm was losing contact with its markets and badly needed a frank and open airing of its decaying policies.[87]

The culture at Digital Equipment Corporation was also becoming insular, and discouraged self-reflection and renewal. Old strategies were never reexamined; and an engineering technocracy remained intact in spite of the pressing need to pay more attention to both customers and marketing. According to *Fortune*'s Susan Fraker, "Some of Olsen's colleagues suspect he has 'founder's disease' and can't see that DEC must become more of a marketing company. Others wonder whether this talented engineer has the skills—or the desire—to market aggressively." It's hard to get a creator to reevaluate the strategy that has made his company great. "How can you tell Ken Olsen that he's doing the wrong thing?" asked one editor of a computer newsletter. "How do you tell him the game has changed?"[88]

Frozen in Time

Tinkerer cultures are mired in the past, in part because their isolation prevents managers from realizing that times have changed. We have seen how the ghost of Walt Disney presided over a corporate mortuary dedicated to the preservation of ideals that froze the firm in a bygone era. Disney's top management, "most of whom had known and worked for Walt for years, had the inbred quality of a small college faculty whose senior members have held tenure for twenty years." Some analysts compared Disney's problems to those of a child prodigy, now full grown but still fanatically adhering to the script written by its parents. In fact, sixteen years after Disney's death, his presence still pervaded the studio in Burbank, California, as well as the corporate headquarters. "His picture was everywhere—in the entrances to buildings, in the hallways, in executive's offices." His name and his abundant homilies were forever being invoked.[89]

Managers were always quoting the departed Disney. Why are the theme parks good business? According to Dick Nunis, who was in charge of outdoor recreation, "Walt said, 'Everyone's a kid at heart—all you have to do is let him find a way to be one.'" Why are there so many beds at Disney World's hotel rooms? "Walt said, 'I want big rooms so that a whole family can stay in a room.'" Disney's original policies were carved in stone. And woe betide anyone who challenged them.[90]

RIGID STRUCTURES

The transition from Craftsman to Tinkerer saw strategies narrowing and becoming mired in a morass of small details. It saw leadership grow more authoritarian, intolerant, and controlling, and cultures grow increasingly rigid and monolithic. However, there is also a transformation in structure as firms become more centralized and bureaucratic. In Craftsmen, the system of bureaucratic control was counterbalanced by small, flexible teams. But Tinkerers are more rigidly structured to prevent any departures from the successful methods of the past. The concern with detail multiplies rules and controls. And conservative production departments come to dominate, making any kind of innovation, or even reaction, exceedingly difficult.

Bureaucracy

TI's management system became ever more bureaucratic and complex, snuffing out the splendid energy and initiative the firm had displayed as a Craftsman. The system now invoked a formal, numbers-dominated strategic planning, which tended to smother entrepreneurship. And headquarters' insistence that operations project in excruciating detail such factors as floor space and manpower needs made TI's planning process more of a liability than a weapon: proposed new projects were swathed in a bale of red tape.[91]

At the same time, TI's confusing reporting structures delayed the design and production of key new products like large-scale memory chips. For example, semiconductor product managers were given marketing responsibilities but lacked control over the labs that developed the chips and the plants that made them. Because they had no power over either engineering or production, their new product ideas were rarely implemented.

Centralization

Over the years, Tinkerers become more centralized as the managers and departments responsible for past successes garner yet more authority.

TI's matrix structure, in which product customer centers (PCCs) reported to both staff and line managers, was intended to force managers to conserve and compete for staff resources. Patrick Haggerty set up PCCs whenever there was a match between a product and a market. The PCC managers were made completely responsible for profits and losses, but were not given enough authority to tell functional departments such as manufacturing what to do. As TI grew, however, the functional departments became larger and more powerful and the small operating units became supplicants—often unsuccessful ones. The digital watch, for example, suffered because the functional managers who supplied semiconductors didn't see a big enough market to warrant making the more appropriate liquid-crystal chips. Also, Hewlett Packard seized 50 percent of TI's programmable calculator market because for over two years TI's calculator group couldn't get updated circuits. In other words, the domination of marketing by manufacturing stifled innovation.[92]

Centralization also occurred at the personal level as Bucy and Shepherd hoarded authority. "The corporate fathers don't have confidence in their people," said one PCC manager. "They're always changing strategies in the boardroom." Planning turned very much into a top-down approach as lower-level managers lost a lot of influence to the executives in the North Building, TI's headquarters. "Proposed products were defined and redefined there ad infinitum. Eventually you were just given a product that was a square peg and told to fit it into the round hole of a market."[93]

The structural problems at Digital were similar. DEC had been divided into eighteen semiautonomous business units. At first, the system worked smoothly because each unit could react very quickly to its customers. Unfortunately, as DEC expanded, the business units began to fight among themselves, arguing about what products to build and competing aggressively for the resources of the centralized, all-powerful engineering and manufacturing departments. Product development could start only after all these parties came to some agreement. Unfortunately, DEC's personal computers became mired in this bureaucracy. Some ex-DEC hands said it took much longer to develop new products than it used to because the engineering department was so insulated from the marketplace. "Six of the last eight major products have been one or two years late," said one former marketer.[94]

Given the centralization, the cumbersome reporting relationships, and the growing bureaucracy, it is not surprising that decision making became slower, more cautious, and more bogged down in staff analysis and quantitative projections. At DEC, head-office planners stole precious time with unreasonable requests for information: product managers were asked to project out ten years for fifteen operating variables. Clearly, the firm was beginning to exhibit middle-age bulge.

MAJOR CHANGES ALONG THE FOCUSING TRAJECTORY

Two types of transformations characterize the focusing trajectory. First, initial strategies are amplified until they become narrowly focused and irrelevant. For example, the goals of high quality or low cost become obsessions that draw attention away from almost everything else—from market needs, product attractiveness, competitors' strategies, and even the working climate of the organization. Tinkering with details takes the place of product-market renewal. And what was a gradually evolving product line becomes a stagnant one in growing danger of obsolescence.

These changes in strategy are in large part products of a second set of transformations: in leadership, culture, and structure. Some leaders become arrogant power hoarders who will not tolerate deviations from their "tried-and-true" recipes. They convert a strong and distinctive culture into one that is increasingly insular and ritualistic. Meanwhile, structures get so centralized and bureaucratic that adaptation becomes impossible.

Paradoxically, success contributes to the very attitudes—overconfidence, complacency, arrogance—that induce momentum; this in turn leads to the strategic, cultural, and structural excesses that promote decline. And indeed, many of the qualities that had contributed to success, when extended, produce failure. Ultimately, many Craftsmen descend on the wings of Icarus to become mere Tinkerers.

CHAPTER 3

From Builders to Imperialists:

The Venturing Trajectory

"A UTOMATIC" SPRINKLER CORPORATION WAS THE BRAINCHILD OF THE enterprising Harry Figgie, Jr., an engineer, lawyer, operations expert, and Harvard MBA. After a brilliant career as a Booz, Allen consultant and turnaround expert, Figgie decided to go into business for himself. In 1963, he raised $6 million in capital to buy "Automatic" Sprinkler, an ailing manufacturer of fire-fighting equipment. Within months he had pared the firm's losing lines, revamped its operations, and cut costs to the bone. Profits tripled during the year. Figgie soon began to acquire firms in related businesses to complement the existing operations, causing sales and earnings to rise even more spectacularly.

Unfortunately, these successes emboldened Figgie to accelerate dramatically the pace of expansion and diversification. He became known as the "Shakespeare" of merger rationales, selling his shareholders, and himself, on an elaborate "nucleus theory of growth" for making acquisitions in unrelated areas. As Figgie's greed grew, AS started swallowing more and more businesses. In mid-1967, the firm completed four acquisitions in twenty-five days; eleven for the year. This frenetic pace invited countless errors and severely taxed finances and managerial talent. Control and administrative systems began to falter under the weight of expansion. Before long, the company's per-share profits had plummeted from $1.43 to $0.10—and Figgie was on his way out.

Builders take their name from their entrepreneurial executives—who do not so much manage their organizations as actively build them, mostly into powerful, diversified corporations. All Builders progress sequentially through two distinct phases: *foundation building* and *diversification.* In the first phase, they create a strong basis for growth by establishing a viable organization; in the second, they boldly expand and diversify, often by acquiring other firms.

The greatest strength of Builders is their entrepreneurial skill: they are able to locate and capitalize on business opportunities better and faster than their competitors. Some Builders find propitious niches in a market and create a new company or division to pursue them; others carry out promising diversification ventures; and still others acquire and thread together a set of complementary businesses to produce a strong, unified enterprise. Builders thrive by amassing and organizing the factors of production—land, labor, and capital. Their imaginative leaders and sharp financial staffs excel most of all at making deals and channeling resources to achieve rapid growth.

Many Builders have become household names—ITT under the brilliant Harold S. Geneen; Tex Thornton's Litton Industries; Gulf & Western Industries during the Charles Bluhdorn years; and the giant Dome Petroleum, run by Jack Gallagher and Bill Richards. Bernie Cornfeld's years at Investors Overseas Services and Roy Ash's Addressograph-Multigraph are also good examples.

The strategy of Builders is rooted in the aggressive personalities, ambitious goals, and entrepreneurial talents of their leaders. Leaders feel driven to multiply the size and scope of their operations. They have a promoter's ability to raise capital, an eye for magnificent opportunities, and the energy to assemble an organization to exploit those opportunities. They also have a knack for achieving explosive growth by taking considered risks.

Builders evolve high-intensity meritocracies that lavishly reward the most enterprising managers and toss out the laggards. They favor decentralized structures that will motivate and harness the initiative of financially driven executives. And they set up sophisticated management information systems to control their burgeoning operations.

Unfortunately, Builders can become the victims of strategic momentum. Their spectacular success contributes to both greed and overconfidence, driving leaders to expand and diversify too aggressively and indiscriminately. Builders, in other words, are emboldened to become wildly venturesome Imperialists. This overtaxes resources, overburdens executives and administrative structures, and spawns a slew of operating problems. Recall that our Tinkerers were punished by their customers when they focused too narrowly and stagnated. Imperialists, on the other hand, punish themselves by ranging too broadly and doing too much. If Tinkerers rust out, Imperialists burn out.

Excessive venturing is caused not only by past successes but also by the transformations that take place in Imperialists' leaders, cultures, and structures. Leaders become arrogant and reckless as they pursue bigger and chancier projects. They soon are so overwhelmed by these grand ventures that they can no longer monitor or even understand their exploding operations. Moreover, their earlier tendency to favor financial over marketing and manufacturing issues intensifies to produce a remote, "bottom-line" style of management that ignores the vital details of products and markets alike.

It is hardly surprising that Imperialists lapse into administrative chaos as a result of their overexpansion. Troubled divisions run wild as control systems falter under the complexity of proliferating operations. The administrative structure and information systems simply cannot keep up. So managers remain oblivious to problems that might otherwise have made them slow down.

We appear to have a vicious circle: expansion overtaxes managers, systems, and structures—and is itself reinforced by this erosion of a firm's infrastructure. It will become clear that many aspects of the Imperialist configuration support each other to create a dangerous momentum, exacerbate problems, and relentlessly drive the venturing trajectory.

THE BUILDER

BUILDER STRATEGIES

As we saw, two major strategies are used in sequence by Builders: *foundation building* and *diversification.* Foundation building sets the stage for expansion in two ways: first, it establishes or revives a healthy core business and creates the financial and administrative critical mass needed to develop it; second, it gives top executives a chance to hone and augment their skills at raising capital, seizing business opportunities, and rationalizing operations—talents so necessary in the later diversification phase. Diversification then extends the product-market scope and the scale of operations by moving into different product lines and markets. The career histories, dreams, and accomplishments of Builder CEOs are described in some detail below

53

as these foreshadow the subsequent phases of the venturing trajectory.

Building the Foundation

Three foundation-building strategies may immediately precede diversification. *Core creation* happens at birth, when the founding entrepreneurs conceive a product-market strategy and muster the capital and resources to create a new business. *Core enhancement* takes place when an owner-entrepreneur purchases a small existing organization and enlarges it by rejuvenating product lines and modernizing operations. And *core revival* is performed within a large and ailing organization by a professional (non-owner) manager, who cuts dead wood, rationalizes operations, and renews product lines.

Core Creation

Some leaders create the core of an organization from scratch. These founders mold people, land, buildings, and machinery into a functioning enterprise—a living, breathing entity, formed for the primary purpose of fulfilling the entrepreneur's ambitious financial goals. Sagas of creation describe the struggle to get financing, to find able workers and decent facilities, and to attract customers. They all start with the vision of a product and a market, and with some semblance of a strategic and financial plan for making the dream a reality.

Bernie Cornfeld, a former social worker from Brooklyn, personally built the legendary IOS financial empire. In 1955, while living in Paris, Cornfeld took up with a liberal, bohemian group of "frustrated intellectuals, mild neurotics, political nonconformists, and cultural misfits." It was Cornfeld's unique vision that these dropouts could be remotivated and made productive by selling mutual funds. He knew that these men, many with a history of defeat and disappointment, would become devoted followers of anyone who could liberate their talents.[1]

Cornfeld soon began exploiting the large market of expatriate Americans in Paris by selling a variety of U.S. mutual funds. A brilliant salesman, he was adept at snapping up and shaping aggressive recruits who had something to prove. And he paid them extraordinarily well. As Charles Raw and his associates have written, Cornfeld "took a bunch of confused young men and convinced them that, after all, what they sincerely wanted was to be rich. Having done that, he dispatched them to scour the earth for money."[2]

Cornfeld was never happy with the status quo. According to one former salesman, "Bernie was always off making bigger deals."[3] He soon incorporated his own fund, Investors Overseas Services (IOS), diversified its set of services, and branched out internationally. Cornfeld was extraordinarily astute in identifying opportunities for IOS— he invented a multiplicity of mutual funds, found the perfect tax havens in which to incorporate them, and branched into investment vehicles that were novel and promising. He also united with financial partners who were among the most prominent in Europe.

Ultimately, IOS was to achieve phenomenal success—and a growth path that was unexcelled by any other fund. By the end of the 1960s, IOS was the largest mutual fund outside the United States. It had almost $2.5 billion to manage in seventeen different funds, and Cornfeld was broadcasting plans to extend that to $15 billion by 1975. Per-share earnings quadrupled between 1965 and 1968 alone.[4] IOS had also made a fortune valued at over $100 million for Cornfeld personally and had turned a hundred of his associates into millionaires as well.[5]

And Cornfeld had seen it all right from the very beginning. In the very first company report of the fledgling IOS, he inserted—rather pretentiously, it then seemed—a section boldly headed "Underwriter and Investment Banker."[6]

Cornfeld created the foundation for IOS—a service company—very quickly. Dome Petroleum, however, under founder Jack Gallagher, took much longer to develop its critical mass of more tangible resources. "Smilin' Jack" Gallagher quit an exceedingly promising career at Standard Oil (New Jersey) in 1950, not to join Dome, but to become it. He set up the firm, a diversification venture of the venerable Dome Mines, for a group of mostly American directors who were entirely devoid of expertise in the oil industry. Gallagher was given an entirely free hand to do as he pleased, a situation that would last for the thirty years in which he ran Dome like the paternalistic owner of a corner grocery store.[7]

Gallagher loved to wheel and deal as he rushed from oil fields to board meetings. He shaped the core of the firm by raising funds and unearthing promising ventures. It was Gallagher himself who "pored for hours over geological maps to select drilling sites, who took investors by the elbow and persuaded them to support his unknown enterprise, and who sweet talked bankers, dazzled politicians, and inspired his employees."[8]

Gallagher became known as a shrewd promoter. "He moves," said another oilman, "a ton of canaries in a half-ton truck by keeping them all flying."[9] He identified glittering business opportunities for acquiring and transporting petrochemicals, and discovered some wonderful new oil properties. But some of his greatest coups came from lobbying the Canadian government for favorable subsidies and tax concessions. It was he who was able to persuade Ottawa to grant super-depletion allowances for frontier oil exploration.[10]

To avoid staking the company's entire future on the results of its wildcatting operation, Gallagher also developed a pedestrian but incredibly lucrative business processing and transporting natural gas liquids.[11]

Dome grew steadily as a respected player in the oil patch. By 1981, from its shoestring beginnings, it had amassed sales of $1.8 billion; Gallagher's personal stake in the venture had risen to over $112 million. Dome also had acquired vast North Sea and western oil and gas properties, extensive pipelines, and a fleet of ships and drilling rigs. For a long time, it led the American Stock Exchange in trading volume as its stock skyrocketed.[12]

The core creation phase supplies these Builders with the product-market, administrative, and financial infrastructure essential for subsequent diversification. But perhaps more importantly, it gives new entrepreneurs the experience and confidence needed to support their later, more substantial ventures.

Core Enhancement

Core enhancement establishes a basis for expansion later in a firm's history than core creation. It occurs when an astute manager takes over an *existing* business that is promising, but small. In order to fulfill his dreams of running a substantial enterprise, the CEO reshapes and revitalizes core product lines and facilities to build a strong foundation for significant growth. Take the case of Litton Industries, the brainchild of Charles Thornton.

"Tex" Thornton was noted for his "cool, financial mind," and was called a great dreamer and entrepreneur. In 1953, he used his celebrated charm to raise $1.5 million in capital from Lehman Brothers to buy the tiny California microwave tube company that was to serve as the core of his subsequent empire.

Thornton's experience as a manager was impressive. He was an expert in management controls—one of the legendary Whiz Kids who moved from the U.S. Air Force to Ford to implement the methods of modern management. Later, he became a vice-president and assistant general manager at Hughes Aircraft, and there he teamed up with his two subsequent Litton partners, Roy Ash, the assistant controller, and Hugh W. Jamieson, a research scientist.[13]

At Litton, the trio began augmenting the product line by developing inertial-guidance systems, radar devices, and computers in their own laboratories. These state-of-the-art products were tailored specifically to the needs of the U.S. Air Force, a customer the principals knew very well. Thornton and his lean staff were careful, at least initially, to stay with complementary technologies and operations—developing lines they knew a lot about. And they made sure to rationalize their operations in order to keep costs in line and avoid duplication. Before long Thornton and company had succeeded in building Litton into a super-profitable high-technology company.[14]

During Litton's first decade, sales rose from $9 million to $540 million by 1963, and earnings per share grew from 9 cents to $2.16 in eight years. A thousand dollars invested at the founding would have been worth $85,000 ten years later.[15]

Some might be tempted to attribute Litton's quick start to its high-tech environment. But "Automatic" Sprinkler (AS), a producer of mundane fire-fighting equipment, built its foundation even faster. AS, under Harry Figgie, Jr., rapidly gained a stellar reputation. Said one investment manager, "Of all the guys running conglomerates, Figgie of AS was the one guy that everybody thought really knew what he was doing."[16] Figgie had a daunting familiarity with the nuts-and-bolts details of running a factory and cutting costs. He also had two engineering degrees, another in law, and an MBA from Harvard.

Even as a teenager, Figgie's dream was to put together his own corporation. So he planned his education and experience accordingly. He was made a partner in Booz, Allen & Hamilton, the management consulting firm, and was appointed head of its cost-cutting unit. Then he became a group vice-president of A. O. Smith Corporation of Milwaukee, and in two years doubled the sales and quintupled the profits of its industrial products division. All the while he was shopping for an affordable company of his own to buy, one that was sufficiently large to have good growth potential. He found "Automatic" Sprinkler in 1963—and by making the rounds of friends and bankers, raised the necessary $5.8 million to buy it within nineteen days. Figgie got AS at below book value.[17]

In what is perhaps the paradigm case of core enhancement, Figgie descended upon AS "like a business school Billy Graham," preaching the gospel of cost reduction. He eliminated unneccesary jobs, refined production methods, and cut the cost of purchases by bargaining shrewdly with suppliers. Figgie also pruned losing products and began to develop more promising lines. His brilliance as a management consultant and production engineer soon restored AS to robust health. During 1964, sales rose only 11 percent, but profits tripled.[18]

From this healthy foundation, "Automatic" Sprinkler was to enjoy explosive growth. Sales catapulted from less than $23 million in 1963 to $325 million in 1968. And profits grew even more dramatically.[19]

A third example of core enhancement is that of Gulf & Western Industries under Charles Bluhdorn. Excitable, brash, and full of fire, Bluhdorn was always single-minded in the merits of his mission. His commodity market capers had made him a millionaire in his mid-twenties. Bluhdorn took over a small automobile-parts manufacturing company and shaped a disparate set of operations into an effective, competitive enterprise. He shaved unproductive units, cut expensive overlap, and honed product lines. And, like Figgie, Bluhdorn felt the need to enhance the core operation he had taken over before embarking upon his bold strategy of expansion. Ultimately, G&W sales moved from $100 million in 1964 to $1.3 billion in 1968.[20]

Core Revival

The third foundation-building strategy takes place mostly in larger and older firms, and is usually performed by professional managers rather than owner-entrepreneurs. *Core revival* occurs as well-established but ailing enterprises recruit promising CEOs in the hope of restoring themselves to health. The challenge facing these new leaders is how to revive and consolidate wayward or outdated operations.

A typical turnaround began with Roy Ash's appointment as CEO of the venerable but languishing Addressograph-Multigraph (AM), a maker of offset printing and addressing equipment. Ash had vast administrative experience, much of it in accounting and control. He, like Tex Thornton, had been one of the Whiz Kids at Ford and Hughes Aircraft, and he had been instrumental in handling operating decisions as president of Litton. Ash quit Litton to serve as President Nixon's director of the Office of Management and Budget. After a private stint managing his own investments, he was invited in 1976 to help turn around AM. Ash invested a sizable proportion of his personal fortune in AM. His reputation and mandate from the board of directors gave him complete control. In effect, he was given the task of rebuilding a troubled corporation and he proceeded to do exactly that.[21]

He began by killing off unpromising products, closing down antiquated plants, and laying off excess personnel. He hired young executives, lowering the average age of his managers from over sixty to about forty. Ash's goal was, as he insisted, "a deliberate attempt to change a corporate culture." He demanded exhaustive financial analyses of everything the firm did or was considering doing, and he made managers personally accountable for the bottom lines of their operations. As he said, "There's nothing like fear of failure to motivate all of us."[22]

Ash's motto at the time was "Rethink, redesign, rebuild, and re-earn—re-question everything." He also began to reshape the product lines at AM, and devised a plan to extend the life of its mature products while simultaneously acquiring new electronic office equipment to replace them.[23]

The actions taken were bold: Ash hired a new president, James Mellor, to serve as his hatchet man. After scrutinizing the Multigraphics Development Center, Mellor terminated two thirds of the work because it was unrelated to the kinds of future products AM now wanted. The entire international division was abolished, and scores of upper-level managers became "dispensable." Factories that had duplicated each other's efforts were now specialized to be more efficient, and the corporate headquarters staff was cut in half. AM also began to push the sale of supplies, as that was where most of its profits came from.[24]

After one year Ash had boosted revenues by 10 percent, and had begun to restore AM to profitability after many losing years. AM shares appreciated by 55 percent in the two years after Ash took over, and the value of his own AM shares climbed by $1.5 million.

Harold S. Geneen at ITT was another master of core revival. Geneen was already a seasoned executive when he took over as CEO of the already substantial ITT. He had been trained as an accountant, and moved up the corporate hierarchy through the accounting and finance areas at Lybrand, American Can, Bell & Howell, Jones & Laughlin Steel, and Raytheon Manufacturing. In 1959, he was appointed president and CEO of International Telephone and Telegraph Corporation, inheriting what was essentially a European and Third World telecommunications company with lackluster performance and secular growth.

Geneen wanted to rationalize ITT—to add more promising lines, enhance efficiency, and reduce vulnerability. He was obsessive in seeking out operations that had to be developed and those that had to be shut down. By analyzing his divisions very carefully, he often found that 20 percent of ITT's products contributed as much as 80 percent of its profits. So, he terminated the weak lines and improved the stronger ones. And he implemented state-of-the-art reporting and information systems to monitor what was going on. New managers were hired to help revitalize sick divisions; and, in many cases, they succeeded in doubling profits within two to three years.[25]

Ultimately, Geneen built ITT into the biggest conglomerate on earth (1980 revenues of $23.8 billion vs. $766 million when he took over). He compiled over sixty quarters of continuous per-share earnings growth, creating a vast group of international companies. Between 1959 and 1977, ITT's profits rose from $29 to $562 million.[26]

Common Patterns

All three varieties of foundation building have a number of things in common that set the stage for expansion. First, in every case managers focus on the *big picture*—on global product-market strategies. They set about to develop entrepreneurial opportunities, broach promising markets, shed millstone products, and close down inefficient facilities. Second, managers devote much attention to *financial strategies*—to raising capital, issuing debt, generating cash flow, and cutting costs.

Both these patterns extend into the subsequent diversification phase. The global strategic emphasis becomes even wider-ranging. Attention to financial strategies increases. And growth and profit goals become still more ambitious, perhaps because of the early successes. In short, the bias toward action—toward building and creating—continues stronger than ever.

Diversification

Having successfully built a strong foundation or revitalized a weak one, Builders are encouraged to expand more aggressively in their quest for growth, money, and power. Such operational matters as quality, efficiency, and innovation are all subordinated to growth financing, diversification, and acquisition. Builders broaden product lines, develop their existing assets and properties, set up new divisions, and buy firms in complementary businesses.

Expansion can take place via both *related* and *unrelated* diversification. Builders may diversify into businesses or markets that are closely allied with their earlier ones, or they may move into more remotely related but complementary fields. But they are by no means content with just any expansion; in fact, they are very selective. First, Builders are careful to look for businesses that they know something about, or at least that strongly reinforce their existing operations. Second, they search diligently for bargains—for example, candidates with hidden assets, patents, good equipment, or highly valued expertise. Third, they do not overextend themselves, either administratively or financially, in making new acquisitions. They expand at a rate that is affordable, and they prime their administrative structures to assimilate and control the new acquisitions or projects. And fourth, Builders very actively manage their expanded operations—they get involved in the restaffing, consolidation, and renewal of their new territories. (As we shall see, during the course of the venturing trajectory this selectivity disappears as success and overconfidence make CEOs both greedy and careless.)

Related Diversification

At Dome, Jack Gallagher sought growth but avoided spending too much to pursue it. Dome's early acquisitions were brilliant: it picked up TransCanada PipeLines and Siebens Oil & Gas at bargain-basement prices. Siebens had rich landholdings in western Canada and mineral titles that allowed it to extract oil and gas without having to pay provincial royalties. Dome acquired the firm through Canpar, a tax-exempt pension fund, which bought the shares of Siebens. Dome then bought the Siebens assets very cheaply from Canpar, which did not have to pay tax on the sale. Since Dome was buying assets, not shares,

61

it was able to claim a fast write-off. It put down only $4 million in cash and floated $396 million in debentures. It was truly a brilliant coup.[27]

The same merciless exploitation of Canada's tax loopholes enabled Dome to acquire 65 percent of Mesa Petroleum, an American company. Gallagher's acquisitions were always integrated with Dome's existing operations in a way that either enhanced market power or saved money. His purchases were also modest in scale and made at rock-bottom prices.

Litton Industries, too, was highly selective in making its early acquisitions. It stuck to the high-tech business machine and medical electronics companies that it knew so much about and which capitalized on its ability to exploit new technologies. These ventures fitted "the Plan" devised by Thornton and Ash. Also, Litton had a superb sense of timing in its acquisitions—it concentrated on defense electronics components rather than the riskier whole military systems; and it stayed out of semiconductors when they were the rage, predicting, rightly, that the industry would be overproduced. Litton kept away from the market for big computers as well, developing instead a promising business in small, inexpensive ones. It designed inertial-guidance devices for the large market in military planes rather than for the more glamorous but hazardous space missile business.[28] Moreover, Litton spotted holes in the market, for example, for attack submarine equipment, and it filled them.

Even the impatient Harry Figgie at "Automatic" Sprinkler made his first acquisitions in related areas—namely, fire protection and construction. Figgie had an explicit plan for his purchases to ensure their complementarity. And his skill as a turnaround expert enabled him brilliantly to revive the fortunes of such ailing acquisitions as the Badger Fire Extinguisher Co.[29]

Unrelated Diversification

Some firms make a conscious effort to broaden their market scope—to enter markets that are entirely new to them in search of more propitious opportunities. This strategy is especially common among Builders who are in sluggish environments or mature industries and who wish to advance more quickly.

In contrast to Dome's strategy of highly related diversification, ITT moved further afield in its search for growth. Harold Geneen firmly believed that acquisitions were the only way to enter new areas. He wanted to diversify ITT in order to reduce its tremendous reliance on foreign subsidiaries and hostile foreign governments. He began first by developing ITT's domestic telecommunications operations, but its near monopoly in the United States limited the scope for expanding this traditional business. So Geneen looked to electronics manufacturing. He soon rejected this avenue of expansion because high price-earnings multiples made potential acquisitions too costly. His painstaking industry studies then unearthed opportunities in the services industries, where P/E ratios were lower and demographics indicated excellent growth potential. ITT's managers started in slowly, familiarizing themselves with the industries by buying small companies such as Hamilton Management Corp. and Aetna Finance Corp. The first big step came when Geneen swapped $41 million in stock for Avis Rent-A-Car in 1965. Heftier acquisitions followed only later as ITT diversified both geographically and into new manufacturing and service fields.[30]

Geneen, however, had been careful to control costs and to avoid the dangers of both redundancy and inefficiency. For its initial acquisitions, ITT minimized debt as it financed most purchases through common and preferred stock rather than debentures.[31] And in 1970, ITT's cash flow still averaged a healthy four times its annual interest charges.[32]

Some Builders shift from related to unrelated diversification. For example, at G&W, Charles Bluhdorn and his staff searched exhaustively for promising candidates—examining fifty or sixty prospects for each contemplated takeover. Even after lengthy preliminary negotiations, 80 percent of the deals fell through because of G&W's demanding terms. From 1958 to 1965, all acquisitions were in G&W's core industry, the making and distributing of auto parts. Bluhdorn was able to put together a solid component manufacturing complex and a distribution system streamlined by modern inventory controls.[33]

Eventually, Bluhdorn was to embark on a broad-ranging acquisition program in his headlong quest for growth. Even then, however, he showed a decided preference for prosaic companies in equally dull industries such as machine parts, cigars, and meatpacking. Indeed, Bluhdorn was most intent upon buying hard assets and stability. He went after well-established companies in conventional, non-cyclical businesses and with underutilized resources.[34]

In short, in Builders diversification takes place energetically but with caution, scrutiny, and an eye for the complementarity of operations.

Creative Financing

All Builders pay a lot of attention to the finance function because they have to raise so much capital for expansion. And of course they need to work out the best financial deals for acquiring or merging with other firms.

Bernie Cornfeld at IOS was not only a master of fund gathering; he also knew how to leverage his capital with different classes of stock in order to obtain the most control with the least money. IOS's financial wizards devised "elegantly complicated, audaciously vast schemes and leverages." Their funds were incorporated offshore to avoid taxes. And IOS's ingenious stock options reduced salary expenses while raising a great deal of capital for expansion.[35]

Dome financed many of its takeovers by exploiting the Canadian tax system, using pension funds to buy shares and then having Dome purchase assets which it could write off. Gallagher also lobbied with the Canadian government for lucrative depletion allowances that would underwrite over 80 percent of Dome's exploration expenses on its most promising frontier sites.

G&W leveraged its capital with borrowings. According to Bluhdorn: "Compare the price of anything twenty years ago and its price today; the best buy you can make today is to put out paper and know that twenty years from now you can pay out the same amount of money."[36] And Litton deliberately kept its growth rate and P/E multiples high in order to make acquisitions for exchange of stock at favorable terms.

ENTREPRENEURIAL LEADERS

Ambitious, aggressive, and independent, all Builder leaders have expansion as their principal goal—and they pursue it relentlessly, especially after the foundation-building phase. It is then that CEOs become generalists, who start to plot out grandiose plans for growth and diversification, and prefer not to concern themselves with niggling operational matters.

Energy and Ambition

These leaders are irrevocably committed to corporate development and the pursuit of demanding financial goals—no matter what the obstacles. They want prominence; they want convincing successes; and they want to get where they're going quickly. Toward those ends, they demand fanatical dedication, both from themselves and from their managers.

Bernard Cornfeld's declared ambition was to make his Investors Overseas Services "the most important economic force in the Free World."[37] A former friend is more realistic: "Bernie's ambition was always to make a lot of money."[38] This was not a passing whim, but a consuming passion that translated itself every day into the pursuit of fund sales and profits. Cornfeld was constantly devising schemes for new ventures, pursuing his goals with remarkable energy and ardor. And he expected his employees to do likewise.

The same was true of Harold Geneen at ITT. According to Geneen,

> The primary difference between an entrepreneur and a profes-sional business manager, generally speaking, is one of attitude. The entrepreneur, especially when he is starting out, knows that he is oper-ating on the threshold of success or failure. A single mistake can ruin him. . . . While others leave the office at five o'clock, he stays behind and works to solve those problems that beset his business. He must manage. He takes his problems home with him. . . . The professional manager all too often loses that sense of commitment, if he had it in the first place. All too often, he manages by the book. He relies upon the knowledge that he is working for a company large enough to ab-sorb a number of mistakes . . . which allows management the luxury of not managing.[39]

Management was an all-consuming business to Geneen—objectives had to be met. And Geneen spared himself least of all, putting in twelve-hour days six or seven days a week, absorbing countless details about ITT's business so that he could keep up with his expanding empire.

Bill Richards, the president of Dome, was a man cut from the same cloth. He was a dedicated workaholic who came to the office on weekends and called many meetings for 8:00 A.M. on Sundays. Jim

Lyon reports that Richards was known to run two or three meetings simultaneously. "Dropping into a subordinate's office for a two-minute conversation, he paces up and down constantly. At times he seems almost like a Hollywood stereotype of a hard-driving business executive, bounding from crisis to crisis, an ever present telephone . . . at his head."[40]

Thornton, Bluhdorn, Cornfeld, Figgie, Geneen, and the Gallagher-Richards team all had enormous ambition—they wanted not only financial success but to build a significant enterprise, indeed, a business empire. This dream gave them the vision and energy to persist in the face of numerous obstacles. Ultimately, it also fostered greed, grandiosity, and strategic imperialism.

"Spare Me the Details"

As they built their firms' foundations, leaders dealt head on with such operating details as production costs, customer reactions, and marketing problems. Afterwards, however, they begin to concern themselves mainly with broader issues such as strategic plans, diversification, and capital structure. They lose interest in the specifics of products and markets and start to concentrate on the bottom line.

This shift is best illustrated by the contrast between Dome's founder, Jack Gallagher, and Bill Richards, who became president in 1974. Unlike Gallagher, Richards had no interest in the firm's technology: he only once visited the Arctic where Dome was engaged in its pioneering explorations. He believed that it was far more sensible and less time-consuming to be briefed by experts in his office than to go "traipsing around looking at a bunch of machinery I don't understand." Field trips bored him, so he avoided them. Richards was at heart a corporate acquisitor, obsessed with the imperative of growth.[41] Ash, Geneen, Bluhdorn, Figgie, and Thornton were cast in much the same mold.

Some leaders adopt a new vocabulary and conceptual framework that reflects their need to expand and diversify. For example, at "Automatic" Sprinkler, Figgie crafted a deliberate plan to erect a corporate giant based on an explicitly articulated business philosophy. As a former management consultant, he certainly knew the language. Figgie propounded a "nucleus theory of growth," both in internal documents and to shareholders, who received a 33⅓ rpm record on the subject in the mail. The theory claims that optimum corporate growth can only be achieved if acquisitions are restricted to industries with outstanding growth potential. The first acquisition in an industry serves as a "nucleus." Other firms are then acquired in the same field to cluster around the nucleus. Eventually, so the logic goes, a group will be developed that is big enough to be a powerful force in its industry. Companies acquired are all subject to a "three part program of cost reduction, sales and market expansion, and product research and development."[42]

These explicit expansion strategies were articulated at Litton as well, and at AM during the Ash years. In fact, *Fortune* reporter Louis Kraar was moved to comment that Ash's "rapid flow of management buzzwords frequently sound more like academic lectures than the marching orders for an ailing corporation."[43]

The point of all this: that CEOs have raised their sights and ambitions; they have articulated an explicit plan of expansion; and they have adopted a corporate (multi-business) rather than a business-level vision. Already the operating details have become secondary in their minds to overarching schemes and long-term programs.

Stretching the Rules

Their ambitions are so all-consuming that Builders are sometimes willing to stretch, elude, or even break the law to achieve them.

IOS, for example, was domiciled offshore in Geneva to avoid U.S. laws and government scrutiny that might have inhibited some rather questionable financial practices. Cornfeld used to refer to the administrators of the SEC as "shmucks." "I like to think our relations with the SEC in future will have all the intimacy of that now existing between [the divorced] Elizabeth Taylor and Eddie Fisher."[44]

ITT under Geneen became infamous for the "Dita Beard" scandal in which the firm was implicated in the overthrow of the Allende government in Chile, illegal contributions to the Nixon campaign, and hyper-aggressive lobbying. Dome's Gallagher was himself a brilliant lobbyist who fairly won many concessions from the Canadian government. But he was also known as an overly shrewd dealmaker who had to be watched very carefully.[45] People of overwhelming ambition, it seems, will stop at almost nothing.

GROWTH CULTURES

Because leaders are so keen to grow, they establish meritocracies that handsomely reward only stars. Laggards are let go. In other words, the corporate culture of the Builder admits no free riders. It is a proud and fierce culture, emboldened by past achievements. But bottom-line financial performance is respected above all else. Bring in the sales and profits, and you will be lavishly paid and rapidly promoted. The sky is the limit. Fail, and you are out.

Pride and Optimism

Within the organization, sagas of creation and growth are recounted with awe and reverence. In a sense, they reflect the "myth of the birth of the venture"—from fragile, tentative beginnings to present prowess—a myth that feeds the ambition of an organization, confirms its strengths, and gives it the optimism to keep pushing ahead. These sagas set the stage for the strategic theme: namely, the Builder as a shaper of, rather than a reactor to, its environment. They reveal, almost from the very beginning, a striving for corporate mass—for influence, for dominance, for control. As time passes, leaders and managers compare their humble start with the dramatically increased scale and breadth of their new ventures. And the resulting sense of accomplishment spurs them on toward yet grander schemes.

Sink or Swim

To better meet his ambitious growth goals, Geneen used to throw young executives in over their heads to see if they could swim. He worried very little about whether his subordinates liked him. According to one former executive, "He sets the standards—you meet them and the rewards are fantastic—responsibility at an early age, always being given opportunity after opportunity. Hal gives you a chance to either strike out or hit a home run in the world series."[46]

The result was a lot of turnover; but Geneen was happy to lose his weaker employees and to have the opportunity to recruit more ambitious and aggressive replacements. In fact, he recruited extensively and paid very well to find the best people, many of whom made their contribution and left because they "wouldn't be career employees in anybody's company except their own."[47]

Financially Motivated

For Craftsmen, the craft is its own intrinsic reward. However, consistent with their adherence to bottom-line standards, Builders motivate their employees with extrinsic inducements: high salaries, bonuses and prizes, promotions, even stock options that elicit longer-term achievement. These all serve as powerful growth incentives.

IOS operated in a cutthroat industry where firms constantly raided each other for salesmen. To keep good men against the schemes of predatory rivals was a considerable feat, which Cornfeld performed through the lure of fortune and fame—or more precisely, with a seductive reward system of great financial and psychological subtlety. He kept his salesmen happy with lavish presents, awards of profitable sales territory, and admirable financial remuneration. Salesmen were always called capital-A "Associates" to confer upon them a sense of membership in a professional elite. Everyone who did a million dollars' worth of business was ceremoniously "decorated" with a Patek Philippe gold wristwatch. Even Bernie's own lavish lifestyle was at least partly intended to give Associates something to shoot for. As he said in "his splendidly arrogant whisper": "I suppose a salesman might find it easier to identify with me, as a symbol of success, than with mousy Jacob Rothschild, fiddling with his pencil."[48]

IOS had a stock purchase scheme that was a further inducement for employees to stay. The plan made it appealing to a salesman to contract for his shares immediately. This placed him in IOS's debt, which he repaid by making more sales and recruiting more Associates. As the head of the British sales force put it, "When you sign up with Bernie, it's for keepsville."[49] The stock plan also generated cash for IOS's expansions into fund management companies, investment banks, insurance companies, and real estate concerns.

All of our Builders devoted a good deal of attention to compensation, particularly compensation that was directly tied to performance. For example, ITT was known to pay generous bonuses tied to a unit's profits. Gallagher at Dome gave his employees juicy stock options which made many of them very wealthy. And the same was true at Litton. Through a foundation set up by Thornton with his own holdings, "you could get Litton stock for a few dollars a share when it was selling in the market for $60. People got very rich, very fast."[50] Recall that most CEOs owned plenty of stock in their organizations; so they wanted their employees also to have a stake that would motivate them to push for growth.

Workaholism in a Meritocracy

Much is offered, but much is also expected. And those who are competent rise through the ranks very quickly. Builders breed workaholics.

As two ITT executives commented about Harold Geneen: "He sets almost attainable standards that either stretch a person or break him," and "He forces people to think who have never thought in their lives; part of it is for survival." Geneen made it clear that he expected a great deal of work and endless amounts of time from his managers—and he got both.[51]

The rewards were commensurate with the Herculean effort. Geneen offered talented managers who were still in their thirties an opportunity to run a major ITT division at salaries most would have dreamed impossible, paying 50 percent more than they could have made anywhere else. He took chances on young managers with apparent potential who had not yet had the opportunity to display it.[52]

At Dome, the workload could be as fierce as at ITT. There were many three-day negotiating meetings in which participants on take-over deals would not sleep for seventy-two hours—functioning on coffee and adrenaline. But people thrived on the energy. According to one former employee, "Getting to work at Dome in its glory days was a bit like taking holy orders, but the worldly rewards were better. To be a Dome employee was to be someone special, a bit like belonging to an elite regiment."[53]

Dome's superb team of headhunters recruited managerial talent from all around the world. The hallmarks of a Dome person were said to be aggressiveness, education, and an assertive intelligence. And Dome hired its fair share of rebels, whom it heeded—again, if they performed well. If someone volunteered to take on extra responsibilities, the work would be heaped upon him.[54]

All these aspects of culture—the sink-or-swim system, the financial incentives, and the workaholism—served the overarching goal of growth: a goal firmly embraced by ambitious leaders and thoroughly reflected in all elements of Builder strategy.

DIVISIONAL STRUCTURES

Because Builders have diversified so extensively and grown so much, they adopt market-based, divisionalized structures in order to facilitate control and free top managers to work on strategic matters. Such structures also spread initiative and responsibility to the divisional heads so as to further stimulate growth. There are three major characteristics that distinguish the structures of Builders. First, firms are usually divided into segments, whose leaders are responsible for the overall profitability of a particular product line or territory. Whereas corporate-level policy making takes place at headquarters, the authority for operating decisions resides with the division heads. Second, sophisticated management information systems are used to monitor and control the divisions. A third characteristic is related as much to decision making as to structure—it is the use of formal analysis by the accounting and financial staff. All of these structural devices are necessary to support the strategy of diversification.

Centralized Policy Making; Decentralized Operations

As Builders expand and diversify, their top managers no longer have enough expertise, information, or time to make most of the necessary operating decisions. So they delegate authority for these decisions to the divisional managers who are most familiar with particular products and markets. Profit centers are established to make the divisional managers responsible for the bottom-line performance of their units. And the division managers report to the corporate head office, which continues to make decisions about major expansions, capital budgeting, potential acquisitions, and large divestments, usually with the help of a staff cadre and a wide-ranging information system.[55] Such a structure motivates those managers with the greatest expertise to use their knowledge and initiative to pursue growth; it frees top managers to make strategic corporate decisions; and it allows quick responses to changes in the environment. Here are some examples of how this structure worked in our Builders.[56]

Geneen gave his divisional executives a lot of room to grow. He

71

accorded managers much authority, but at the same time prodded and questioned them. As one divisional manager at ITT reported, "He expected me to put my neck on the line," insisting on specific targets and evaluating performance accordingly. "Geneen would assign responsibility and expect you to do it and not run back to him for any little question. He makes you make the decisions and get the job done. He doesn't care how you accomplish something: as long as it is running according to plan, you'll have very little communication with the man. [Otherwise] you'd better prepare to have a good reason why not and a good suggestion about how to get it back on track."[57] On the one hand, executives had a good deal of freedom; on the other, Geneen was always there probing for weak spots.

Evidently, however, authority was not all that decentralized. To help monitor the divisions, Geneen employed eight staff product-line managers, who divided product planning and marketing into international groups such as telecommunications, components, avionics, and consumer products. They reported directly to Geneen and made frequent recommendations to operating officers. Also, ITT's newly acquired firms had to channel all changes in personnel, engineering, marketing, and so on through a central ITT staffer. They were indoctrinated in ITT standards and procedures, and slotted into an industry group, where functions such as marketing and R&D were centralized, and where related ITT companies pooled resources to serve one broad market.[58]

Dome's Bill Richards had a looser management style. He once said, "I don't want to see tedious rows of figures. I assume the arithmetic is right and the work has been done properly. I want a proposal and an analysis and options and a reasonable review of the assumptions. My view of a well run company is that you always delegate the maximum amount of responsibility to the lowest possible level."[59]

The same attitude prevailed at Litton. At meetings and in corporate documents, Litton tirelessly enunciated its principles of decentralization and control. Roy Ash as president ran the day-to-day internal affairs, while Tex Thornton as chairman handled external affairs. Said Thornton: "No division reports to me directly, but the point is that anybody can walk into Roy's office or my office any time." He created a loose, informal style of management that kept everyone moving; the centralizing of major investment decisions was combined with a decentralizing of everyday operating matters. Headquarters employed a staff of ninety people, which was pretty lean given the size and diversity of the firm.[60]

The point of decentralization was to allow adequate control at head office without extinguishing the advantages of local expertise and initiative. It also freed up top managers' time for their expansion ventures.

Sharp Intelligence Systems

Builders implement smart management information systems to provide them with revealing information about their decentralized divisions. In fact, such systems become a primary means of control.

Thornton and Ash, the ex-Whiz Kids, had legendary expertise in designing control and information systems; indeed, they had almost invented the book.[61] At Litton, they installed a highly regarded system of internal forecasting and reporting under which every division's performance was measured at least once a month against detailed plans and projections.[62]

Control could be tight. Operating managers prepared monthly financial statements describing their progress toward established goals. Before each fiscal year, every division had to produce a detailed annual plan and forecast, which managers had to justify not only to the head of their group but also to the "murder squad" of corporate executives, usually including Roy Ash. All plans were revised and updated every three months.[63]

But it was ITT under Harold Geneen that devised the most sophisticated and celebrated control system. Geneen's approach was three-pronged, with a powerful central management group, semiautonomous divisions, and a highly refined system of goals and controls. Here's how the system was described in *Dun's Review*:

> Each ITT manager throughout the system sends to world headquarters in New York a monthly report detailing all facts affecting the performance of his unit. Often running to twenty single spaced pages, the report must contain financial analyses of sales, profits, return on investment and virtually every other measurement used in the business. What is more, it must describe every existing and potential problem affecting the operation. "All hell breaks loose," confides one ITTer, "when a problem that should have been put into the report has not been put in. That's when Geneen gets really livid." . . . The report also must explain exactly how the problem will be solved.[64]

Reports from all of ITT's operating units were mimeographed, collated, bound into sets, and airmailed to each manager, who had to prepare for the monthly management meeting held soon afterwards at world headquarters in New York. Ten times a year, the massive looseleaf books were emptied and the whole process began anew. The six-inch books were the heart of ITT's system of management around the world. "There's more intelligence in these books over a period of time," said Geneen, "than you can buy from 100 services."[65]

The monthly meetings in New York were marathon events lasting up to three days and running late into the night. Geneen presided and was the principal interrogator. Reports were picked apart, discussed, and molded into "action assignments." In addition to these monthly rituals, once a year each ITT company had to develop an exhaustive five-year business plan, which was reviewed annually by regional and headquarters staff. "These are real working meetings," boasted Geneen. "There's no substitute for getting the facts."[66]

ITT also used a distinctive system of financial control: "The controller of an ITT subsidiary has two direct bosses: the president of his business and the corporate controller at world headquarters. Both get the controller's reports, a system ensuring that operating results aren't fudged by the president."[67]

Analytical Decision Making

Because of the risk and expenditure involved in their major new investments, Builders characteristically analyze before they act. They diligently scan their environments and carry out thorough financial assessments before making any final commitments.

For example, when Roy Ash took over as a major shareholder and CEO of Addressograph-Multigraph, he undertook a highly detailed analysis of all its operations, identifying precisely which products and units were profitable, who was the competition, which development projects had the best chances of succeeding, and so on. Instead of immediately starting to rebuild AM, Ash spent a few months visiting its widely dispersed facilities and asking a lot of searching questions. "He wanted to get a handle on all the operations and assess the key people who ran them."[68]

In studying AM, Ash "kept jotting down what he saw as the issues that had to be resolved." They made up what he referred to as his "brick pile" for redesigning AM, and included some two hundred items, ranging from problem products to organizational difficulties. It was Ash's intention to make the company's executives "re-question everything."[69]

To recap, the Builder configuration revolves around the theme of growth: firms build their foundations to prepare themselves for the subsequent period of diversification and expansion. Entrepreneurial leaders then formulate and carry out strategic grand plans and establish up-or-out cultures that push managers to achieve ambitious financial goals. And they set up decentralized, divisional structures to control their burgeoning empires and assimilate new divisions. These structures energize lower levels and free top managers for their entrepreneurial projects. They also give rise to a cadre of financial and accounting staff that begins to play an increasing role as the venturing trajectory unfolds.

THE TRANSITION TO IMPERIALIST

Builders are so very successful. Their painstaking foundation building and selective diversification have borne extraordinary rewards and have transformed them into major enterprises. Although it is apparent that caution, control, and periodic consolidation all contribute to a Builder's success, leaders give the chief credit to diversification and expansion. The fruits of growth are all too visible: dramatic increases in revenues and profits, skyrocketing price-earnings multiples, and CEO fortunes that attract worldwide attention. But such success breeds overconfidence and an urge for still quicker growth—especially among leaders who are eternally optimistic and financially aggressive. Our Builders are now primed to become Imperialists.

Imperialists increase their pace and range of development, straying far from familiar businesses and incurring much onerous debt. In a classic case of strategic momentum, Builders recklessly extend and amplify the strategy of diversification. Instead of carefully orchestrating their growth and being selective about how they branch out, they grope for size and start to chase after alien and even crippled acquisitions. What is worse, their former fascination with the big picture makes them neglect the vital details of their products and markets.

Such overexpansion strains both the company's managerial and its financial resources. Overtaxed managers who must cope with businesses and issues they don't understand tend to make serious errors; unassimilated acquisitions render the culture chaotic; and severely proliferating operations overwhelm the crucial reporting and information systems.

Of course, with an inadequate system of controls and a structure that is already overburdened, leaders will not be warned of the perils of such overexpansion. So the problem only gets worse. (Figure 3 summarizes the venturing trajectory.)

IMPERIALIST STRATEGIES

Imperialists escalate the very strategies that served them so successfully as Builders. First, they increase the already considerable pace of expansion, taxing company resources and making mistakes. Second,

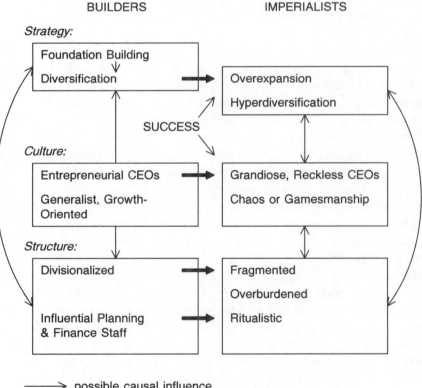

FIGURE 3
The Venturing Trajectory

in continuing to diversify, they move further and further afield, getting into markets and product lines they know too little about. Third, they increasingly neglect strategic details as they worship the bottom line. And fourth, they accelerate an already substantial tendency toward risk taking, and often take on massive borrowings.

Hyperexpansion

Like Builders at the diversification stage, Imperialists have as their major objective the conquest of more territory. Whereas Builders were careful to balance selective growth with consolidation, however, Imperialists show no such restraint. They simply move as fast as possible into colossal projects and grandiose schemes. Mistakes increase with the pace and scale of expansion as managerial and financial resources and the infrastructure of control are all stretched paper-thin.

In the late 1970s, Dome Petroleum launched an uncontrolled burst of furious expansion, probably unequaled in Canadian economic history. According to Dome historian Jim Lyon, "For a while, it seemed that the company was being driven by an irresistible urge to become the dominant force in the Canadian oil industry overnight, with just a few throws of the dice."[70]

Dome, under the expansionary Bill Richards, leveraged itself to the hilt, borrowing too much money to do too many things. Its managers were described as "buying everything in sight and doing it on credit, a hell of a risk." Soaring interest rates and collapsing oil prices exacerbated the problem of mounting debt. By 1977, Dome had acquired Arctic assets of nearly $1 billion. And over the next five years, it purchased Canada's biggest natural gas pipelines; oil interests in Texas, the North Sea, and Indonesia; gold mines; and even a shipbuilding company.[71]

But the final blow was to come in the form of a seductive opportunity. In 1981, the Canadian federal government introduced an incentive plan for frontier exploration whose benefits were proportional to a firm's degree of Canadian ownership. As Dome was mostly owned by Americans, it set up a new company, Dome Canada, which sold its shares to Canadians in the biggest stock offering in the nation's history. The new Canadian policy depressed the value of foreign oil and gas holdings, making them cheaper for Canadian firms such as Dome Canada to buy. The firm gorged itself, abetted by the Canadian banks who were only too eager to lend money for such "fire-sale" acquisitions.[72]

Dome, in 1981, went after Conoco, the tenth largest U.S. oil company, in an effort to capture its 53 percent of Hudson's Bay Oil and Gas (HBOG). First, Dome bought 22 of the 53 million shares of Conoco; then it paid $245 million for Conoco's HBOG interest—the total cost came to $1.68 billion. Even before the Conoco deal, Dome was more than $2.2 billion in debt. But by 1982, Dome loans amounted to $5.8 billion, six times equity and about half of the total capital of Canada's three biggest chartered banks. And the company could not repay in time.[73] The government of Canada had to come forward with a rescue package.

"Automatic" Sprinkler was to meet with a similar fate, and CEO Harry Figgie's overly hasty acquisition program was largely to blame. AS exploded with multiple acquisitions in industries new to its management. Figgie bought four companies in 1965 and another four the next year, almost doubling AS sales both times. But the pace was to accelerate still further. As we have seen, in mid-1967, four acquisitions were completed within a twenty-five-day period, eleven for the year. This was just too fast to allow for an adequate examination of merger partners before deals were made, or for the acquired firms to be properly assimilated before management's attention was diverted by yet other purchases. Between 1967 and 1968, AS's per-share profits fell from $1.43 to $0.10, and the share price plummeted from $70 to $19.[74]

Roy Ash at AM moved at a somewhat more measured pace, but only barely so. Having turned his firm around, Ash's growing extravagance promptly propelled it, once again, into decline. Said one security analyst: "Ash's big blunder was his failure to build a solid foundation on profits before making acquisitions. Roy Ash was building a skyscraper on sand." He acquired a slew of companies manufacturing electronic office equipment. According to one analyst of the day: "Ash sped ahead with his plans. First, he plopped down $3 million of cash for Infortext, a Chicago producer of terminals for monitoring the use of paper copiers. Then he hired 120 salesmen to market the products, but 18 months later the division was virtually shut down."[75]

Ash also invested $18 million in Jacquard-Systems, a manufacturer of word processors, and bought out ECRM, which made text-editing machines, for $5 million. These again were costly acquisitions that proved unrewarding because of their bloated marketing staff, sloppy financial controls, and high management turnover (Jacquard alone lost $22 million in 1980).

AM lost $16 million in the first two quarters of 1981; debt as a percentage of total capitalization had shot up from 34 percent when Ash took over in 1976, to 55 percent in 1981; cash dwindled from $42 million to $4 million during the same period; and inventories as a percent of sales grew from 23 to 29 percent. Not surprisingly, the turnover in staff also soared.[76]

Such hyperexpansion drains Imperialists of their resources, leaving them with a bunch of ailing, underperforming units and wads of debt. Often the very survival of these organizations is threatened as expansionary zeal turns into naked greed.

Diversifying into Areas of Ignorance

Not only is the pace of expansion a problem, but so is its scope. In extending a once complementary diversification strategy, many Imperialists move ever further away from their own areas of expertise as they try to encompass a hodgepodge of operations. Cohesive strategies are destroyed as firms blindly pursue growth for its own sake.

Litton had done very well in its military markets. But it started to move into businesses such as office furniture that it did not understand. Litton also knew nothing about the shipbuilding business it had just entered, and it badly underestimated the costs of some of its large contracts.[77]

Fortune's Tom O'Hanlon described the problem: "[Litton] sought to project itself as unique, staffed by executives who could successfully manage any business. But its acquisitions orgy bought [it] a lot of duds. And it lacked operating managers for the good businesses it retained. In the early 70's it gave the appearance of an outfit that was being managed with clumsiness, if not desperation."[78]

In fact, Litton made over a hundred acquisitions, purchasing troubled firms that demanded a lot of attention. It was so sure of its ability to turn around its subsidiaries that their condition at the time of purchase was slighted. Tex Thornton's high-tech experience and his legendary prowess at management control, "Whiz Kid style," led him to think of business in the broadest, boldest terms. Said O'Hanlon: "Bigness was an integral part of the plan which led to the astonishing burst of acquisitions in the 1960's. Thornton believed that technology could improve virtually any business. [As he raced] to build a big company in a favorable political climate, he sometimes seemed to be picking off businesses at random."[79]

By 1968, earnings and share prices had fallen over 50 percent from the previous year. Litton stock, which was at $92 in 1967 (an astronomical forty-seven times earnings), was below $3 seven years later, "giving it all the glamour of a Czarist railroad bond."[80]

Charlie Bluhdorn, who had begun with systematic and related expansion, similarly started to stretch his Gulf & Western Industries to the limit with far-ranging diversification projects. He made seventy-two corporate acquisitions in a single decade. Bluhdorn tried to swallow behemoths that he couldn't properly digest, and amassed an incongruous collection of companies ranging from apparel to sugar refining to zinc mining. Bluhdorn's was truly a pell-mell acquisitions policy. He tried to buy Armour & Co., whose sales were three times G&W's. Other Brobdingnagian deals brought in Paramount for $125 million, and Desilu Productions. What's worse, Bluhdorn was so intent upon maintaining his empire that he was emotionally bound to his acquisitions, hanging on to even the least rewarding ones.

His purchases drove sales up from $180 million in 1965 to $1.3 billion in 1967.[81] But by 1983, Bluhdorn's hodgepodge of unrelated companies was still earning only $169 million on revenues of $5.3 billion; return on equity was a dismal 7.7 percent. The new CEO, Martin Davis, was forced to sell off sixty-five subsidiaries with over $4 billion in revenues to revitalize G&W.[82]

Bernie Cornfeld's diversifications were even more unfelicitous than those of Bluhdorn. IOS embraced a free-floating, almost directionless strategy as it branched into underwriting and banking, fields it knew nothing about. President Ed Cowett was fond of saying, "The best corporate planning is a lack of planning in the formal sense. . . . We [only] have an overall plan to do business on as broad a basis as we possibly can." In other words, we'll go anywhere and do anything, as long as it makes us bigger.[83] In 1969, the share price of IOS fell from $19 to $1.50 and the firm was losing $12 million per year. The dying company was soon to be taken over by the now fugitive financier Robert Vesco.[84]

Even the brilliantly analytical and rather more cautious Harold Geneen ran into trouble by expanding the ITT empire too widely. Despite its sophisticated structure and magnificent information systems, ITT's acquisitions finally became unwieldy. One former colleague suggested: "Three things should be written on Hal Geneen's tombstone—earnings per share, 15% growth per year, and size." From 1967 to 1970, just six of ITT's larger acquisitions—Sheraton, Levitt, Rayonier, Continental Baking, Grinnell, and Canteen—brought in combined sales of $1.8 billion. And Hartford Fire, the sixth largest U.S. property and casualty company, was about to be added. This stretched management capabilities almost intolerably, increasing the number of executives from 450 to 2,200 between 1959 and 1970.[85]

When Geneen retired in 1978, ITT was left with "an incredible hodgepodge" of firms—of mature properties, such as Europe's tele-communications groups, and new ventures such as Eason Oil and Carbon Industries, a coal company for which ITT paid $269 million but which, according to one expert, "would never have sold for much over $100 million to anyone with coal expertise."[86]

By 1977, ITT had grown to 375,000 employees in 80 countries, operating in 250 diverse profit centers. Three of its eight major indus-trial groups—natural resources, telecommunications, and consumer services and products—were plagued by operating problems. Be-tween 1971 to 1979, there was virtually no growth in earnings per share, and the market accorded ITT stock a price-earnings multiple of just over 6 when the individual industries it was in averaged multi-ples of 9. The need for consolidation was becoming obvious.[87]

Evidently the headlong rush for growth pulled each of these Im-perialists into a messy collection of unrelated businesses. A number of acquisitions faltered because remote top managers and head-office accountants simply hadn't the industry expertise—the knowledge of actual products and markets—to create or maintain any truly distinc-tive competitive advantages. This problem was compounded by the frenetic pace of expansion and the drawing down of cash reserves.

Many of our Imperialists got into trouble because they embraced a so-called conglomerate rationale that led them into a vicious cycle. It goes something like this. Firms with a high price-earnings multiple can more cheaply buy those with a lower multiple, purchasing a controlling share of a target's stock by offering their own, more expen-sive stock in return. The price of the conglomerate's shares is in turn supported by the rapid growth it achieves via such takeovers. The firms taken over are reorganized to enhance divisional profits, thereby boosting overall profits—and hence share price. In other words, firms try to increase the price of their shares to make acquisitions *by making* acquisitions. To make matters worse, many buyer firms also increase their financial leverage, deliberately restricting the supply of common stock that benefits from increased profits. Imperialists thus take on much debt to finance their expansion. One false move and growth levels off, debt becomes onerous, and the house of cards comes tumbling down.

Neglecting Strategic Details

The deemphasis of operational details that begins when Builders are diversifying becomes outright neglect in Imperialists—whose leaders are often bored with, and remote from, operations. Leaders skirt technological, design, and marketing concerns and are ignorant about many of the new businesses they have entered. They are so busy expanding and acquiring firms that they haven't the time to tend to or learn about their existing operations. In addition, an exclusive concern with the bottom-line "big picture" by managers and their head-office accounting and finance staffs allows devastating oversights at the micro levels.

Litton's executives, for example, were so intent on looking into the future and pursuing grandiose growth plans that they bungled the more immediate operating challenges.[88] They failed to cut the ponderous workforce in Litton's staggering business equipment group, they were late in introducing electronic calculators, and they tried to compete against Xerox in copiers with a bland machine that had no advantages. Indeed, Litton was often left far behind in business machine technology, perhaps because by tying incentives to a division's return on gross assets it discouraged managers from spending enough on R&D.[89]

While Roy Ash was diversifying AM, he both created and neglected key operating problems. His haphazard and violent restructuring of the key duplicator division alienated the salesforce and caused many top salesmen to quit. A faulty $2 million inventory control system caused severe production foul-ups. And an unpopular move of the head office to Los Angeles angered employees, cost a bundle, and severely disrupted operations. As *Fortune* reported: "Ash tripped over his grandiose dreams for the future. He preferred to talk about where AM would be in five years rather than where it was at the moment. Everyday problems bored Ash, even as they multiplied."[90]

It is hardly surprising that aggressive conglomerators such as Figgie, Bluhdorn, and Thornton should have run into trouble with operational problems. But Harold Geneen at ITT was known as a manager's manager—a man whose command of detail was legendary. It is a testimony to the hazards of imperialism that even such a genius could be overwhelmed. Geneen's concern with expansion, and with the bottom-line performance of ITT's divisions, caused him to neglect such important details of strategy as product quality, customer needs, manufacturing cost, competition, and marketing effectiveness. Because of its lackluster marketing and inadequate R&D, ITT lost its leadership role in telecommunications, which still accounted for 33 percent of its sales volume.

"ITT has blown more telecommunications opportunities in the past ten years than any other company," said Harry Newton, president of Telecom Library, Inc., a telecommunications research group. "ITT has faced the same opportunities that hundreds of newcomers have faced in this industry. But ITT has not had the resources or management focus or attention or discipline to do anything."[91]

Most of ITT's telecommunications sales were in simple telephones. At the high end of the market, its products were few and dated. And Northern Telecom, Western Electric, and L. M. Ericcson left it way behind in critical product areas. In fact, ITT put out only one low-end PBX automated switchboard. "They offer products of old design and they haven't been quick to react," said analyst William Ambrose. ITT was used to marketing to governments through lobbying but was very poor at selling to end-user markets. It never seemed to be in touch with what customers wanted. Also, ITT's XTRA personal computers proved to be just another product in an already overcrowded field.[92]

According to one analyst, "Harold Geneen was an absolute disaster as an operating manager . . . you have only to look at the record—he could acquire companies but not manage them. And his further failing was that he could not recognize this."[93]

An intimate knowledge of processes, goods and services, and markets is necessary to run any business. But as our Imperialists expanded, this knowledge began to disappear. Many firms were dominated by generalist CEOs and their accounting and finance staffs, rather than by engineering, manufacturing, or marketing people. This drove an abstract variety of "management-by-numbers" that failed to grapple with the substantive issues.[94]

Financial Risk and Extravagance

In order to expand and diversify, Imperialists classically over-spend. They take on too much debt, purchase cash-hungry operations, and indulge themselves in corporate luxuries. The "conglomerate rationale" mentioned earlier is one reason why Imperialists try to grow as quickly as possible and refuse to dilute their equity. Instead, they issue costly debt. Ailing acquisitions also drain away precious resources. And perhaps most fatally, a good growth record fosters a sense of wealth that extinguishes cost-consciousness.

President Bill Richards at Dome was obsessed by growth, as he charged boldly from one acquisition to another. According to one critic, "His idea of capital budgeting was to tell a manager that he wasn't spending enough money."[95] When Jack Gallagher argued that Dome was growing too fast, Richards always overwhelmed him with his enthusiasm. Dome's buying sprees and Gallagher's reluctance to finance them with equity created a huge appetite for debt, which Canada's overoptimistic banks were glad to accommodate.[96]

Incredibly, even after Dome had piled on its backbreaking debt, it did more borrowing to buy Cyprus Anvil Mining Corporation, a firm that mines lead and zinc. Dome stuck to its plans for lavish spending in 1982, budgeting for state-of-the-art drilling ships in the Beaufort Sea. And in spite of looming problems in servicing the debt, Gallagher refused to sell off any assets. As soon as oil prices eased and interest rates rose, Dome became, for all purposes, insolvent.[97]

Thornton at Litton and Bluhdorn at G&W also amassed enormous borrowings that would burden their respective operations for years to come. Surprisingly, even ITT with its legions of accountants took on too much debt. Geneen became an avid borrower, expecting that long-term inflation would allow ITT to repay its obligations with cheaper currency. He also needed leverage to finance the growth he craved so strongly. By the early 1970s, ITT's debt was close to 50 percent of total capitalization; indeed, the firm was taking on the financial profile of a public utility.[98]

ITT's far-flung operations also represented an enormous cash drain. According to Brian Fernandez of Nomura Securities, "Nobody realizes the terrific strategic box that Geneen built for the company by not clearly thinking through the future cash requirements of all the businesses."[99] Even Geneen himself loaded up on extravagances such as a Boeing 727 with a forward cabin that, according to one passenger, "made airline first class look like a freedom flight." Among other creature comforts, ITT purchased hunting and fishing lodges and a corporate houseboat in the Florida Keys.[100]

Sometimes, rapid growth itself engenders the illusion of wealth and prompts lavish expenditures. Bernie "I-like-the-good-life" Cornfeld's grandiosity made IOS a high-living company. A former Montreal sales manager gives one explanation for the big-spending mentality. "We decided we were rich and just started spending . . . bigger offices, better locations, more expensive furnishings . . . more secretaries, a new intercom system. If we were going to hold a meeting, let's do it in some nice place." Cornfeld himself bought a BAC-111 to serve as his flagship, and acquired a lakeside château in Geneva to complement his French château, Paris apartment, and London townhouse. The money just hemorrhaged from IOS.[101]

EUPHORIC LEADERS AND CULTURES

Overexpansion and excessive diversification are caused not only by past success but by a natural evolution in the styles of leaders and the impact this has on corporate cultures. Indeed, Imperialists' strategies derive in large part from their leadership styles, cultures, and structures—and vice versa.

Imperialist cultures have three central characteristics. First, the lofty ambitions of leaders, coupled with their brilliant track records, make them inherently aggressive and arrogant. They establish a culture of hyperoptimism, even euphoria, which both creates and obscures emerging problems. Second, CEOs become increasingly busy administering their megaventures and mushrooming operations. They concentrate too much on grand strategies and have too little time for, or knowledge of, vital details. Third, two disparate control cultures grow up: either chaos predominates because managers are simply too overloaded or too preoccupied with their grandiose projects to cope, or, in a desperate attempt to control their proliferating empires, top managers impose financial control systems and appoint head-office analysts who breed suspicion and engender political gamesmanship.

Arrogance and Euphoria

Tremendous success gives managers a feeling of power. They become used to having their way; used to winning against all odds; and used to succeeding at grand ventures. It's hard for them to stop grabbing for more.

We noted that Litton executives prided themselves on being able to run *any* business. At ITT, this confidence grew to the point of arrogance. According to Geneen, "We knew we were Number 1. We would fight to sustain that belief: we were the best business managers in the world."[102] In the lobby of ITT's Park Avenue headquarters there sat an immense sculpted bronze globe. The message engraved in capital letters on its marble base read: THE HAROLD S. GENEEN CREATIVE MANAGEMENT AWARD. (The globe has since been moved.)[103]

Figgie at AS was fond of asserting that he could gauge the condition of a company simply by walking through its plants. He ridiculed standard measures of value as "toilet paper," preferring to assess potential acquisitions almost exclusively by his judgment of how much they might contribute under *his* management to earnings per share.[104]

Imperialist leaders feel they can do no wrong, and this cockiness contributes to a climate of heightened optimism, indeed, of pure euphoria. At IOS, for example, it was an article of faith that, as before, sales and earnings were going to double every year, and that meant expanding facilities to get ready for the new business. In 1969, when IOS was already in trouble, sales boss Allan Cantor was making predictions of unprecedented growth, while President Ed Cowett exclaimed: "New IOS activities have so much profit potential that I can no longer predict earnings precisely. I can predict a minimum but not how much they will exceed it. I've lost the top half of my crystal ball."[105]

This euphoria was reflected too in expectations about the price of IOS stock—insiders, officers, and sales representatives scurried to buy the shares on margin (the buyer had only to put up 20 percent of the price). Many of the margin loans were made by IOS-owned banks, soaking up large amounts of liquidity. In effect, IOS managers and sales reps were mortgaging the farm to buy shares, even as IOS teetered on the verge of insolvency.

When oil prices reached their all-time peak and Dome was saddled with excessive debt, Jack Gallagher remained feverishly optimistic about Dome's future and the prospects for dramatically rising oil prices. He refused to issue more equity to reduce the staggering debt because he believed his firm was undervalued, even at its astronomical peak price of $21 per share. So he let the last chance for rescue pass him by. Within a year the stock had fallen to a dollar. Clearly, it was not false bravado but a true sense of invulnerability that so doomed our Imperialists.

The One-armed Paper Hanger and the Big Picture

As operations become larger and more complex, they demand more of a leader's time. Geneen was busy as a one-armed paper hanger. He put in a superhuman effort at ITT. His sixteen-hour days and two hundred meetings days per year were legendary. And he absorbed thousands of facts about ITT's operations. Yet even this valiant effort was not enough to manage his empire. He was forced to rely, more and more, on staff experts; to focus on the bottom line rather than the vital strategies that determined it.

So leaders manage only the big picture, making use of accounting controls, capital budgets, financial measures, and strategic plans for diversification. The head-office staff reinforces this focus on the abstractions of management. And all the while the details are lost—details needed to understand customers, to renew product lines, or to hone production and service methods. At Dome, for example, a cadre of strategic planners was brought in. According to Jim Lyon, "The new men were sharp as a pin, lean overachievers in three piece suits, who seemed to be far more intimate with the subtleties of corporation law and the arcane working of the Canadian tax system than the routine business of land acquisition and drilling, producing, and transporting oil and gas."[106]

Chaos vs. Gamesmanship

Imperialists usually display one of two very different cultures: *chaos* or *gamesmanship*. Chaos occurs when top managers are too busy with grand ventures to monitor their operations. Gamesmanship results from head-office attempts to control vast operations by means of staff inquisition. Although chaotic cultures are the most common among Imperialists because of the expansion craze, in a way, gamesmanship cultures are the more revealing. They show the weaknesses of imperialism even when it is accompanied by sophisticated financial control systems and brilliant analysts.

CHAOS In some firms, top managers are so preoccupied with large-scale ventures and their operations have become so complex—so rapidly burgeoning and extensive—that there is hardly any control at all. Major problems remain hidden as very little information filters up to headquarters.

This was certainly the case at IOS, where top management so overestimated their abilities and the strengths of the company that they failed to monitor expenses. They allowed severe cost overruns to doom IOS; no one knew how badly the firm was bleeding from its extravagance and misguided ventures until it was too late.[107] Recall that we saw similar examples of chaos in the strategies and operating problems of AS, Dome, and Litton. The structural manifestations of such disorder will be discussed below.

INQUISITION AND GAMESMANSHIP Some Imperialist leaders try desperately to control their far-flung empires with sophisticated information systems and a crack staff of accountants and financial analysts. They bring divisional personnel into the head office on a regular basis to grill them and make them accountable. Leaders and their staffs then ask tough questions in order to display their command of details and to make the divisional line managers "come clean."

Geneen at ITT implemented what is perhaps the best known culture of suspicion. "Although Hal was ready to be presented with the facts, opinions were not as well received," said Herbert C. Knortz, ITT's controller and executive vice-president. Geneen questioned his managers aggressively, exhaustively, and, sometimes, brutally.[108]

Another source of terror at ITT were the corporate staff princes. Line managers worked with the disconcerting knowledge that their work and reports were being picked over by hit squads at headquarters; by a control staff who could further their own careers by torpedoing reports and snagging—maybe even exaggerating—problems within the divisions.[109]

According to Professor Kirby Warren of Columbia University, Geneen "created one of the most complete contention management systems in American business. Conflict was considered not only acceptable, but desirable . . . it smacked of Gestapo tactics."[110]

The result was a pressure-cooker atmosphere, which many managers could not tolerate. Here's what some of them said: "[Geneen] either fires [managers] or drives them so hard that they finally decide that no amount of money is worth it" . . . "I left because of hellish pressure I could not endure" . . . "I did not want a premature heart attack" . . . "The pace, the pressure was frenetic. I couldn't see ITT as the sole purpose in life" . . . "He goes too far—drives people to the wall. Then, suddenly, no matter how much he pays them, the money becomes unimportant."[111]

Clearly, the climate is one of great stress. Divisional people are so busy writing reports, and preparing to cover their backs for meetings at head office, that they have little time to look after their own units. In his book *Managing,* Geneen estimates that his managers spent thirty-five weeks a year going to meetings and preparing budgets and reports. After four weeks of vacation, there remained a scant thirteen weeks in which to run the company—to attend to business rather than just talk about it.[112]

When divisional managers must subject every project to terrific head-office scrutiny, they often take the easy way out and do what is safe rather than original and inventive. They also begin to use various forms of gamesmanship and subterfuge in order to work to rule and get around the system. Gamesmanship is, after all, the stock in trade of many of the financially motivated employees so eagerly sought out by Imperialists.

According to Peters and Waterman, "At ITT there were countless rules and variables to be measured and filed. But the dominant theme there was gamesmanship—beating the system, pulling end-runs, joining together with other line officers to avoid the infamous staff 'flying squads.' Too much overbearing discipline of one kind will kill autonomy."[113]

And, of course, one man, even Geneen, cannot be expected to think of everything. Formalistic initiatives took the place of projects based on a thorough understanding. It was as though internal performance at meetings was as important as external performance in markets.

OVERLOADED STRUCTURES

Imperialists grow so large and diversified that their structures just cannot keep up. As was true of the corporate culture, two problems are most common: chaotic structures, with confused reporting relationships, inadequate controls, and too few guidelines; and cumbersome, bureaucratic structures, in which so much effort goes into financial control that initiative is stifled and substantive operating issues are neglected. In either event, these overburdened and disorganized structures fail to stem the overexpansion and excessive diversification.

Chaotic Organization

The most typical structure among Imperialists—if you can call it a structure—is chaos. Expansion has outstripped the capacity of managers to manage. Communication founders, lines of responsibility are confused, and control systems are simply too primitive to cope.

CONFUSED, OVERLOADED STRUCTURES At IOS, management overlooked the fact that the practices that worked so well when IOS began were no longer suitable for a large firm. So, the lines of responsibility were poorly drawn. Ed Cowett as president and Bernie Cornfeld as chairman had unclear but overlapping responsibilities, with Cornfeld having the last word. Cowett, for his part, concentrated much information in his own head, trusting no one. While Cornfeld "wanted to run the company or be seen to run it but was bored by day-to-day decision making," neither leader delegated enough authority to middle management, and managers were preoccupied to an extraordinary degree with trying to sense the mood at the top and play to it.[114] Indeed, there was very little communication between top management and the rest of IOS.[115]

At AS, Harry Figgie's minuscule head-office staff proved totally inadequate for the range of businesses. It was impossible for so compact a group to monitor the operations of a multidivisional company with sales in the hundreds of millions of dollars. Therefore, the benefits of having an operating expert such as Figgie at the top vanished as AS expanded.[116]

Ironically, Figgie prided himself on running AS as an operating company rather than a financial edifice. But of course the main links between corporate headquarters an the divisions were financial. The reporting system, on the rare occasions when it functioned, could only alert top management to aggregate outcomes and symptoms, not to actionable problems. Small wonder that subunits continued to deteriorate and expansion went on unabated.

POOR CONTROLS Control systems fail to keep up with the growing scale and complexity of Imperialists or to rein in their expansionary binges. What was most surprising about the IOS crisis was the stunning simplicity of its causes and the fact that it took management so long to discover them. The financial system was hopelessly unsophisticated. Not only were costs not related to IOS's businesses in a way that could allow managers to identify problematic sectors, but even the most essential expense figures were late in coming through.[117]

Costs mounted rapidly as the IOS salesforce pursued ever more marginal businesses. There were fewer paid-up programs, more installment investment plans, and more lapsed payments. Management remained mesmerized by misleading record "face-value" sales figures. After the fall, Cornfeld grumbled: "We never knew we were operating at a loss. How the hell do you know unless the financial people tell you?"[118]

Controls were not quite so primitive at Litton Industries, but its example serves to illustrate some of the weaknesses of the conglomerate form. Litton's system of control failed to catch most of the operating problems that had begun to emerge in the late 1960s. Asked industry analyst Ernest Stowell: "Was management getting the right information? I would say they were not. Litton has very fine quantitative reporting techniques, but not qualitative. They must rely on their divisional managers to tell them that they are taking care of things qualitatively—whether they are keeping up with the field, with their customers' needs, with technology."[119]

In fact, Litton's top managers were strongly implying that the information filtering up to them from the business equipment group was misleading. According to one commentator, "Doubts raised by recent troubles strike at the heart of Litton's concept of conglomerate management: the idea that talented general managers, applying modern management techniques, can effectively oversee diverse businesses in which they have no specific experience."[120]

Ritualistic Bureaucracy

Even when Imperialists try diligently to organize and control their vast operations, they usually fail. Top managers simply do not understand enough about their operations. And they are too busy with grand projects and too remote from the scene to manage substantive issues. So rituals of interrogation by a head-office staff take the place of effective controls.

ITT did in fact devise extremely elaborate control and reporting systems. As we saw earlier, these made for a confrontational style of management that stifled creativity and engendered gamesmanship. They also reinforced a bottom-line mentality that skirted key operating issues, causing ITT to fall behind in its more dynamic markets. Eventually, the control systems turned management into ritual.

The ITT control system became far too unwieldy, especially the three-day monthly management meetings, which most executives came to regard as numbing and a waste of valuable time. "There would be a dialogue between Geneen and two other guys on the far side of the table," recalls one executive, "and everybody else would sit there and make bets on when the meeting would break up."[121]

The huge staff group at ITT headquarters were thought by almost all of the operating officers interviewed by *Fortune* to be incompetent and short on realism. When they looked at the bottom line, they couldn't explain it—and by the time problems showed up there, they were already well advanced. As in most bureaucracies, the staff in time became bloated and ineffective. But Geneen stuck faithfully to the system, which came to play him as much as he played it.

MAJOR CHANGES ALONG THE VENTURING TRAJECTORY

The venturing trajectory shows four major changes in strategy, all amplifications of previous tendencies. First, ambition and spectacular success encourage entrepreneurial strategists to become still bolder and more venturesome. Expansion speeds up, while rationalization and consolidation are neglected. Second, cautious and selective diversification becomes an unbridled, impulsive expansion into businesses managers know little about. Third, an emphasis on global "grand" strategies becomes a neglect of substantive operating issues. And fourth, intelligent risk taking becomes recklessness as more debt is taken on and more resources are squandered.

This strategic momentum is supported by—and itself induces—changes in leadership, culture, and structure. For example, past success converts ambitious and confident leaders into hyperoptimistic and extravagant ones. This further fuels overexpansion and degrades corporate cultures, which either become chaotic or rife with games-manship. Meanwhile, corporate generalism turns into management-by-numbers, a pseudo-science practiced by remote executives and staff experts who have never talked to a customer or visited a plant.

Overexpansion also proves too much for organizational structures that simply cannot keep pace with the scope and complexity of operations. Managers get overburdened, reporting relationships become muddled, and controls falter. This erosion of control permits still further overexpansion. Growth has become a cancer.

The venturing trajectory has occasioned strong reactions from the popular press. The spectacular rise of Builders attracts a great deal of attention from journalists, who then publish stories celebrating such firms and their leaders. When, years later, the businesses run into trouble, often under the same management, media attention is again lavished on these organizations. The tributes to executive brilliance turn into brutal critiques of managerial stupidity. The heroes, it seems, have become bums. Their true status, of course, lies some-where in between. Indeed, imperialism is so natural an extension of building that the transition represents a subtle shift of emphasis rather than any vast deterioration in the quality of management. Here, as with the other trajectories, changes are very much ones of degree rather than orientation.

CHAPTER 4:

From Pioneers to Escapists:
The Inventing Trajectory

THERE WAS COMPLETE CONSENSUS IN THE INDUSTRY: ROLLS-ROYCE was the most progressive, state-of-the-art aircraft engine manufacturer—period. A history of engines reads like a litany of Rolls firsts: the first jet engine design, the first turbofan engine, air-cooled turbine blades, thrust reversers, vertical takeoff engine, composite materials to cut weight, and the first commercial supersonic engine. Rolls led the pack with its superb design teams and its willingness to take risks on bold new development projects. Marketing and cost control took second place.

But the company's quest for unparalleled breakthroughs ultimately went too far. In its zeal to obtain the engine contract for Lockheed's TriStar airbus, Rolls bid very aggressively. It undertook to develop an engine with a very unusual "three-shaft" construction that employed 25 percent fewer parts, reduced noise, used less fuel, and was lighter and less costly than the competing GE model. This demanded that Rolls discover new composite materials never before tested on an engine. The design was brilliant in conception but too far ahead of its time, hopelessly costly to develop, and impossible to implement. Tremendous delays, daunting manufacturing problems, and massive cost overruns plagued the project. Rolls' utopian brainchild pushed it to the brink of bankruptcy.[1]

For Pioneers such as Rolls, innovation is a way of life that becomes an obsession. In the transition toward escapism, intelligent invention escalates into technological grandiosity. Myopic strategies come to focus on science and technique, but ignore customer needs and economic constraints. And optimistic, inventive cultures turn into chaotic, scientist-dominated cabals.

Pioneers are best at opening up new markets and creating new technologies—they lead; the competition follows. Their visionary leaders and R&D Whiz Kids push back the frontiers of an industry, plowing tremendous resources into state-of-the-art products that they can develop better and faster than anyone else. And Pioneers artfully ply their innovative skills on an appreciative, precisely targeted niche of the market.

These strategies are inspired by visionary leaders and powerful R&D groups. Indeed, many Pioneers are run by brilliant innovators, who excel at spotting technological opportunities and establish knowledge-based cultures that encourage people with exciting new ideas to pursue them. Their flexible structures further nurture innovation by eschewing bureaucracy, empowering creative experts, and promoting intensive collaboration.

Unfortunately, many Pioneers get carried away with invention and turn into Escapists who too eagerly chase after whopping breakthroughs. They introduce a host of products that are impractical, too far ahead of their time, and dreadfully expensive to develop. The periodic, well-targeted innovation of Pioneers becomes a plethora of new products in Escapists; sensible development projects mushroom into extravagant R&D megaschemes; and focused, intelligent marketing degenerates into a myopic fixation on irrelevant technical details.

Missionary leaders and utopian corporate cultures drive this one-sided strategy. Escapists' powerful R&D staffs fervently pursue technological ideals, peering so far into the future that they overlook pressing operating matters. Their inefficient structures get so chaotic that no one knows who is responsible for what. And, as if these problems weren't enough, they are compounded by growth and mounting competition.

THE PIONEER

PIONEER STRATEGIES

There are two sequential components to the strategy of Pioneers: Taking the Lead and Staying in Front. The titles are self-explanatory, so let's just proceed.

Taking the Lead

Pioneers employ three common ways of taking the lead. I call these *routing, reaming,* and *ramming. Routing* creates a completely new market using existing technologies. For example, Federal Express established the market for overnight package deliveries using existing methods of air transportation. *Reaming* expands an existing market by advancing new technologies. Polaroid's Edwin Land, for instance, broadened the camera and accessories market by creating instant photography—an exciting new film development process. Finally, *ramming* batters into established markets with the boldest technological innovations of all. Control Data Corporation built the most powerful, technologically advanced computers in the world for an existing niche of scientific, research, and government clients.

Figure 4 plots some of the innovations of our Pioneers along two dimensions. *Technological novelty* refers to the newness of an actual design or product technology; *market novelty* is the newness of the customer need being served. As we can see, there seems to be an interesting inverse relationship between how well established a market is and the amount of technological innovation needed to conquer it: the more established the market, the more novel the technologies. Also, firms tend to progress gradually from routing to reaming, and sometimes even to ramming, as their markets mature.

Routing

The routing strategies of Federal Express and Apple Computer both incorporated unique visions of market needs and novel ways of meeting them. These firms were able to grow very rapidly by routing out, indeed creating, "jackpot" niches in which there was absolutely no competition.

Federal Express Corporation (FEC) used time-tested technologies to satisfy an undiscovered need. FEC was founded in 1972 by the twenty-eight-year-old Fred Smith, who pioneered a system of rapid small package delivery, an ingenious scheme he devised while working on a term paper as an undergraduate at Yale. The product was attractive: FEC covered all population centers in the United States, guaranteed delivery before noon the next shipping day, and was extremely reliable. It afforded clients door-to-door pickup and delivery,

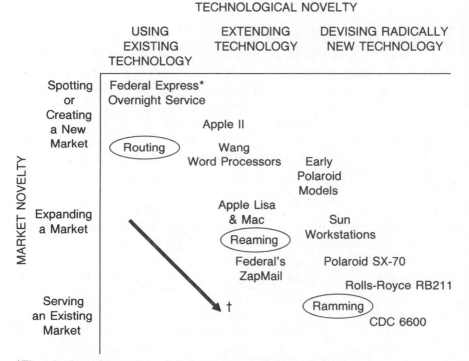

TECHNOLOGICAL NOVELTY

FIGURE 4
The Inventions Compared

*The plotting of inventions is approximate and illustrative only.
†The arrow indicates a tendency over time for firms to move toward more novel technologies.

accurate and timely billing, and equitable rates. FEC employed a hub concept in which all planes flew into Memphis around midnight. Parcels were then sorted, and by 3:00 A.M. the planes departed once again to make deliveries. Smith chose the most economical small aircraft for the distances and payloads involved, and insisted on a single-entity system in which FEC would control the parcel every step of the way. Package sizes were limited to fit easily into the planes and to allow drivers and sorters to handle all materials manually; and flight, servicing, and routing operations were among the most efficient in the business. The economies behind Smith's system were staggering. Imagine how many slim Fed Ex letters, at approximately $10, $20, or $30 apiece, would fit into the space that would be occupied by a single passenger on most other flights. Smith's little parcels didn't need legroom, didn't need to be fed, and never ever complained.

Because FEC's overnight delivery service was so new, the company embarked upon a catchy and very major national ad campaign for sending packages that "absolutely, positively" had to be in another city the next day. Routing, it seems, often requires that as much effort be aimed at creating demand as at developing a product.[2] After a slow beginning during which much money was spent on building hubs, collection centers, and a fleet of aircraft, FEC began to grow explosively. Sales of $76 million in 1976 rose to $1.5 billion by 1983, and FEC's profits increased correspondingly.

The legendary Apple Computer undertook somewhat more technological innovation than FEC, but its primary feat also was to identify a propitious new market niche. Apple not only pioneered a new product, it single-handedly created a new industry. Its challenge was to convince people to use personal computers which until then had been cumbersome machines suited only to high-tech hackers. Apple's founder, the mercurial Steve Jobs, has been called the Johnny Appleseed of personal computing, "the leading broadcaster of technology for the people."[3]

In 1976, Jobs, at age twenty-one, and design prodigy Steve Wozniak started Apple from scratch. Wozniak built a primitive homemade computer system around a microprocessor—a computer on a chip invented by Intel in 1971. When several friends expressed interest in the crude machine, Jobs saw its sparkling potential. Almost immediately, he sold a hundred machines to a Palo Alto store that marketed kits for microprocessor-based computers. He arbitrarily selected a price of $666.66. Wozniak sold his HP calculator and Jobs his VW van to raise the $1,500 to buy parts. The business was profitable from that moment on.[4]

When the founders raised $600,000 in equity capital, they spent it on promotion—to design a logo, advertise, and create a professional, polished image. Their first job, they felt, was to generate demand, not to hone technology; that could come later. Apple was given the image of a $100 million company at a time when it had precisely twelve employees.[5]

Routing strategies strive to make a product as useful as possible to the customer—the purpose is to create a market. And this was especially the case at Apple. In May 1977, the user-friendly Apple II was introduced. Commands were simplified, a monitor and keyboard were added, and an operating system was installed to manage the computer's internal operations and executive programs (thus an owner no longer had to write his own programs). Apple also provided customers with captivating user instructions that had attractive graphics and a humorous text. With marvelous foresight, the firm published the Apple II's technical specifications—an unprecedented step in the industry—so that other companies could develop programs for its machines.[6]

By January 1983, 650,000 Apple IIs had been sold—more than any other personal computer. Sales grew from $8 million in 1978 to $583 million in 1982; net income from $793,000 to $61 million. Annual unit sales increased from 7,600 to 350,000.

Reaming

A more common Pioneering strategy develops a new technology or product to expand an existing market. By reaming, a Pioneer devises a unique offering that enhances and broadens that market.

Polaroid Corporation, founded by the brilliant Edwin H. Land, startled consumers by introducing an entirely novel camera and film development process that could produce a picture in seconds. Because instant photography provided a very different kind of enjoyment from standard picture taking, the Land camera was not so much a substitute for other cameras as a breakthrough that enlarged or "reamed" the market for photographic equipment.

Polaroid initially built much of its reputation and almost all of its sales around its camera. Although Land's invention was announced in 1947, it wasn't until 1976 that any other company devised a similar product. Indeed, by 1959, Polaroid's continual pioneering had earned it 238 U.S. patents in one-step photography—122 of them the work of Land himself—and these protected the firm from troublesome competitive incursions.[7]

Instant photography caught on very quickly. Ten years after its invention, Land's sixty-second camera was the best-selling model in the world. And its buyers used much more film than anyone else because of the fun and curiosity involved in taking instant pictures. Sales of $1,500,000 in 1948 had vaulted to $65 million by 1958, and to $800 million by 1976. Between 1947 and 1975, revenues had grown by an average of 25 percent per year, profits by more than 17 percent per year. Polaroid had become the second largest photographic products company in the United States after Eastman Kodak.[8]

Other reaming strategies pursue still more radical substitutes for products on the market. Sun Microsystems, for example, built systems that would take business away from firms making microcomputers and minicomputers. Its pathbreaking strategy would completely change the direction of the computer industry: Sun's machines were one step above the most powerful PCs, yet far more economical than the minicomputers of firms such as DEC. Sun almost single-handedly captured the burgeoning market for computer-aided design and sophisticated networking. In addition to workstations—the superpowerful desktop computers geared to technical tasks—Sun also made computers that could be shared by an entire department. The consensus in the industry was that the products were well designed and especially suited to technical users who did not require the bedside manner of an IBM.

As an added advantage, Sun's compact machines used software that embodied widely accepted industry standards (such as Ethernet networks and AT&T's UNIX operating system). These made it simple for customers to switch to the fledgling firm. They also gave Sun the edge over its major competitor, Apollo Computer, Inc., whose proprietary operating system made it difficult both to change brands and to link up with different systems.[9] In short, Sun had found a wonderful, lucrative niche, and the brilliance of its strategy was amply confirmed by its performance: sales climbed to an astounding $2 billion in Sun's seventh year of operation.[10]

Sometimes reaming combines independent products and components to create highly original networks or systems. In 1966, Wang Laboratories took a "new-fangled machine called a word processor, carved out a market, and changed the office forever." Wang also developed a successful minicomputer line and a personal computer, both key elements in its local area network called Wang-net. The company's approach was to mesh five separate technologies—word processing, data processing, voice transmission and storage, image processing, and networking. "It's the premier vendor of office automation," said one high-tech research analyst.[11] Wang achieved one of the most impressive growth records in the industry: ten years of quarterly earnings increases and a 39 percent compounded growth rate from 1980 to 1984, when revenues reached $2.2 billion.

Ramming

Now we come to the heavy artillery. Ramming Pioneers innovate via megaprojects: expensive, long-term ventures to introduce complex, pathbreaking products. They serve well-established markets but invent new technologies and state-of-the-art products that are the envy of their industry.

Control Data Corporation was born in 1957. Founder and president William Norris and chief designer Seymour Cray had as their overriding ambition to design the world's most powerful and most sophisticated computer—and at this they succeeded more than once. CDC's first model, the 1604, was finally introduced after three years of intensive development work and a series of scientific and engineering breakthroughs. It was the first solid-state computer ever built, many times more powerful than any competing model and years ahead of its time. The comparatively diminutive CDC was to become famous for its perennial leadership in supercomputers and for catching rivals such as IBM and Sperry Rand by surprise. As soon as the 1604 was introduced, research labs and universities fought to get their hands on it. Sales volume shot up to $25 million almost immediately after the machine came out, and it grew rapidly to reach $160 million by 1965.[12]

Rolls-Royce also went in for massive development projects. By the late 1960s, the venerable British producer of luxury automobiles was deriving 80 percent of its revenues from the sale of jet aircraft engines. It entered the industry during World War I with a twelve-cylinder piston engine, and in World War II it gave birth to the jet era with its turbojet Welland model (all the engines were named after rivers in the United Kingdom). By 1947, Rolls had licensed the design of the first jet power plant to Pratt & Whitney, which like every aircraft manufacturer had concentrated its wartime efforts on traditional piston engines. Rolls-Royce, clearly, had been a pioneer for a long time.[13]

In 1969, Rolls was headed by two accomplished engineers, CEO Sir Denning Pearson and Aero Division head Sir David Huddie, whose major objective it was to stay technologically ahead of the pack. They succeeded with advanced engines such as the reliable Spey, and innovations such as the turbofan jet. It took years and many thousands of employees to design, build, and market a new engine; and Rolls typically incorporated many first into its designs—new kinds of materials, different propulsion techniques, and other engineering breakthroughs. Rolls grew to become Britain's seventeenth largest firm by 1969, with 87,000 employees and gross sales of $720 million (up from $269 million in 1959).[14]

Whatever their differences, all of our Pioneering strategies—routing, reaming, and ramming—have one thing in common: they create novel offerings that attract a clearly defined segment of the market. But a single innovation is not enough to maintain excellent performance in the face of competition. The lead must be preserved. And this Pioneers are able to do very well by upping the ante—by innovating even more boldly.

Staying in Front

Pioneers prevent competitors from copying their initiatives by accelerating the pace and scope of their product improvements. Routing turns into reaming as newly discovered niches are defended against encroaching competition with new product designs and innovative technology. Reaming strategies pursue more far-reaching technological improvements. And ramming strategies continue the quest for technological revolutions. In short, to protect their lead, Pioneers move down the arrow of Figure 4 toward more novel technologies and more established markets.

Apple's routing strategy gave way to one of reaming markets with technical breakthroughs to defend against new entrants such as IBM. In 1978, Apple was the first to offer the immensely convenient floppy-disk drive—a storage medium that was compact, reliable, and easy to use. The customer could also buy packaged programs sold on floppies. Between 1980 and 1983, Apple introduced the II+, IIe, and III models, increasing memory, operating system sophistication, keyboard flexibility, and the convenience of the display.[15]

Pioneers that began with a reaming strategy start to make still more inventions to update and broaden their product lines. They introduce many new items to stay ahead of their rivals, and invest fortunes in R&D in order to do so. In 1948, Polaroid sold a chunky five-pound, $90 camera that produced, after a seemingly endless exposure, poor-quality brown-and-white pictures in one minute. In 1950, true black-and-white film was introduced and its speed was to increase every few years—at an increasing rate. By 1960, development time had fallen from sixty to ten seconds and automatic exposure control was invented.[16]

When, in 1962, the market for black-and-white instant cameras appeared to be just about saturated, Polaroid awakened consumers by introducing a color-print film. Next year it pioneered convenient film packs and an attractive new Colorpack camera. In 1965, to broaden

103

its distribution to drugstores and supermarkets, Polaroid developed the sporty "Swinger" model for $19.95, quickly selling millions of units. Again, the camera was later improved and adapted to use faster film. While rival Kodak tinkered with incremental improvements, Polaroid kept up a steady stream of pioneering advances.[17]

It is interesting that Edwin Land believed design changes should come mainly in large lumps and at well-spaced intervals. This would prevent Polaroid from squandering its resources and prematurely antiquating its own products. But as periodic innovations met with success, their frequency, and even their scale, began to increase.

The same arduous updating of products and technologies was in evidence at Wang Labs and Sun Microsystems. By constantly upgrading its product lines, Wang was able to dominate the market for clustered word processors. And Sun spent 14 percent of revenues on R&D, compared to the industry average of 8 percent, in its scramble to get products to markets quickly.[18]

Ramming Pioneers continue to maintain their lead by embarking on periodic technological revolutions that require long development times and major resource commitments. Rolls-Royce, for example, was forever engaged in improving its engines and introducing new models. Its spending on R&D almost doubled during Pearson's first year as CEO and grew to 23 percent of the company's budget by 1969; R&D staff came to account for one quarter of total personnel, a staggering 22,000 people. Such investments bore much fruit: over the years, Rolls-Royce achieved so many technological firsts that it took a six-page booklet to list them. Examples include: air-cooled turbine blades (1957), thrust reversers for airlines (1958), silencer jet exhaust nozzles (1958), a vertical takeoff engine (1958), composite materials to reduce weight (1962), and the first commercial supersonic engine (1964). The company also pioneered the first turbofan engine in the late 1950s. By introducing its pathbreaking line of Spey jet engines in the early 1960s, Rolls was able to boost its sales by 16 to 20 percent annually for the rest of the decade.[19]

It is important to bear in mind that Pioneers initiate product improvements at a measured pace and in response to changing client needs and real challenges from their competitors. As we will see, the same firms, once they become Escapists, bury themselves in a proliferation of new products and irrelevant technology.

Auxiliary Strategies

A Well-Defined Target Market

Pioneers, unlike Builders, usually sell to a well-defined market to which they have precisely tailored their product. Like Craftsmen, they design with a particular customer in mind. In fact, many of their ideas for innovations come directly from discussions with clients.

Control Data Corporation marketed its powerful machines mostly to scientific users, such as universities, government research labs, and large, scientifically oriented corporations. By focusing on this niche, CDC was able to avoid head-on competition from IBM, Honeywell, and Sperry, which had targeted mainly the business management and process control markets. Also, the scientific market did not require much handholding or software support, which CDC could not provide; but it did value computing power, which was CDC's strong suit.[20]

Federal Express Corporation, for much of its history, concentrated on overnight delivery of small, light packages only to significant population centers. That was it. No heavy freight, no intercity trucking, no telecommunications. Federal's was a deliberate niche strategy.[21]

The same was true of all our Pioneers. Sun marketed mostly to engineering users rather than to those seeking machines for commercial data processing. Apple initially designed and marketed its models for the home market and the inexperienced user. Polaroid focused solely on the instant photography market. And Rolls made most of its revenues from two or three jet engines.

The only way to innovate successfully is to be intimately familiar with specific technologies and with the exact needs of a particular set of customers. Too broad a market or range of offerings would prevent the concentration and sharpness of focus so necessary for true pioneering.

Focused Marketing

Because Pioneers have such tightly circumscribed target markets, their marketing efforts can concentrate on specific kinds of customers and product features. For example, Apple kept stressing simplicity and convenience in its attractive print advertising. Federal Express's memorable "fast-talking" television commercials touted speedy and reliable delivery. And CDC and Rolls sent their sales engineers out in teams to a select few clients to analyze their operations and discuss their concerns, and later these teams helped incorporate suggestions from customers into actual designs. Such precisely targeted marketing is not only economical; it also appeals very directly to the potential buyers to whom it is so closely tailored.

Flexible Production

Because Pioneers innovate so much, they cannot be caught with rigid, capital-intensive production facilities. These would simply be too costly to change. At the same time, Pioneers must keep their manufacturing expenses down in order to have enough resources left for R&D. Moreover, they have to avoid overtaxing their administrative structure with complex production problems. So, firms like Apple, Wang, and Polaroid farmed out their manufacturing. This kept them small and agile, and delayed the hardening of the creative arteries that so often is a by-product of size.

VISIONARY LEADERS

The Leaders of Pioneers are often visionary inventors, and most have backgrounds in science or engineering. Their principal interest is in technology, and what it can do to improve life; money is rarely a primary motivation. Because many of our Pioneers are young, they are still run by their founding fathers, who retain significant ownership and have enormous personal influence. These leaders garner much respect for their expertise, and they energize their firms with their values as they spread the gospel of innovation.

Scientist-Bosses

Edwin H. Land founded Polaroid Corporation of Cambridge, Massachusetts, in 1937 and was for four decades its president, chairman, and research director. Land was a supremely gifted inventor and an inspired scientist. By 1959, he held 240 patents for polarizing filters and instant photography. His wide-ranging scientific capabilities earned him an appointment as an institute professor at MIT's School for Advanced Study, and he was made a member of the highly influential Science Advisory Committee that reported directly to President Eisenhower.[22]

Most of our other Pioneers also had leaders with impressive technical backgrounds. Rolls-Royce was run by Denning Pearson and David Huddie, two accomplished engineers. CDC's Seymour Cray (not a CEO, but a prime CDC strategist) was the preeminent computer designer in the world. And An Wang of Wang Labs was a brilliant applied physicist who had made a fortune on his patents for computer memories.

Land, Wang, and Cray each had a pervasive knowledge of every aspect of their business, especially research and design. They were masters of invention and had stellar professional reputations. And their personal styles had an enormous influence on their companies. Land, for example, had his own laboratory directly next door to his book-lined office. Throughout the day, his associates would bring him the results of experiments and discuss findings.[23] The atmosphere was very much that of a research lab or a think tank. Cray at CDC got even closer to his work. According to T. A. Wise, "At the lab he is likely to be found on the floor—like any garage mechanic—trying to rework the wiring in the panels of a computer."[24] Such hands-on management, and the myths that grow up to celebrate the leader's genius, ensure that the values of invention and creation predominate for Pioneers.

The Visionary Element

Scientist-leaders believe that technological advancement is an intrinsic social good, and they inspire their managers to pursue it. Indeed, there is a missionary and visionary element to their leadership—an urge to change the world with their new technologies and products. The bottom line is quite secondary.

The proselytizing Steve Jobs was more a missionary bringing Apple's technology to the people than a businessman. He wanted to introduce personal computing into every home by creating some of the most attractive, interactive, user-friendly products in the world. Jobs and Wozniak focused on the product and its customers—not on financial issues.[25]

Edwin Land saw Polaroid as a problem-solving, research-based organization that continually develops new products to meet important human needs—frequently needs that were not even recognized.[26] Michael Porter reports that

> Annual meetings at Polaroid were always a unique experience for stockholders; sales and earnings figures were hardly ever mentioned. At typical meetings Land would demonstrate one or more new products or processes he and his large team had developed. Most often, these demonstrations, which . . . were much like seminars or lectures, were totally unrelated to the products the company intended to introduce in the future. According to Land: "Our function is to sense a deep human need and then to satisfy it. . . . Our company has been dedicated throughout its life to making only those things which others cannot make. . . . We proceed from basic science to highly desirable products."[27]

The zeal of such leaders gives them the energy to persevere and the personal magnetism to motivate their employees. But, as we will see, it can also produce stubbornness.

"R&D" CULTURES

Pioneer cultures are energetic, flexible, and often centered on R&D. They promote free-flowing interaction, creativity, and debate. And they foster innovation by engendering a climate of optimism, by encouraging teamwork and participation, and by reinforcing a sense of mission and commitment.

Optimism

Because Pioneers undertake such far-reaching innovations, they require a healthy dose of optimism to give them the courage to proceed in the face of myriad design obstacles and to invest in major projects with highly uncertain payoffs. "Optimism is a moral duty," said Edwin Land, who has demonstrated over a quarter of a century of innovative boldness.[28] Land, An Wang, Steve Jobs, and Seymour Cray seldom hesitated to back risky, long-term product development projects; they were all true believers in their firms' abilities to conquer all obstacles, technological, human, and financial.

But optimism can also breed cockiness. At Sun Microsystems, the sheer chutzpah of CEO Scott McNealy and his team has outraged some competitors. Sun, the newcomer, tried to impose new microchip standards that would make senior statesmen in the computer industry conform to its own design specifications. And Sun's track record imparted to some employees a sense of supreme confidence. According to co-founder Vinod Khosla, "A lot of Sun's newer managers think they're infallible."[29]

Receptivity, Participation, and Teamwork

Because they demand so much originality and inventiveness from their employees, Pioneers must create a very special working climate. Innovation requires reflection and discussion, freedom and challenge, all of which can be elicited only by a "laboratory" atmosphere in which managers and scientists are encouraged to think, collaborate, and experiment. The Pioneer's R&D culture is therefore based on a keen receptivity to new ideas; on the participation of many in making decisions; and on close teamwork in design and implementation.

RECEPTIVITY   Land knew that his brilliance could be potentially intimidating to his subordinates. So he was careful to make sure not to outshine or discourage them. "Instead, he has a rare gift for inspiring them to high achievements of their own. He is careful . . . not to spoil anyone else's joy in creating. 'Any intelligent man,' said Land, 'can finish another man's sentence. We are all careful never to do that.' "[30] Polaroid created a climate that encouraged the open expression of ideas.

PARTICIPATION   Sun tried to instill passion in its employees by giving free rein to their creativity and inviting broad participation. Major decisions were made in noisy, table-pounding meetings, but they typically reflected a consensus among all the senior executives. Product strategy percolated up from independent divisions rather than being imposed from the top. Significantly, two of Scott McNealy's favorite slogans were: "Consensus if possible, but participation for sure," and "To ask permission is to seek denial."[31]

TEAMWORK   Pioneers confront technical problems that are simply too complex to be solved by one individual or even one unit. So, they set up multidisciplinary teams. For example, at Polaroid, the "photographic scientists" and the "chemical scientists" worked very closely together. In developing new films, the chemists dreamed up and synthesized many new molecules, which the photographic people then incorporated into their experimental films. Teamwork also figured very prominently in An Wang's management philosophy. Indeed, observers considered the close working relationship among Wang's scientists and managers to be one of the primary factors in its success.

Professional Commitment

Pioneers have more than their share of professionals—scientists and engineers who are guided by the aspirations and codes of their disciplines and who are committed to the pursuit of scientific excellence. These people innovate to reshape a part of the world. They want to make a difference. And this infuses them with a terrific sense of purpose.

Apple, Sun, Polaroid, Rolls-Royce, CDC, and Wang all embraced such goals in their quest for better products. Their R&D departments were energized by the values and guided by the professional protocols of applied science: elegant, powerful designs and beautiful solutions were taken to be the highest rewards. And technical obstacles were seen as enemies that had absolutely to be vanquished.

Even Federal Express, our sole Pioneer without an R&D-based culture, showed a remarkable commitment to getting the job done. This was because of the powerful sense of mission infused into the company by its CEO, Fred Smith. According to one report, Smith "and a handful of loyal employees were willing to do almost anything to keep the planes going. Smith once sold his personal aircraft to buy enough fuel to keep the Falcons flying. A driver pawned his watch to buy gasoline for his delivery truck when the company's credit cards were cancelled."[32]

ORGANIC STRUCTURES

Pioneers have "organic"—that is, loose, flexible, non-bureaucratic—structures. They favor small, informal groups, whose members have broadly defined tasks and in which authority is a function of knowledge, not rank. Moreover, independence and self-sufficiency are promoted to multiply the number of discoveries. And firms facilitate linkage between departments to help in implementing innovations.[33]

Flexibility

Pioneer leaders try to keep their companies spry in order to maintain creativity. They make their divisions, departments, and teams small and agile, and do their best to free R&D departments of the pressures of everyday operations.

CEO McNealy of Sun kept his business units small and responsive, splitting the firm into autonomous divisions to cater to specific markets, such as workstations sold to government agencies. These flexible units performed brilliantly because they could get close to a single market and product and develop inventions without having to go through a series of hierarchical approval hurdles.[34]

Sun also scorned the bureaucratic strictures that slowed down many of its competitors. But it was careful to effect some balance between freedom and discipline at the very top. The hard-nosed Bernard Lacroute, Sun's number-two man, served as a counterfoil to the sometimes overenthusiastic McNealy. Still, the balance leaned toward flexibility. As Vice-President Eric E. Schmidt put it: "Sun is controlled chaos."[35]

R&D departments particularly need flexibility and freedom from bureaucracy. When sales at CDC reached $25 million in 1960, systems architect Seymour Cray began to get uneasy. He disliked paperwork and was distracted by the noise and confusion at CDC's headquarters in Minneapolis. So he was permitted to set up a lab near his home in Chippewa Falls, Wisconsin.[36] Polaroid's Edwin Land always used to say that men perform best the jobs they create for themselves—and he allowed his managers the flexibility to do this.[37]

Distributed Power

Pioneers foment creative initiative by endowing the most knowledgeable and talented of their employees with a good deal of power. Scientists and engineers are usually given the freedom to make major decisions on their own. At Sun and Wang, for example, top management heaped responsibility on R&D experts and provided them with as little direction as possible. Land's associates at Polaroid cannot recall his *ever* having issued an order. He guided his firm sensitively, managing by a mix of persuasion and delegation. Apple also was very decentralized, reflecting the entrepreneurial nature of its employees and their business. In fact, to disperse operating authority, Apple adopted product divisions for its different models and the components that went into them. And authority was sometimes more a function of expertise than of rank.

Close Interaction

Generating ideas calls for flexibility and independence. Implementing them, by contrast, must produce close interaction among specialists from R&D, marketing, and production to hammer out mutual problems. Such collaboration was especially close at Wang, which was known for its intense, open internal communications. The interaction among functional heads was frequent and free-flowing. And informal task forces and project groups were used to ensure that the views of experts in marketing, research, and manufacturing were brought to bear on every complex project.[38]

VENTURESOME DECISION MAKING

Pioneers employ a unique style of decision making. They have to make major decisions rapidly in order to stay technologically ahead of their competitors. And they are not afraid to take considerable risks.

The Importance of Speed

Our Pioneers typically deal in turbulent environments—or at least in niches of the market that change rapidly and unpredictably. Their innovations may take them into uncharted territory, not only in terms of what they are inventing, but whom they are inventing for and what the competition will be like. This was especially true in the computer industry, where things moved so quickly that there just wasn't the time, or even the information, available for exhaustive analysis. So at CDC, for example, decisions sprang more from managerial vision and intuition than from long-range studies.[39]

Wang, too, was known for its speed in making important decisions. Said the prominent high-tech analyst Howard Anderson: "[At Wang] when there is a problem [managers] all get together and make decisions. Things happen quickly. There is no wasted time and energy. And that shows up on the bottom line."[40]

Two further slogans from Sun's Scott McNealy nicely summarize the theme of decisiveness: "Agree and commit, and: disagree and commit—or just get the hell out of the way," and: "The right answer is the best answer. The wrong answer is second-best. No answer is the worst."[41]

Taking Risks

All of our Pioneers took risks by investing in the development of products that might easily fail. And they did so in part because of their ambitious leaders. Beyond its finely tuned strategy and technological prowess, Wang's dramatic growth was fueled by the entrepreneurial style of its founder, An Wang. According to one source, "the Doctor," as he was known to all staffers, "imbued management with an audacious, risk-taking willingness to challenge competitors many times Wang's size" (especially the giant IBM).[42]

Industry conditions may also demand that firms take risks. The jet engine business is a highly competitive and very complex crapshoot. It requires huge investments, long lead times, and the courage to undertake perilous gambles to introduce a new machine. Development projects inevitably tax capital resources, and prospective returns are by no means guaranteed. When Denning Pearson took over at Rolls-Royce in 1957, it was necessary to shift the product line to turbofans—the new engine of choice. Pearson took the plunge. As he said then: "Building a new engine would not guarantee that we stayed in business. Not building one would certainly guarantee that we went out of business." He invested $78 million, a huge fortune at the time, to develop the highly advanced and ultimately very successful Spey turbofan engine.[43]

Risk taking was just as common at CDC. According to Gregory Wierzynski of *Fortune* magazine, "Computer manufacturers live dangerously, and [CDC] lives more dangerously than most. Having gained one ambitious goal, its management marches on toward another, still more ambitious, with scarcely a pause for consolidation."[44]

It took CDC many years and tens of millions of dollars to develop a supercomputer. Countless imponderables had to be met, and innumerable insidious bugs and scientific obstacles were the norm. Then a huge slice of earnings had to be plowed right back into developing pioneering features for the next generation of machines. This was no business for the faint-hearted.

In sum, the Pioneer configuration is a wonderfully cohesive and harmonious one, with many complementary parts. Strategy, leadership, culture, and structure all seem to fit together nicely. Pioneers lead their industries with novel technologies, products, and services; sometimes they even establish new markets. They safeguard their lead over the competition by continuing to innovate, occasionally quickening the pace of discovery and redefining the state of the art. And to get the most out of their inventive skills, they go after price-insensitive customers who most appreciate the latest technology. These innovative strategies are strongly supported by the scientific expertise and the missionary zeal of Pioneers' leaders, as well as by the prevailing optimistic and participative corporate cultures. Pioneers' structures further underwrite creativity and invention with their flexibility, their expertise-based authority, and their collaborative techniques, all of which encourage decisiveness and intelligent risk taking.

THE TRANSITION TO ESCAPIST

Because Pioneers are so magnificently rewarded for their innovations, many continue inventing until their momentum turns them into Escapists. We use the term "Escapist" to describe firms that in some sense retire into themselves—into a world of utopian ideals, futuristic technologies, and warm and friendly corporate cultures. The primary concern of Escapists is invention—coming up with new products and new ideas. But invention gets out of hand. It becomes an end in itself—the embodiment of a central mission. Constraints are lost sight of, resource limitations and client needs are ignored, and competitors are scoffed at. Escapists retreat into their own game as their inventive zeal breaks free of market requirements and economic rationality.

The controlled, periodic innovations of Pioneers become, in Escapists, a constant stream of gratuitous novelties that cannot justify their costs of development or that prematurely date existing offerings. Mistakes are made, costs blow out of control, and delays erode market share. To make things worse, some Escapists move into environments with which they are unfamiliar, myopically selling expensive, sophisticated, high-tech products that are unsuited to their new markets.

These problems are fed by missionary leaders, think-tank R&D cultures, and loose structures that seize upon innovation as a way of life. For example, Escapists actively seek out and lionize R&D types who thrive on basic invention—useful or not. Loose, decentralized structures give these people the freedom to embark on ever more ambitious projects. Meanwhile, the marketing and production personnel who might recognize the dangers of such excesses aren't given the power or credibility to stop them. And, unfortunately, financial controls tend to be so primitive that the dangers are slow to be detected. To make matters worse, in many ways Escapists are trapped: their cultures and structures are inappropriate for implementing any strategy *other* than innovation. So firms innovate, in part, because this has become their only significant skill.

Things deteriorate further as the environment changes. Pioneers' successes often attract new competitors into the market. At the same time, as firms grow, their simple, informal structures become less and less adequate. The result is chaos. (Figure 5 summarizes the inventing trajectory.)

ESCAPIST STRATEGIES

All Teched Up with Nowhere to Go

Escapists are run by technology freaks who see invention as an end in itself—even when it's expensive and superfluous; even when customers are not ready for it. Some products are technological marvels that have only a limited market. Others are too expensive vis-à-vis competing lines. And still others are just plain impractical in spite of, or even because of, their advanced technology.

Steve Jobs, the genius behind the popular Apple II, now wanted to go further—this time by paying more attention to technology and less to the needs and resources of users. His innovative Lisa computer could do a lot; however, its price tag, at $10,000, was just too steep. The Lisa was attractive, convenient, and highly sophisticated, but it did not have much of a market. Most hobbyists and homemakers simply could not afford it. Yet the Lisa was too inflexible for engineers and professionals, and not very well suited to the business market because it was hard to write software for and could not be expanded. Apple was losing touch with its customers.[45]

115

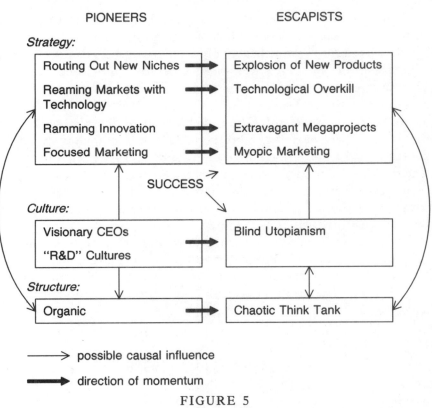

PIONEERS   ESCAPISTS

Strategy:

Routing Out New Niches → Explosion of New Products

Reaming Markets with → Technological Overkill
Technology

Ramming Innovation → Extravagant Megaprojects

Focused Marketing → Myopic Marketing

SUCCESS

Culture:

Visionary CEOs → Blind Utopianism

"R&D" Cultures

Structure:

Organic → Chaotic Think Tank

——→ possible causal influence

━━▶ direction of momentum

FIGURE 5
The Inventing Trajectory

And that is a recurring problem. Escapists tend to become stubborn; they design the products they want rather than those that cater to genuine markets. Missionaries, no matter how astute, do more preaching than listening. And this was again the case at Apple when it first introduced the Macintosh, a sequel to the unfortunate Lisa. According to CEO John Sculley:

> Steve [Jobs] felt that with the Macintosh he would change the way people would view the computer. He didn't see the need for anyone to be able to modify the machine—you could order any color as long as it was black, to use the Ford analogy. And what it meant was that, as Apple began to compete in a marketplace where there were lots of alternative products from competitors that offered a wide range of openness, the Macintosh became more and more isolated because it still focussed on the internal vision of the founder rather than on the needs of the customers.[46]

While IBM was seen as a company turning out quality products and excellent services, the Apple staff wanted to be seen as pioneers; as innovators. They wanted the opportunity to create significantly different products from those that might be turned out in a larger, more structured environment. But when taken beyond a certain point, innovation had its disadvantages. For example, because of the uniqueness of the Macintosh, getting programs written for it was very difficult. In fact, only three programs were ready when the computer was introduced. Early demand flagged.[47]

And yet, as Sculley reminds us, we find the source of Jobs's, and Apples, attitude in its history: "You have to remember that Apple had become an extraordinarily successful company by going against conventional wisdom—that it was successful because it had followed its own instincts rather than listening to the market. That product-driven strategy worked well—as long as there wasn't much competition and Apple was, in effect, creating the industry."[48]

But times had changed, and Apple's strategy failed to reflect this. Disappointing sales and bloated inventories in the Mac division caused the layoff of 20 percent of the workforce. Apple's stock fell to a three-year low as earnings per share dropped from 64 cents in 1983 to about 50 cents in 1985 and 1986. In 1985, Steve Jobs, Apple's thirty-year-old co-founder and chairman, was stripped of all operating authority.[49]

Edwin Land was also increasingly driven toward technological overkill as he ignored market demands and money pressures. Polaroid's earlier cameras had been incrementally honed to make them more convenient, powerful, and cheap. But by 1976, its new products had become more arcane and less practical. For example, at its 1976 annual shareholders' meeting Polaroid announced an 8- by 10-inch instant camera, instant color movies, and a camera the size of a room, for making full-color, instant, lifesize copies of museum paintings that, in Land's words, "will change the whole world of Art . . . make great paintings available in every high school . . . [and] bring museums into the home." These products seemed a bit too futuristic; they were extremely expensive to develop and had very limited market potential.[50]

Megaprojects

Their past successes at innovation induce Escapists, especially those pursuing a ramming strategy, to embark on ever more grandiose development projects. These become so costly, complex, and risky that they drain resources, require high prices, and entail long payback periods. Polaroid's SX-70 camera project is a case in point.

Instead of basing the SX-70 on the successful $30 Colorpack camera, Land insisted that Polaroid start from scratch with a totally new design. The design criteria were simply this: that the photographer need only compose his or her picture and press a button. The parameters that followed from this were startling—single-lens reflex, collapsible for purse, totally automatic exposure and processing, and litter-free film. The reflex viewing system alone cost millions; a single mirror, one of three in the camera, took over two and a half years of computer work to develop; and the eyepiece cost $2 million to design.[51]

According to Dan Cordtz at *Fortune* magazine, the SX-70 project "involved a series of scientific discoveries, inventions, and technological innovations in fields as disparate as chemistry, optics, and electronics. Failure to solve any one of a dozen major problems would have doomed the SX-70."[52]

The total cost of the eight-year program for developing the SX-70 was staggering as Polaroid, for the first time, decided it would have to manufacture the radically new camera itself. It is estimated that over $500 million was spent developing a single product whose sales potential was believed to be only about 1.3 million units. Even an impossible price of $400 per camera would barely recoup the investment in R&D, let alone cover the costs of production and marketing. And, indeed, sales were slow in coming. This was because Polaroid charged $180, or six times the price of its Colorpack, and also because of the competition from its own cheaper models. Clearly the SX-70 represented one of the biggest gambles ever taken on a consumer product. Its gargantuan costs caused earnings per share to fall from $1.90 in 1971 to 86 cents in 1974.[53]

Rolls-Royce got into even more trouble than Polaroid with its massive development effort because it was under more time pressure and had fewer resources. Rolls, a past master at creating new products, pursued nothing less than technological revolution when it undertook the development of the RB.211 engine. With an air intake 8 feet in diameter and 40,000 pounds of thrust, the 211 was designed to be substantially cheaper, more advanced technologically, and more efficient than competing products. Indeed, it was far ahead of the rival engines of Pratt & Whitney and General Electric. CEO Pearson and his staff endowed the RB.211 with three special advantages—each of which presented its own problems. First, the 211 employed an unusual three-shaft construction that required 25 percent fewer parts, reduced noise, and used less fuel. But the novelty of the design entailed numerous costly corrections. Second, the fan blades were to be made of Hyfil, instead of the usual titanium, saving about 300 pounds. But Rolls spent $2.5 million just developing Hyfil, and was having problems machining it. Third, Rolls's price of $575,000 per engine was appreciably lower than GE's $630,000. But this price did not cover costs.[54]

Between 1963 and 1969, Rolls's debenture obligations increased from $36 million to $133 million—to an astounding 84 percent of equity. Resources were doubly strained by severe technical difficulties and cost overruns. The firm reported a $115 million loss in the first half of 1970, which required a $144 million loan package from the Tory government to stave off bankruptcy. Financially oriented executives were ultimately installed to replace engineers Pearson and Huddie.[55]

Ahead of Its Time

Another problem with Escapists is that they are tempted to develop promising products prematurely. They rush headlong into expensive development efforts before either the technological or the market infrastructure has evolved sufficiently to support the innovation.

As Federal Express began to move into electronic mail, it did so in its typically bold and decisive way, spending $100 million to develop, advertise, and promote its new service. FEC offered *ZapMail*—facsimile transmission of messages supplemented by hand pickup and delivery of all documents.[56]

But in 1983 the service seemed premature. For all but the shortest documents, the facsimile technology was far too slow to meet the promised two-hour delivery deadline. Also, low volume and high costs made the service very expensive—$35 for documents of up to five pages, and a dollar for each additional page.

Volume remained low—one tenth of that needed for break-even operation. To boost business, prices were slashed to $25 for up to twenty-page documents, but this didn't help much.[57] So, FEC turned to high technology—sinking $200 million more into ZapMail capital expenditures in 1985. To speed up ZapMail, the company assembled a complex network. Tandem Computers, Inc., and Harris Corporation were hired to install the first part of the system. Thirteen satellite earth stations were linked with more than thirty Tandem computer-switching centers across the country. ZapMail customers leased a ZapMailer state-of-the-art facsimile machine that transmitted documents to other ZapMailers in seconds, instead of the minutes it took for traditional facsimiles.[58]

Unfortunately, even once machines were installed on the premises of customers, they tended not to be used as clients thought no one else had a machine to receive their messages. Further, because the satellite network was not fully operational, FEC had to lease expensive telephone lines, which couldn't handle the speed of the facsimile machines. Garbled messages resulted, and word of this got around. To add to the problems, Tandem's switches developed software troubles due to the slower phone lines. FEC was forced to declare a moratorium on new ZapMail installations. Costs and losses continued to climb, however.[59]

For fiscal 1986, ZapMail lost $132 million on sales of only $33 million. FEC decided to abandon ZapMail and take a $190 million after-tax write-off. Because of the ZapMail losses, profits fell from $2.52 per share in 1984 to $1.61 per share in 1985, and this at a time when FEC's main overnight package delivery business was thriving. It seems the firm had jumped the gun, introducing a radical new service too early and too boldly.[60]

New Product Proliferation

Some Escapists innovate because that is, quite simply, what they do best. In response to problems, they just introduce new products. Whereas rammers go in for megaprojects, routers and reamers pursue numerous smaller product introductions—but they pursue too many of them in too short a time. This is costly, it confuses customers, it makes existing lines prematurely obsolete, and it needlessly complicates operations.

Sun Microsystems was so successful with its workstations that it now saw innovation as the answer to all its challenges. To fight increasing competition, firms like Sun tried to build up as much market share as possible by introducing a slew of new products—at a breathless pace. "Sun's not only trying to grow faster than any other company, but it's trying to do it with one of the broadest lines. It's unprecedented," said Laura Conigliaro, an analyst with Prudential-Bache Securities, Inc.[61]

Sun's product portfolio proliferated wildly, as new products conflicted with old ones and lines became technologically incompatible, making it impossible to shift software between machines. Many customers delayed ordering existing products while awaiting the new ones. And instead of protracting new product introductions over a period of months, Sun, with its usual "full-speed-ahead" style, elected to revamp its entire product line all at once. Furthermore, there was far too little selectivity in new product introduction. Said one employee: 'It was a high excitement, high burnout environment with few review committees. There was no one around at Sun telling me I couldn't do things." Profits fell sharply for the quarter ending June 1989.[62] The same reckless new product proliferation took place at Wang Labs—with the same results.

Delays, Errors, and Cost Overruns

Monstrous development projects and proliferating new products have a way of taxing financial and managerial resources. They make Escapists susceptible to errors, delays, and budgetary lapses. In fact, economic constraints and financial objectives, which had been of only secondary interest to Pioneers, become ignored entirely by Escapists.

During the early 1960s when the CDC 6600 supercomputer was being developed, assumptions about the machine's manufacturing costs, the time to get it to the market, and its reliability of operation all proved too optimistic. Delivery of the 6600 to the Atomic Energy Commission's Livermore Labs was scheduled for February 1964. But the machine had more bugs than anticipated, and delays cost CDC $90,000 per month in penalties. IBM took advantage of the delay to announce its ultra-powerful 360-90 computer, with traditional IBM service support and software. Although IBM was to run into fatal snags creating the 360-90, its announcement blunted CDC's initiative. Many 6600s developed severe problems even after delivery. And because the computers were so complicated, they were hard to troubleshoot. So, during 1964 and 1965, CDC engineers were flying all over the world trying to get their machines to work.[63]

Control Data's performance oscillated wildly. Earnings of $1.06 per share in 1965 became a loss of 98 cents in 1966 as cost overruns from new product development and late delivery penalties took their toll. The stock price fell from $74 to $23.

Almost identical problems occurred at Rolls-Royce while it was developing the RB.211 engine. Delays, snags, bugs, and cost overruns were the order of the day. Rolls was far too optimistic in pricing and scheduling delivery of its pioneering engine. First, it estimated the cost of development to be $156 million—a figure that by 1970 had reached $324 million. Technical difficulties had bedeviled efforts to build a compressor fan out of Hyfil carbon resin. Rolls had done insufficient research on the fiber—which was hard to machine and susceptible to damage from bird strikes. The design team was finally forced to use titanium instead. Second, Rolls had signed fixed-price contracts and could not pass on its increased costs. And third, financial controls were woefully inadequate—they failed to alert managers to the cost overruns.[64]

Similarly, the SX-70 project at Polaroid saw costs soar from a projected $150 million to estimates of well over $500 million (the actual figures were never disclosed).[65]

Myopic Marketing

Recall that as Pioneers, Apple, FEC, and Polaroid were all energetic, albeit highly focused, marketers. But as they move along the inventing trajectory, such firms begin to neglect marketing and to concentrate mainly on technical issues—those that preoccupy the dominant power-holders and are credited with past success. The severity of this error is compounded by two factors. First, their many new products have brought Escapists into different markets, which they do not understand—markets for which they must adapt their products. Second, as Pioneers age, so do their industries. Although novel technology was enough to sell products when an industry was young and Pioneers were protected by their patents, this is no longer true. With the coming of competition, convenience, price, and service begin to count more and more. Marketing becomes increasingly important. And yet, if anything, Escapists pay less attention to marketing. They fall down particularly in the areas of customer support, distribution, pricing, promotion, and above all, relevant design.

POOR CUSTOMER SUPPORT Sun Microsystems, which had sold its workstations mostly to engineers and scientific users, was beginning to sell to less technically sophisticated customers. But it didn't know how. It offered customers too little service support and inadequate software. Furthermore, Sun's many product introductions left it without enough time to develop the kind of bedside manner that IBM and DEC were famous for. This weakness was especially serious when Sun tried to capture commercial customers. In fact, Schlumberger, the oil field services company, was so dissatisfied with Sun's after-sale support that it replaced half its two hundred Sun workstations with DEC machines. "They don't have the expertise in the [oil technology] field," said a Schlumberger vice-president.[66]

Sun also neglected its software operations. It had agreed to distribute some mathematical software made by Wolfram Research, Inc., a small software company in Champaign, Illinois. But Wolfram backed out of the deal after complaining that Sun had taken too long to begin shipping. "We fielded hundreds of calls from Sun customers who tried to contact Sun about our software and were very unhappy with the responses they got," said Wolfram's president.[67]

NEGLIGENT DISTRIBUTION Because Escapists believe that their novel designs alone will sell products, they neglect their distribution channels. Polaroid, for example, viewed its dealers and distributors merely as vehicles for delivering its products to the final customer— as passive rather than active participants in the selling process. Rarely did the company employ sales incentives for its retailers: it avoided introductory specials and cooperative advertising programs. Worse still, it often surprised dealers with new products, leaving them too little time to dispose of the old models before the new ones arrived. Michael Porter comments that Polaroid "never appeared to be concerned over the high turnover in its sales staff, which, in the opinion of many observers, it treated more as 'order takers' than as true salesmen."[68]

Sometimes Escapists fail altogether to mount a selling campaign appropriate to their new target markets. Apple, for example, made little effort to sell its Macintosh computer directly to corporations, and as a result, stood little chance of competing with the sales force of IBM.

UNREALISTIC PRICING   Another problem is that their costly innovations force Escapists to sell their products at too high a price. Polaroid misjudged customers' willingness to pay for the convenience of the SX-70 when its own economical models were already doing a good job. A price of $180 scared away customers. In order to obtain sales, Polaroid had to keep redesigning the camera so that it could drop the price to where customers would buy. In 1974, an SX-70 model with a cheaper case was introduced for $140. Sales rose hardly at all. In 1975, the SX-70 Model III was introduced for $99; it replaced the reflex viewing arrangement with a viewfinder. Again, only a modest increase in sales resulted. In 1976, the SX-70 "Pronto" was introduced for a list price of $66—which was heavily discounted to $49 (only a few dollars over cost). Finally the product began to move.[69] Recall also that Apple's Lisa computer was priced at $10,000, placing it well beyond the reach of most customers.

VANISHING ADVERTISING AND PROMOTION   Many Escapists neglect advertising, preferring to spend more on R&D. Although Apple had allocated a significant fraction of its starting capital to advertising, it did not continue this policy. Its machines sold so well at first that advertising seemed superfluous, so Apple spent its money on research instead. "Historically, marketing at Apple was regarded as an expense rather than an investment," said one Apple marketing director.[70]

IRRELEVANT DESIGN   Perhaps the most serious marketing deficiency is one of product design—the first of the four P's of marketing: product, place (distribution), price, and promotion. Escapists design products that are technically advanced—but not what the customers want. This error stems in part from the attitude that "we alone will decide what's good for the customer." Escapists tell their clients what they *should* have rather than listening to them to find out what they really need and designing their offerings accordingly.

Wang Lab's R&D department became supremely arrogant. Almost all its customers used IBM as well as Wang equipment, and therefore wanted compatibility between the two types of machines. But Wang pressured customers into using products that could be hooked up only with other Wang equipment—and that attitude began to erode their sales once the industry started to slow down.[71]

As we noted earlier, Apple also affected a "we-can-do-no-wrong" posture that many critics blamed for the failure of the Apple III and Lisa. Although the Lisa was intended for a business market, it lacked what corporate clients wanted most—an ability to communicate with other computers, mainframes in particular. The Lisa could not use the software intended for any other machines; to compound the problem, its design made it hard to develop software for. Similar problems existed initially with Apple's Macintosh computer; potential corporate clients tended to view the Mac as a "cutesy, avocado machine intended for yuppies and their kids."[72]

Underdiversification

The term "underdiversification" is a bit misleading. Although Escapists do tend to move into new markets, they do so without really adapting their products. They diversify, or try to diversify, into niches in which their innovative skills are less relevant. But they continue to focus too heavily on the technologies and methods that were appropriate only for their former clients. For example, Apple's computers were fine for personal use but less appropriate for the office. Sun Microsystems' products were suited only to sophisticated customers even though Sun was trying to market them more broadly.

Some Escapists don't even attempt to diversify. Thus Polaroid stuck to instant photography, which it had introduced in 1948. It steadfastly refused to apply its considerable skills to advantage in the traditional market for photography or video technology. When Kodak invaded the "instant" market in 1976, this obsessive focus proved very dangerous. Polaroid launched a series of lawsuits to challenge Kodak's supposed patent infringements but it refused even to consider entering Kodak's market in retaliation.

The Competition

It is worth reiterating that all of the problems described above are aggravated by the mounting competition that commonly occurs after Escapists have created an attractive new product or market, or after their patents expire.

A hazard of pioneering is imitation by efficient competitors who economize on development costs. And, indeed, Pioneers are often copied by their larger rivals. Sun's territory was invaded by Apollo Computer, Polaroid was confronted by Eastman Kodak, and CDC had to face IBM.[73] In fact, the mere announcement by IBM of its competing 360-90 series put a great deal of extra pressure on Control Data and its 6600 computer project. So did IBM's easing of its leasing terms, which forced CDC to respond with price cuts of its own.[74]

Yet instead of countering this competition by responding more sensitively to their markets, most Escapists simply accelerate the pace of invention.

MISSIONARY LEADERS AND UTOPIAN CULTURES

The leadership styles of Pioneers remain essentially intact when they become Escapists. Bosses continue to prize technology and invention above all else; they still see new products as vehicles for improving the quality of life; and they continue to insist upon a loose, informal style of management. But all of these tendencies are amplified along the inventing trajectory. As a consequence, cultures become more missionary, R&D-dominated, and insular. And this strongly reinforces the strategic escapism that we have just described.

The Sacred Mission

Escapists approach their product-market strategies with considerable zeal. Leaders view their markets as their turf—as holy ground that must be defended at all costs. When Kodak began to invade Polaroid's instant photography market in 1976, Edwin Land was moved to comment: "This is our very soul that we are involved with. This is our whole life. For them its just another field. . . . The only thing that keeps us alive is our brilliance, and the only thing protecting our brilliance is our patents. . . . We will stay in our lot and protect that lot. [It is] an overlap of their way onto our way."[75] Products are the means to fulfill a leader's vision of what the world needs. Market preferences and profits are secondary.

At the 1977 shareholders' meeting, after having demonstrated Polaroid's instant movie camera, Land said: "There's a rule they don't teach you at the Harvard Business School. It is, if anything is worth doing, it's worth doing to excess." Land stressed the symbolic importance of technology, without mentioning its implications for Polaroid's business or getting into the specifics of strategy. He spoke only generally and philosophically. Finally one shareholder interrupted to ask: "All of this is well and good. But what about the bottom line?" "You think that the only thing that counts is the bottom line!" retorted Land. "What a presumptuous thing to say. The bottom line," he added, "is in Heaven."[76]

Such missionary fervor can also result in a perfectionism that depletes resources. For example, a story is widely circulated about Control Data's former chief engineer, Seymour Cray. He was known for building a new sailboat each spring, "sailing it over the summer, and then burning it at the end of the season so that he wouldn't be bound by that year's mistakes when he sets about designing a more perfect craft for the following year." That, for better or for worse, was also the costly way in which he approached computer design.[77]

The Primacy of Designers

The prime objective is to innovate, and the greatest rewards and prestige go to the innovators. Everybody else is a second-class citizen. This fine distinction within Pioneers becomes a full-blown caste system within Escapists. Marketing, finance, and manufacturing units all are given short shrift, as are the departments producing older, more established products. Such gross imbalance becomes especially dangerous given the increasing competition and the administrative complexity that comes with growth.

Rolls-Royce has been described as "a company of engineers, remote and self-contained, intensely proud of its reputation, and embarrassed by the fact that it must promote its products." The engineers and designers were the heroes; the marketing and finance people the drones.[78]

Under Steve Jobs, Apple had acquired a near-maniacal focus on novelty: the chairman electrified Apple's corps with talk of "insanely great" new computers. He made stars of new product designers but was very wary of his marketers. According to one of Jobs's lieutenants, "Steve was genuinely frightened that a blue-suited marketer with an MBA wouldn't understand Mac's technological capabilities. He didn't want any bozos around whom he couldn't control."[79]

Jobs's attitude created much friction between the Mac and Apple II divisions. Mac's managers had been publicized as superstars, the firm's corporate elite. "The Apple II division was producing more of the company's sales and most of the profits, yet the Mac division seemed to get all the perks. For a time these included free fruit juice and a masseur on call."[80]

According to several managers, Jobs, a devout believer that "new technology should supersede the old," couldn't stand the success of the venerable Apple II. He did not conceal this fact. Jobs addressed the Apple II marketing staff as members of the "dull and boring product division." Said one Mac staff member, "He was so protective of us that whenever we complained about somebody outside the division, it was like unleashing a Doberman. Steve would get on the telephone and chew the guy out so fast your head would spin."[81]

A former employee of the Apple II division remarked, "We used to say that the Mac people had God on their team." In February 1985, Steve Wozniak—co-founder, designer of the original Apple computer, and an engineer in the Apple II group—finally quit in anger.[82]

CHAOTIC STRUCTURES

Escapists adopt structures that are simply too informal, too loosely controlled, and too primitive for the growing scope and complexity of their operations. They are so concerned with creating a comfortable seedbed for creativity that they neglect the need for control, coordination, and integration. They become think tanks instead of functioning organizations.

Excessive Informality

Most Escapists are too loosely organized to shape and implement strategy in an orderly way. That is one of the reasons why their projects, costs, and product lines get so out of control. It is also why the controlled chaos of the Pioneer degenerates into the unmitigated chaos of the Escapist.

Take Sun Microsystems. According to many industry analysts and former employees, Sun needed to strengthen its management to allow it to continue to grow and to meet the increased level of competition. But "they literally do not have the management in place to make that happen," said one analyst. Sun employed a seat-of-the-pants management style that lacked discipline. Supervision was lax, and managers were trying to do too many things at once. In 1989, founder-CEO Scott McNealy, thirty-four, conceded that Sun had been adding 250 employees a month, too many to assimilate successfully. "Things would inevitably fall through the cracks, sometimes angering customers and business partners."[83]

At Control Data, one of chief designer Seymour Cray's cardinal rules had been to avoid formal meetings and planning sessions. His insistence on informality was legendary. When a vice-president asked Cray to produce one- and five-year development plans, the genius responded in his unique way. The next day, the vice-president found two three-ring binders on his desk, each containing a single page. In the first binder had been written: "Five year plan: To build the world's fastest computers." In the second, the sheet read: "To complete one-fifth of the five year plan."[84]

As Pioneers grow, their informality becomes excessive. At Apple, the lines of responsibility were unclear and communication among divisions got cumbersome. Overtaxed managers began to spend more time deciding who was to do what than actually doing it. As one high-level executive admitted: "I have a top ten list of priorities . . . and there's 19 items on it. That should tell you something. That's a real good example of what Apple is."[85]

Apple's loose structure failed to coordinate the efforts of its principal divisions. Each computer had its own operating group—its own independent clique. So employees lacked a sense of the company's general direction. It was widely held also that Apple's structure had grown remote from any overall logic.[86]

According to John Sculley: "Oh I suppose we used to celebrate the fact that you could do anything you wanted at Apple, if you thought it was a better idea. That was fine when the company was a handful of people trying to invent new things. But it became very destructive when there was no focus or process for people to work together. After awhile, what it meant was that we were treading water."[87]

Poor Controls

The problems of such chaotic organizations were exaggerated by a lack of effective controls. For example, Sun's internal data-processing operation was "so fouled up that the company could not keep track of incoming orders or of what it was producing."[88] The former number-two man, Bernard Lacroute, has criticized Sun's management for trying to do too many things at once. Even Scott McNealy conceded that the company was so bent on achieving rapid growth that it had neglected to invest in internal computer systems and controls. "Any time you don't know how much money you spent last month you're not in control," one Sun official said. "We didn't know how much we spent in May."[89]

Poor controls also cause delays and erode the quality of services. Take the case of Wang Labs. According to analyst Arthur Louis, "As Wang expanded, it became notorious for making promises to customers that it couldn't keep—product deliveries were delayed for months, the billing department became hopelessly snafued, and maintenance and support services just about collapsed."[90]

Bureaucracy vs. Adhocracy

Some Escapists do in fact make an effort to formalize, coordinate, and integrate their operations, and to give the production, marketing, and finance people some parity with the omnipotent R&D group. But this inevitably creates conflict. The R&D people want to preserve the informal "adhocracy" configuration of the Pioneer while the other groups press for a tighter, more bureaucratic structure.

This conflict is reinforced by the administrative realities. As a small organization grows, it begins to require a certain amount of structure. But the pressure from the competition also demands a continual flow of innovations. So firms are in a dilemma. They must balance control with innovative chaos. And, all too often, Escapists opt for the latter.

This, in large part, is because scientists and engineers dominate Escapists—they hold all the power, have the most say about what will be produced, and prefer to work without too many formal plans or controls. Just as the production managers of our Tinkerers preferred bureaucratic structures, and the financial managers of Imperialists loved controls, the scientists in Escapists gravitate toward organic, loose operations, in which spontaneity is encouraged and informality prevails. After all, they reason, such a climate *did* foster successful innovation when Escapists were Pioneers.

But with growth, more formality is needed: integrative devices to foster collaboration among R&D, marketing, and production personnel; and plans, programs, and controls to monitor large-scale ventures, keep them on track, and avoid delays and duplication of effort. As projects escalate in complexity and cost, financial controls also become more essential. Unfortunately, Escapists remain far too informal to properly assimilate these practices.

MAJOR CHANGES ALONG THE INVENTING TRAJECTORY

As Pioneers become Escapists, strategic momentum is everywhere in evidence. Innovation turns into gratuitous invention. Intelligent risk taking becomes grandiosity; and selective and periodic product introductions accelerate to become a constant flow of new offerings. Firms also begin to sell to markets that they no longer understand, using only technology as their major selling point. Meanwhile, R&D and engineering concerns drive out those of marketing, manufacturing, and cost control—aspects of strategy that are increasingly neglected.

Missionary leaders and utopian corporate cultures very much contribute to this transformation by focusing so exclusively on innovation. Moreover, the R&D and new product development groups become ever more powerful, promoting looser, more informal structures that are far too primitive for the increasing size and complexity of operations.

A QUALIFICATION   There is a good deal of variation in the severity of the problems afflicting the firms on our inventing trajectory. Some companies, such as Rolls and Wang, experienced life-threatening deficits. Others, such as FEC, CDC, and Polaroid, were hit with large but survivable losses on a major project. And others still, such as Apple and Sun, faced less severe problems but seemed to be following paths that could get them into more trouble down the road. In spite of these differences, however, the roots of the problems seemed to be the same; and all firms started out as Pioneers, then to varying degrees became Escapists.

CHAPTER 5

From Salesmen to Drifters:
The Decoupling Trajectory

ITS COMPETITORS HAD TO GET UP VERY EARLY INDEED TO GET THE BEST of Procter & Gamble. For decades, P&G was the nation's quintessential mass marketer and its number-one advertiser. It planned its ad campaigns the way a clever general charts out a major battle. With legendary zeal and thoroughness, P&G performed exhaustive marketing research on how best to reach the most promising markets. But it also took great pains to discover consumers' needs—and then to design a highly selective and attractive array of offerings to meet them.

P&G's parade of marketing victories—Crest, Tide, and Pampers, to mention just a few—eventually left some of its managers with the distinct impression that they could sell the sizzle without the steak. To take advantage of its powerful marketing channels and reputation, P&G began to offer a proliferation of mediocre products. An exclusive preoccupation with form and image had begun to drive out substance and quality; and this enabled competitors to steal market share in disposable diapers, detergents, even toothpaste, with fresher, superior products. Meanwhile P&G's growing complexity, complacency, and bureaucracy made it slow to respond to these new challenges.[1]

P&G, IBM, GM, A&P—all are easily recognized by their initials alone. These Salesmen are famous for their forceful mass-marketing strategies, their ample distribution networks, and the household names that make them market-share leaders. Indeed, Salesmen cover their industries deeply and broadly, capitalizing on their reputation by offering a wide array of goods and services. They compete with intensive advertising, fine service and warrantees, and attractive styling and packaging, all of which build—and build on—their image and reputation.

Because Salesmen are so large and diversified, most are structured into energized, semiautonomous divisions that each specialize in a particular product or market and are run by executives with much local authority.

Unfortunately, many Salesmen gradually transform themselves into unresponsive Drifters. They extend their tradition of appealing mostly via image until the package becomes more important than its contents. Product quality and relevance declines; and lines become dated. Also, because Salesmen have so successfully penetrated their markets, they come to believe that they can sell anything. They introduce an ungainly proliferation of conflicting models, enter too many new market niches, or open too many sales outlets.

This disorderly expansion makes for confused, disparate operations and creates labyrinthine structures. Top managers become so distanced from their vast empires that they can no longer either motivate or control their troops. Budgets, planning systems, and bureaucratic rules replace rich cultural values as the central tools of management. And divisions turn into politicized fiefdoms whose frequent turf battles make a coherent strategy impossible to attain. In this gridlock of relationships, the dangerous trends in strategy, structure, leadership, and culture all seem to feed off each other.

THE SALESMAN

SALESMAN STRATEGIES: IMAGE DIFFERENTIATION

Salesmen are behemoths who dominate their industries through *image differentiation*—by cleverly managing the impressions their products and services make on potential customers. They use attractive styling and packaging; provide friendly, dependable service; and devise brilliant marketing strategies—that is, captivating advertising campaigns, forceful direct-selling programs, and well-planned distribution systems. Pioneering designs, low prices, and exceptional quality, however, are alien to a Salesman's competitive arsenal.

Attractive Styles and Designs

Salesmen are very much concerned with making their products attractive and stylish—with giving customers exactly what they want by appealing to their physical senses and their needs for value and security.

Firms like General Motors devoted a great deal of attention to *styling.* Indeed, Alfred P. Sloan, the austere chairman who in the 1920s shaped GM's strategy and structure for decades to come, believed that styling was a cornerstone of success. He thought demand could be created by changing automobile styles every year, in effect making cars into fashion goods. In July 1926, Sloan pressed home the importance of styling to the general manager of Buick: "I am sure we all realize . . . how much appearance has to do with sales; with all cars fairly good mechanically it is a dominating proposition and in a product such as ours where the individual appeal is so great, it means a tremendous influence on our future prosperity."[2]

By 1963 this thrust was still very much alive at GM. Semon Knudsen, who ran the Pontiac division, propelled it to success by creating a hot, spirited stable of cars. He publicized the powerful "wide-track" Pontiac's youthful, sporty looks, and lauded its performance at stock-car races. Knudsen introduced sports coupes, bucket seats, and the elegantly aggressive Grand Prix with its "clean expensive look." A *Fortune* article about GM in 1963 tried to account for GM's brilliant record of success. It referred to the *sporty* Pontiac; the *elegant* Olds; and the *classic* Cadillac. Engineering, the dull stepchild, was hardly ever mentioned. The formula worked. GM consistently outperformed its U.S. rivals in return on sales, return on investment, and market share. It regularly captured over 50 percent of the market, almost twice Ford's share and four times Chrysler's.[3]

The Chrysler of the early 1960s was also a strong proponent of style as CEO Lynn Townsend undertook his dramatic turnaround. One of Townsend's first acts was to recruit a new chief stylist to bring models more into line with what the public wanted. Townsend hired the Ford stylist who had designed the exemplary Lincoln Continental to spruce up Chrysler's car lines. This helped boost sales from 1.2 to 2.2 million units per year between 1963 and 1969. Market share increased from 10 to 18 percent and worldwide sales tripled to $7.4 billion.[4]

For other Salesmen, styling is not so much guided by the artistic proclivities of designers as by the tastes of customers. Procter & Gamble, for example, achieved brand recognition from the distinctiveness and quality it built into its consumer goods. But this was not quality in the sense of superdurability or high-tech design; there were only modest differences between P&G's soaps or diapers and those of its rivals. Quite simply, P&G's products had an edge because they were so painstakingly tailored to the wishes of customers. Elaborate market research ensured that to most people, P&G's products would look, smell, feel or taste better, and be more fun to use.[5]

P&G's ex-chairman, Ed Harness, described its version of consumerism as "giving customers what they want."

> P&G reaches a verdict on its own innovations by rigorously testing them against the competition. A development team begins refining the product by trying variations of the basic formula, testing its performance under almost any conceivable condition, and altering its appearance. . . . Then they start testing variants on hundreds of P&G's own employees. . . . [If the product passes these tests] P&G presents it to panels of consumers picked at random. In all, P&G queries 250,000 consumers a year, asking whether this or that product fills their needs and whether they would buy it.[6]

P&G's designers created bright packages that would stand out on the shelf. In a make-believe supermarket at headquarters, art directors compared their containers with competing brands. Then they thoroughly tested customers' reactions before introducing the design. This kind of attention helped P&G to overtake all of its competitors: Revenues grew at 8 percent per year for over 125 years. And profits and dividends expanded commensurately.[7]

Recall that for Craftsmen, quality was usually a matter of creating products that were objectively excellent; products that lasted longer, performed faster, or whatever. In contrast, Salesmen want to create an image—to appeal to the senses—so subjective quality is most important. Customers are wooed with styles, colors, fragrances, and packaging.

Salesmen who are primarily retailers must obviously create attractiveness differently from manufacturers. Sears, Roebuck & Co., from its beginnings, was known for its shrewd selection of merchandise and its attractive and exciting presentation. Sears obsessively studied what customers wanted and how they wanted it displayed; its managers pored over consumer surveys and tinkered relentlessly with displays until they yielded the maximum returns. And for decades it succeeded brilliantly in attracting millions of shoppers and making them happy.[8] Sears got the inside track on its aggressive competitors by anticipating, interpreting, and catering to the public's tastes. It made the right offer, at the right time, to the right people, and as a result it developed a massive following. Sears outgrew its rival Montgomery Ward tenfold in over a century of competition.[9]

Excellent Service

Salesmen enhance their image and reputation, and differentiate themselves from their rivals, by offering exceptional service. Some variations on this theme include helping customers to use and maintain a product, supplying courteous and unusually informative personnel, and pursuing scrupulously ethical conduct. Such services build up the confidence and loyalty of the customer when products alone will not do the job.

PRODUCT USE AND MAINTENANCE   IBM exhibited stunning profitability and growth in revenues from the early part of the century until 1984. Its long-term performance is, quite simply, without equal. And much of the credit for that performance goes to superb service. According to ex-Chairman Thomas Watson, Jr., "We want to give the best customer service of any company in the world. . . . IBM's contracts have always offered, not machines for rent, but machine services, that is, the equipment itself and the continuing advice and counsel of IBM's staff."[10] IBM, more than any of its rivals, helped its customers to get the most out of their equipment. It provided support software to perform specific jobs, and had a team of servicemen on site within hours of hearing of any problem.

Peters and Waterman tell the story of one witness who observed IBM patriarch Thomas J. Watson, Sr., at a meeting of his officers. The managers were discussing customer complaints, which they had categorized under engineering, manufacturing, and so on.

> After much discussion, Mr. Watson, a big man, walked slowly to the front of the room and, with a flash of his hand, swept the table clean and sent papers flying all over the room. He said, "There aren't any categories of problems here. There's just one problem. Some of us aren't

paying enough attention to our customers." He turned crisply on his heel and walked out, leaving twenty fellows wondering whether or not they still had jobs.[11]

According to IBM's long-time sales manager Francis "Buck" Rogers, "IBM is customer- and market-driven, not technology-driven; salesmen [should] act as if they were on the customer's payroll . . . getting the order is the *easiest* step; after-sales service is what counts." In fact, IBM sales branches were kept to a maximum of one hundred people to make them as quick and responsive as possible.[12]

COURTEOUS PERSONNEL AND ETHICAL SALES POLICIES Salesmen ensure that those employees who are in direct contact with the customer will be unusually helpful. Buck Rogers insisted that every sales proposal be overwhelmingly cost-justifiable *for the customer.* Salesmen were always instructed to recommend the cheapest product that would get the job done. IBM also answered customer complaints—all of them—within twenty-four hours.[13]

The Great Atlantic & Pacific Tea Company rose to prominence to become the biggest retailing chain in the United States, and it maintained this position against all comers for decades, until the 1960s. Many believed that the quality of its service and its ethical policies were largely responsible for A&P's success.[14]

A&P employees scrupulously adhered to the policies displayed very prominently in the front window of each and every store. They knew the policies by heart—"Do what's honest, fair, sincere, and in the best interests of every customer"; "Extend friendly, satisfying service to everyone"; "Give every customer the most goods for her money"; "Cheerfully refund the customer's money if for any reason any purchase is not satisfactory."[15] Customers never had to worry if there was any problem with a purchase. A&P would honor its guarantee. A&P generated an enormous volume of sales by providing competitive goods, honest dealing, and courteous service at a reasonable price. (Sears's service policies were almost identical.) In the process, A&P ruined so many competitors that the U.S. government tried for years to dismantle its operations. By 1950, A&P's sales of $3 billion exceeded the combined volume of its two largest rivals.[16]

Brilliant Marketing

The name says it all: marketing is more important to Salesmen than to any of our other successful types, perhaps because the products themselves are unexceptional. Marketing is the principal means of competing—of enhancing reputation and differentiating offerings. Outstanding advertising and promotion, aggressive direct selling, and well-planned distribution are the major components of the marketing campaign.

ADVERTISING AND PROMOTION Salesmen very actively manipulate the public's perception of their goods and services. Often this is done by mass advertising—copious amounts of it, on television, on radio, or in magazines and newspapers. Because Salesmen deal in gigantic national, even international, markets, they can use the mass media more economically than smaller businesses with sparser constituencies.

Procter & Gamble, for example, is considered the quintessential mass-marketing company. By 1974 it was the nation's number-one advertiser, spending $200 million on TV and providing, by itself, 10 percent of the networks' total revenues. P&G used nonstop advertising to build its brands: it ranked first in the United States in laundry detergent (Tide), shampoo (Head and Shoulders), toothpaste (Crest), disposable diapers (Pampers), shortening (Crisco), and toilet paper (Charmin).[17]

P&G tested its marketing methods as painstakingly as its products. In some cities with cable TV, one advertisement went to homes on one side of a street and another to homes across the road. Researchers then polled residents about what they remembered. P&G constantly ran such tests to discover the most economical combination of ways to reach its customers.[18]

Advertising is even used by Salesmen to rebuild confidence destroyed by past mistakes. When Lynn Townsend took over at Chrysler in 1960, the firm was in a mess. The previous CEO, Lester "Tex" Colbert, had introduced a line of enormous, low-slung gas guzzlers that were overpowered and underengineered. After a brief interval of popularity, the market got wind that there were serious quality problems. It fell to Townsend to patch things up. He immediately took out ads that were unusually frank in order to reverse Chrysler's tarnished image. These admitted to past goofs and made a pledge to do better. They read in part: "We intend to fix what's wrong, keep what's right, and move ahead."[19]

DIRECT SELLING   Many Salesmen complement their mass media efforts with vigorous personal selling. IBM deployed exhaustive sales-training programs, most lasting fifteen months, and salesmen were sent regularly on advanced training follow-ups, where they dissected the psyches of various types of clients. One thousand people a year went through specially designed presidents' classes, taught by fourteen professors from the Harvard Business School and from IBM itself. These instructed salesmen how the presidents of potential customers might think and react. Another thousand salesmen went through the financial officers' course—to learn about the concerns of financial executives. IBM insisted on fifteen days of sales training per year for every employee, no matter how senior.[20]

Sales are also boosted by other methods. For example, GM introduced installment plans and company financing to push its cars. A&P provided money-back guarantees. And Sears strongly pursued convenient catalogue marketing. At Chrysler, ploys such as the five-year, 50,000-mile warranty and even the use of the blue and white Pentastar trademark were smashing successes.[21]

DISTRIBUTION   Some Salesmen aggressively force sales through their distribution channels. "Sales just aren't made, sales are pushed," Chrysler's Lynn Townsend used to say. And push he did. Taking care to find out exactly which models were selling, which styles and colors, Townsend then used computers to establish production schedules for each model for each plant. He monitored where the various models were sold and shipped cars to his dealers accordingly.[22]

Townsend rebuilt the flagging distribution network by recruiting new dealers and realigning dealerships that were competing in marketing areas that were too small. And he set up a system of auditing dealers to spot trouble early. During Townsend's early years, Chrysler added numerous new dealers at promising locations and pared away unproductive dealerships. The boss had shaped a disorderly assembly of car salesmen into a coordinated army of marketers—at least for a time.[23]

AUXILIARY STRATEGIES

Product image and styling, fine service, and brilliant marketing are the foundations of "image differentiation." But there are some support strategies that Salesmen use to complete the picture. These include delaying innovation to conserve resources; selling broad and full product lines to capitalize on reputation and marketing facilities; integrating vertically to achieve economies of scale; and boosting sensitivity to customers to improve styling and marketing.

Not the First to Market

Salesmen are not Pioneers. They cannot introduce many new offerings, as this would overtax their resources and fragment their marketing budget. Also, they have to take time to ensure that a new product is not a bomb that will erode their precious image. Therefore, Salesmen prefer to imitate a new trend rather than establish one.

IBM was seldom the first with state-of-the-art products. UNIVAC and others led; IBM learned from their mistakes, introducing its new products only after much testing. Having decided on a course of action, however, IBM moved decisively. This was true, for example, of its PC microcomputer, which came out only after Apple and others had established the potential for such a product.[24]

P&G also took "this farsighted view, rather than jerking the company from one course to another in response to breezes in the market." From 1970 to 1974, P&G introduced only two new products, even though it was spending over $100 million per year on research. It often took a decade to fine-tune an item before bringing it to market.[25]

In the early 1960s, GM lagged behind its competitors in developing compact cars. It let Ford move first. GM's strength was stylish imitation, not novelty. Furthermore, Chairman Frederick Donner saw that GM had much to lose from any mass defection from large to small cars, so "it wasn't of a mind to lead the stampede."[26]

We will see later that this cautious adaptation on the part of Salesmen can easily turn into the sluggish unresponsiveness of Drifters.

Full Lines

Salesmen seek broad market coverage by offering full lines that take advantage of their size, reputation, and marketing prowess. At GM, for example, the Cadillac name and image helped to sell a number of different models. Full and varied lines also satisfy a wide range of customers and increase market share. And fortunately, Salesmen are big enough to achieve economies of scale even for highly elaborate lines.

GM Chairman Alfred Sloan's motto was "a car for every purse and purpose." He articulated this policy as follows: "[GM] should produce a line of cars in each price area, from the lowest price up to one for a strictly high-grade-quantity production car . . . the price steps should not be such as to leave any wide gaps in the line and yet should be great enough to keep their number within reason, so that the greatest advantage of quantity production could be secured . . . there should be no duplication by the corporation in the price fields or steps."[27] Sloan's innovation was a major reason why GM was able consistently to trounce both Ford and Chrysler. GM simply covered the market more thoroughly, earning excellent margins in niches neglected by the competition.

Townsend knew this. He believed he too could increase Chrysler's market share vis-à-vis GM and Ford by selling as full a line of cars as possible. He wanted to deny his competitors the huge gaps that Chrysler had left in the marketplace.[28] By the mid-1960s, the line in Chrysler's showrooms had increased by 50 percent. Plymouth and Dodge were segmented into four different price lines. However, to hold down costs and ensure maximum sales, Townsend, at least initially, rationalized his lines—ensuring, for example, that Dodge and Plymouth would complement each other instead of competing as they had in the past.[29]

A&P spread its reputation and sales expertise not only across different lines of food, but geographically as well. By 1925, A&P had fourteen thousand stores scattered over twenty-nine states; its dairy and grocery products numbered more than six hundred items, and fruits, vegetables, and fresh meats had been introduced in select locations. A&P's managers felt they could use their good name to market a full line of food products in the most promising markets of the country. Complete lines also increased store sales, bringing customers "one-stop shopping," 1920s style.[30]

Many Salesmen use *related diversification* to extend and build upon their reputations and to make more use of their marketing and manufacturing abilities. For example, Chrysler invaded the world market with Simca and Rootes Motors, as well as starting up operations in Mexico, Venezuela, Greece, Spain, and elsewhere. Sears continued to explore the potential of lines it wasn't yet selling to see if it should branch out; it also moved into promising new fields such as travel, insurance, and financial services. GM expanded abroad to buy Opel and Vauxhall, and it ventured into the manufacture of trucks, refrigerators, and army vehicles.

Backward Integration

Salesmen want to control the quality of their supplies in order to protect their reputations. They also seek economical parts and products that they can sell to build market share. Therefore, given their tremendous sales volume, many Salesmen "integrate backward," that is, they start to manufacture items for themselves. This provides economies of scale and enhances profit margins. It also allows retailers to trade upon their reputations for quality by selling their own store brands.

When suppliers offered prices that A&P's bosses saw as being too steep, as soon as volume warranted it, A&P began to manufacture those products itself. Such backward integration assured consistently high-quality supplies at reasonable prices.[31] Chrysler and GM manufactured many of their own parts simply to benefit from the economies in manufacture.

Sensitivity to Markets

To provide the most attractive products and services, Salesmen must find out what their customers want. This they do by thoroughly studying their markets and by adapting in light of what they learn.

SCANNING Salesmen adopt elaborate sensing mechanisms to get close to their customers. Their best ideas come from clients; not, as was true of Pioneers, from a staff of "rocket-scientists." Salesmen scan their markets both to get ideas and to test new products.

Even Peter Drucker was impressed with Sears, commenting that "True marketing starts out the way [Sears, Roebuck] starts out: with the customer, his demographics, his realities, his needs, his values. It does not ask: 'What do we want to sell?' It asks: 'What does the customer want to buy?' It does not say, 'This is what our product or service does.' It says, 'These are satisfactions the customer looks for.' "[32]

P&G, with its "testing fetish," constantly subjected all of its new product ideas to potential clients. According to one frustrated competitor, a Crown Zellerbach executive, "P&G tests and tests and tests. . . . They leave no stone unturned, no variable untested." The knowledge P&G gleaned from its surveys and tests was immense.[33] Peters and Waterman point out that "P&G was the first consumer goods company to put the toll-free 800 phone number on all its packaging. In its 1979 annual report, P&G says it got 200,000 calls on that 800 number, calls with customer ideas or complaints. P&G responded to every one of those calls and the calls were summarized for monthly board meetings. Insiders report that the 800 number is a major source of product improvement ideas."[34]

IBM, too, was careful to poll customers about problems with existing systems, and top executives received *daily* tabulations of customer complaints and lost orders. To learn still more, the top corporate officers at IBM personally made sales calls with great regularity.[35]

ADAPTATION   Polling customers would not mean very much unless firms did something with their discoveries. And Salesmen do respond, designing and redesigning products and updating their product lines accordingly.

IBM obtained most of its new product ideas directly from its customers. It was driven toward its "distributed processing" system by one large customer, Citibank. Most of its early innovations, *including its first computer*, were developed in collaboration with a lead customer, the U.S. Census Bureau.[36]

GM at one time had an eerie knack for sensing changes in customer preferences. In the early sixties, when buyers began to hanker for more variety and luxury in automobiles, GM had the most desirable merchandise in this class, and captured 66 percent of the market. It found out what appealed to car buyers in the most rapidly growing market segments, and it designed and powered its lines—fins and all—to match.[37]

A&P responded not only to customer tastes but to demographics and the strategies of competitors. In 1936, the giant became aware of its rivals' successes with "supermarkets." A&P responded by becoming the first major grocery chain to convert its total operations to the new retailing format. By 1938, A&P had opened an astounding 1,100 supermarkets across the nation. By 1950, the conversion was complete—the company operated only 4,514 large stores (compared to its former 14,000 small ones), of which 4,000 were supermarkets. One reason for A&P's adaptability was its one-year store leases, which gave the colossus the flexibility of its smallest competitors.[38]

According to Harvard Professor Roy Johnson Bullock, "The keynote of A&P's progress has been adaptability . . . this concern has consistently ridden the crest of the wave."[39]

One former A&P executive, William Walsh, sums it up nicely: "A&P's true genius was the adaptability to change the outward form swiftly, efficiently, and en masse, without deviation in the basic underlying policy upon which the business was founded—namely, providing the most good food for the money."[40]

"ORGANIZATION MAN" LEADERS AND CULTURES

Salesmen favor sophisticated, decentralized operations that are animated by intense values and loyalties but monitored by professional management. They blend formality with informality, that is, *cultural with administrative control*, and this is a tough balancing act.

A Legacy of Strong Cultural Values

Most Salesman companies were built up by visionary marketers with a fierce commitment to serving their customers honestly and well. Executives such as Julius Rosenwald at Sears, the Watsons at IBM, and the Hartfords at A&P propounded service and performance values that they infused into the corporate psyche, producing strong, coherent organizational cultures. These cultures clearly engendered esprit de corps. They gave employees something special to believe in and shoot for—something that went beyond the mere drudgery of making a living.[41]

However, cultural values not only shaped product/service policies; they also affirmed the importance of the individual employee, molded the style of management, and created pride in the uniqueness of the organization. Such culturally based values motivated everyone to create better goods and services.

Take Peter Schisgall's account of the P&G culture: "They speak of things that have very little to do with price of product. . . . They speak of business integrity, of fair treatment of employees. 'Right from the start,' said the late Richard R. Deupree when he was chief executive officer, 'William Procter and James Gamble realized that the interests of the organization and its employees were inseparable. That has never been forgotten.' "[42] The involvement among P&G employees was truly intense; they showed a positively religious commitment to doing things the company way. Recruits either embraced P&G's values or they got out. There was no middle ground.

IBM had an equally strong culture, which stressed the overriding value of the individual employee. According to Thomas J. Watson, Jr., "This is a simple concept but it occupies a major portion of management time. We devote more effort to it than to anything else." To prove it, IBM avoided layoffs and firings at all costs; promoted from within; and established IBM day-care centers, running tracks, and tennis courts. IBM also trained and indoctrinated its employees intensively, promoting an open-door policy to give everyone access to the top executives. It even circulated an IBM songbook. Watson Senior's enshrined homilies and celebratory hoopla also played a role. Perhaps most ingeniously of all, sales quotas were set so that most employees could meet them—and thus perceive themselves as winners.[43]

John and George L. Hartford at A&P indoctrinated all their employees in their core policy: "Always do what is honest, fair, sincere and in the best interests of our customers." They drummed in this message relentlessly. Their policy booklet was the A&P bible: it stressed courteous, prompt, attentive, patient service; instant refunds; best values; no cutting corners.[44] The Hartfords met with dozens of store managers every week to reinforce A&P values and to express their appreciation to employees for their services. Pensions were introduced when these were rare in the industry. And since most of A&P's profits were donated to the Hartford charitable foundation, many A&P'ers felt they were contributing to a good cause. All of this inspired intense loyalty.[45]

In fact, the Salesman culture breeds "organization men"—in the best sense of the word. Managerial ranks swell with devoted individu-

146

als who have spent long years with the organization and are extremely well versed in many aspects of its business. GM, for example, was usually run by automobile men—leaders who had lived their entire professional lives in the firm or one of its divisions. The same was true at IBM, Chrysler, and P&G.

According to William H. Whyte's classic, *The Organization Man,* company men not only work for the organization, they belong to it. They "have taken vows" of organization life, "and it is they who are the mind and soul of our great self-perpetuating institutions."[46] Michael Maccoby, in *The Gamesmen,* elaborates on this: "Company men equate their personal interest with the company's long-term development and success . . . their belief in the company may transcend self-interest."[47]

Professional Administration

Salesmen's cultures were established years ago by their visionary leaders. The present leaders, in contrast, are professional managers who certainly maintain the culture but do not alter it much. They devote most of their time to strategic and financial issues, not ideological ones.

The professional managers who run Salesmen tend to have backgrounds in marketing or finance. Like the leaders of Builders, they manage the bottom line and pursue growth. On the other hand, they are really more concerned with profitable increases in market share than with growth per se; they are far more familiar with the details of their more focused businesses; and they are aided by a strong culture, a solid company reputation, and a clear, concerted strategy.

Leaders concentrate on the major issues: capital budgeting, introducing new product lines, vertical integration, and diversification. The operating details are left to subordinates. CEOs devour accounting reports, request endless market research studies, and some even talk to customers. But unlike the bosses of Craftsmen and Pioneers, they shy away from manufacturing and technical issues.

Chrysler's Lynn Townsend was trained as an accountant. He said: "You control the company by a knowledge of figures." The reports were what excited him.[48] He didn't understand much about engineering—but he did know which lines were moving, where, and to whom. He also knew where much of the profit came from. Townsend's interests were the facts, plain and simple. According to Michael Moritz and Barrett Seaman, "The head of automotive sales would know that he would have to come up with a good excuse if he didn't meet his sales targets. In the 'war room' at Highland Park, the charts of market share for each model, which hung on the walls, would be watched nervously. In the plants, managers were grimly determined to meet their production targets and zone sales managers would concentrate on shoving the new cars onto dealers."[49]

Salesmen's top executives, however, are usually familiar with more than just the financial side of operations. At GM, Sloan wanted executives to be knowledgeable about a wide range of functions. He encouraged young managers, usually graduates of the General Motors Institute, to progress through engineering, manufacturing, and marketing. Many would start in a plant, then work their way up.

There were differences among our Salesmen in the balance between cultural and administrative control. Over the years, there was a gradual dilution of cultural values and a movement toward professional administration as operations became larger and more diffuse. And perhaps because of their age and complexity, the car firms tended to emphasize bureaucratic, professional administration, whereas the simpler retail operations, especially in their early years, relied more on cultural values. As we will see, this substitution of bureaucratic for cultural controls becomes even more pronounced in the transition from Salesmen to Drifters.

DECENTRALIZED STRUCTURES

Much of the substantive task of management takes place at the second tier. Because of their size and the range of their products and markets, Salesmen are split into product-market divisions or regional profit centers. Significant discretion is given to the divisional heads, who understand their customers best and take responsibility for the overall performance of their units. Head office mostly sets the general policies and guides major capital allocations and changes in product lines.

"Decentralized Operations . . . with Coordinated Control"

Alfred Sloan was canonized for the system he conceived in the 1920s for administering GM's far-flung empire. Advocating a balance between financial oversight and operational autonomy, Sloan split GM into major car divisions—Chevrolet, Pontiac, Cadillac, and so on—each with its own design, manufacturing, and marketing departments, and with a divisional vice-president responsible for both market share and profitability.[50]

Sloan believed that overall policies should be set at the top of the firm, usually by a committee of executives. But the heart of Sloan's system was "decentralized operations and responsibilities with coordinated control—Give a man a clear-cut job and let him do it." This balance between centralization and decentralization helped GM remain responsive in spite of its complexity and size. According to Robert Sheehan, in 1963, GM's structure, on the one hand, permitted "the maximum exercise of initiative by relatively autonomous division managers, thus fostering throughout the units of GM all the beastly aggressiveness you would expect of a small, hungry company. On the other hand, the system provides, through the subtle ministrations of the GM governing committees and general staff, the centralized planning, policy direction, [and] specialized services . . . so necessary to a large scale enterprise."[51]

Chrysler and IBM were set up in much the same way. But retailers such as A&P were split into geographical operating divisions to boost their responsiveness to local markets. These divisions were subdivided by region into units, each with its own directors of sales, warehousing, and administrative staff. Each division was headed by a president who served on the A&P board. This decentralization allowed the Hartford brothers who ran A&P to move away from routine problems and focus on strategy.[52] A comparable structure was adopted by Sears.

That concludes our look at the formal aspects of structure. The informal aspects are every bit as important, however, as they contribute to the energetic commitment of managers. Salesmen strive to minimize the effects of departmental barriers, hierarchy, and bureaucracy by encouraging corporate entrepreneurship, and by promoting flexible task forces and internal competition.

Corporate Entrepreneurship

CONTROLLED INITIATIVE   We saw that Salesmen take care to push authority down to the line managers in closest contact with particular products and markets. These managers are given as much authority as is needed to work for results within their control—market share, productivity, and profit. Such accountability and freedom drives them to be entrepreneurial. At the same time, strong corporate cultures, clear values, and well-known role models ensure that managers will act in the company way.

According to Peters and Waterman, at P&G "the brand manager is anything but a swashbuckling entrepreneur. On the other hand, the entire socialization process of . . . the P&G system is aimed at making him believe that that's exactly what he is: a hero. Time and again, the system of myths and tales lauds the valiant brand manager who has challenged those many years his senior and repositioned his brand against all odds."[53] Although P&G's brand management structure strongly guided the way decisions were made, managers still felt that they had a great deal of independence.

TEMPORARY TEAMS   Salesmen use project teams to build initiative and get around departmental and hierarchical barriers. To develop the 360 computer, IBM established a giant task force with a fluid structure. Reorganizations took place with great regularity; contact among team members was intense; everyone had the authority to make binding commitments; and there was a widespread sense of shared responsibility.[54]

GM encouraged ad hoc groups that cut across lines of authority to start small development projects. Divisions were given seed money precisely for such purposes. One such group, under Ed Cole, gave birth to GM's first compact car, the Corvair. The group contained members from engineering, manufacturing, research, styling, and distribution, all of whom met once a month to guide the project.[55]

LOCAL IDENTIFICATION AND INTERNAL COMPETITION   Competition is encouraged among divisions to increase their initiative and ingenuity. This forces managers to identify with a smaller, more immediate, more involving group. At GM, it produced a cadre of "Pontiac men," "Chevy men," and so on.

P&G instigated the idea of competition among its brand managers in 1931, encouraging "a free-for-all among brands with no holds barred." Management decided, even then, that internal competition was the best way to promote initiative among its employees. According to Peters and Waterman, brand managers were "encouraged to compete. There is even a special language to describe their competition: 'counterpartism,' 'creative conflict,' 'the abrasion of ideas.' . . . A large share of new P&G products is likely attributable to the intensity of brand managers' desires to be judged winners. Each year's brand managers become a 'class,' and competition among classes is fierce."[56]

IBM also used multiple approaches to the same design problem. Then, at some point, it had "shootouts" among the prototypes of competing groups to make real performance comparisons. Unfortunately, when Salesmen become Drifters this energizing sense of competition escalates into heated turf battles and a destructive factionalism.

Cautious, Analytical Decision Making

For all their initiative, Salesmen are cautious decision makers. In order to protect their image, they screen all proposals very thoroughly, taking care to gather reams of facts before acting.

P&G did crisp, penetrating studies that confounded its competitors. Its staff were stars at getting the numbers, analyzing them, and using them to solve problems. Said one financial analyst of P&G, "They are a very deliberate, exacting company." Added another, "They are so thorough it's boring."[57] Peters and Waterman go on to comment: "Outsiders wonder how they can be all that thorough, deliberate and exacting if reports are only a page long. Part of the answer lies in the struggle to get it all on that one page. Tradition has it that the typical first memo by an assistant brand manager . . . requires at least fifteen drafts. Another part of the answer is that they have plenty of back-up analysis available, just like everyone else. The difference at P&G is that they don't inflict all those pages on one another."[58]

Lynn Townsend at Chrysler was a great believer in such management tools as computers, statistics, operations research; his computer installation grew to be the biggest in the industry.[59] Every day when Townsend arrived at his Highland Park office, he received detailed up-to-the-hour reports on retail deliveries in the field, a summary of each plant's output, the number of units shipped from each plant, as well as cumulative monthly totals, a report on new orders, and a report that compared orders, production, and retail deliveries. He would not move before knowing all the facts.[60]

To recap, all of our Salesmen pursued a primary strategy of image differentiation, with carefully honed mass-marketing campaigns, penetrating distribution networks, and superb services. But they were careful to support this effort with a "secondary strategy" of designing up-to-date offerings and tailoring them to the needs of their customers. Also, although our Salesmen adopted formal, divisional structures and financial controls to oversee their complex operations, they managed to avoid the stultifying effects of bureaucracy by infusing these structures with meaningful cultural values. In the trajectory from Salesman to Drifter, the original marketing strategies and formal structures are extended, but unfortunately the essential "secondary" product-design strategies and cultural values disappear.

THE TRANSITION TO DRIFTER

Momentum drives many Salesmen to become Drifters by amplifying four of their most prominent practices. Each of these begets its own type of "decoupling."

First, Salesmen capitalized on their reputations and marketing abilities, and successfully increased their scale and scope by adding to their lines—offering more models and opening up new outlets. Overconfident Drifters extend this strategy by expanding their lines and outlets too broadly and indiscriminately. The result: the first type of decoupling, in which product lines are no longer either complementary or cohesive. Strategic focus and integration are lost, and a sense of aimlessness ensues.

Second, Salesmen are primarily marketers and image builders, not high-quality producers or innovators. Their past successes and abilities encourage them to continue to stress image over substance, while engineering, marketing, and product renewal are increasingly neglected. Hence the second kind of decoupling—that from markets. Drifters' lines fall behind the times and cease to have much appeal.

Third, massive operations, line proliferation, and a lack of strategic focus can give rise to bureaucracy and "management-by-numbers," with its arid leadership and politicized corporate culture. Conversely, weak leadership and politics can induce divisions to pull in opposite directions, thereby further blurring strategic focus. Such conflict continues to erode the organization's cultural values, which then are replaced by more stifling controls. And this gives us our third type of decoupling: that of leaders and significant cultural values from the organization.

Fourth, decentralization and remote leadership can fragment the organizational culture and promote turf battles. In this fourth type of decoupling, individual units become disconnected, which further diffuses strategy and inhibits adaptation.

In short, dangerous extremes are reached as full lines widely proliferate; as an emphasis on marketing leads to the triumph of packaging over contents; as professional administration becomes insipid bureaucracy; and as decentralization becomes fragmentation. (Figure 6 summarizes the decoupling trajectory.)

DRIFTER STRATEGIES

Drifters' strategies are subject to two major tendencies: the drift toward product proliferation; and the drift away from markets. We shall deal with these in turn.

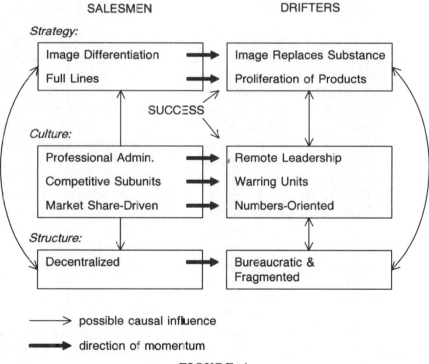

FIGURE 6
The Decoupling Trajectory

Product Proliferation

We saw that our Salesmen were able to broaden their product lines very successfully to extend their market coverage. They capitalized on their reputations, their extensive distribution channels, and their powerful mass-marketing apparatus to expand their array of offerings and outlets. But past success induces Drifters to take this strategy too far. Product-line proliferation begins to wipe out economies of scale, to dilute quality, and to confuse the customers with meaningless brand distinctions. It also pulls firms into niches of little promise, and for which they have inadequate expertise. In short, product lines become diffuse, disjointed—*decoupled*.

Strategic Drift

Product-line proliferation creates a number of problems. It prevents managers from focusing clearly; it escalates costs, reduces quality, and confuses customers; and it destroys the distinctiveness, even the identity, of the products themselves.

Product profusion may *prevent Drifters from focusing attention* where it is really needed. At IBM, for example, the system of competing projects had begun to generate far too many marginal items. Engineers frittered away their talent on small ventures instead of concentrating on the projects that really mattered. IBM introduced minor product variations that vied against each other in the marketplace, instead of bringing out significant new products that could really make a difference. For example, it left huge gaps in the growing workstation business and in software for networking computers.[61] By 1986, IBM's profits were down for the second year in a row, the first double drop since the 1930s. Revenues were flat, and return on equity was down to 14 percent from the recent average of 20 percent.

Proliferating lines may also *drive costs too high*. What started as a rational attempt to produce a fuller line of cars blew out of control as Chrysler's already substantial array of models ballooned from 244 to 370 between 1960 and 1967. Plymouth and Dodge alone rolled out 160 styles with countless combinations of options. This explosion of models escalated costs. An enormous variety of parts had to be manufactured in uneconomic quantities as mercurial stylists came to dominate manufacturing. A Chrysler speedometer, for example, had twenty-two parts, a Buick's only two.[62] By the time Townsend left Chrysler in 1975, the firm was on its way to its biggest loss in history—$282 million—and market share had fallen from 18 percent in 1969 to 12 percent in 1976.

Product proliferation also absorbs time and resources, and *reduces average quality*. P&G, which as a Salesman had gradually and successfully introduced new products, now grew too liberal with its line expansions. It brought out many nondescript, mediocre items, taking "its eye off the ball of superior performance in the early 1980s," according to a senior vice-president at the advertising firm of Ogilvy & Mather.[63] "[P&G] is bringing some products to market more quickly, with little or none of the test-marketing that used to be mandatory. It is introducing me-too products that aren't distinctive in performance. It no longer disdains the low-priced end of the marketplace, and has developed bargain brands. It is bringing out product-line extensions—different 'flavors' of dishwasher detergent and cleansers . . . that follow consumer trends instead of leading them."[64] In 1985, P&G's profits fell 29 percent, its biggest decline in thirty-seven years. Sales showed a meager, erratic growth that averaged only 4 percent per year from 1980 to 1985.

At retailers such as A&P and Sears, proliferation took the form of too many types of stores and selling policies that *confused the customer*. A&P's strategy over the years had been to expand by gradually opening stores and broadening its lines. But it began to do this far too quickly and indiscriminately. "A-stores" and "WEO superdiscount" stores, a myriad of manufacturing establishments, and a trading-stamp operation all appeared within a short space of time. The large variety of retail operations, each with a different policy, confused shoppers who no longer knew what the A&P logo stood for. It also induced top managers to lessen their escalating administrative burden by splitting A&P into thirty-three autonomous geographic units. But these units, unfortunately, proceeded to head off in different strategic directions—with different pricing, merchandising, and inventory policies. As the company became more and more fragmented, with no central strategy, its customers no longer knew what to expect. In the 1950s, A&P started on a steady road to decline that was to bring it to the brink of bankruptcy by the early eighties. Competitors stole its business, resources bled away, and A&P was forced to sell off most of its stores in order to survive.[65]

Sears was into everything—stock brokerage, superstores, boutiques, children's stores, real estate services, appliance marts, and much more. Gradually, slowly, it drifted ever further afield, obliterating both its core strategy and its market identity. Sears became a jack-of-all-trades, master of none, as it began to confuse and alienate its customers. Increasingly, it was squeezed by specialty boutiques from above and by mass discounters from below. Growth slowed to a crawl—less than 3 percent from 1983 to 1988; Sears's share of U.S. general merchandise sales fell from 18 to 13 percent between 1978 and 1988; and return on equity averaged 12 percent as against the industry average of 15.5 percent.

At GM, almost all of the above disadvantages of proliferation could be found, plus one more—the *destruction of product-line differentiation*. Between 1950 and 1983, the number of major lines of cars increased almost sevenfold, from five to thirty-four. This confused customers and escalated costs. Many models were so alike in style, price, and size that GM "lost the marketing advantage of differentiation and they still had poor costs," said Maryann Keller, an auto analyst.[66] Buick and Chevy models were only a few hundred dollars apart.[67] This was also true of the look-alike J-cars—the Chevy Cavalier, Olds Firenza, Cadillac Cimarron, and so on. The A-cars—Pontiac 6000, Chevy Celebrity, etc.—too were similar to each other and to GM's G and X lines.[68]

Line proliferation also made GM the highest cost producer in the industry. Toyota produced fifty-eight passenger vehicles per employee, Ford sixteen, and GM only 11.7; labor costs per vehicle for the three firms were $630, $2379, and $4148, respectively.[69] GM's profits hit the skids in 1979 as earnings per share fell from $6.00 to a loss of $1.33 (GM's first loss since 1921) in 1980. By 1982, GM was still earning only $1.50. Its market share fell from almost 50 percent in 1978 to 33 percent in 1987.

Diversification

We saw how Salesmen diversified to take advantage of their size, reputation, and superb marketing abilities. Drifters, again, take this strategy too far, moving into areas that are not very promising and that fail to mesh with their existing businesses.

P&G, for example, moved into the low-margin food industry with its Citrus Hill orange juice and Duncan Hines cookies. It took over dishwater-dull Crush International beverages in 1980, which had little success in selling its soft drinks. Norwich Eaton Pharmaceuticals was acquired in 1982, and it too could not come up with any product winners. P&G did not know how to manage these firms, so it abandoned them—to flounder unsuccessfully.[70]

The same was true of GM's takeover of Hughes Aircraft, which made it one of the largest U.S. defense contractors, with an array of military technology that included lasers, missiles, airborne radar, and advanced aerospace electronics. GM left Hughes pretty much alone.[71] But it took more of a hands-on approach with Ross Perot's Electronic Data Systems (EDS), a data-processing company which it acquired in 1984. GM thought that EDS could help computerize car manufacturing—something EDS knew nothing about. Friction developed between the two very different corporate cultures, making GM managers reluctant to use EDS services. Said one GM executive to another: "It will be a cold day in hell before I make those bastards from Texas richer."[72]

Sears bought Western Auto Supply (a chain of paint and hardware stores), some freestanding children's apparel stores, the Coldwell Banker real estate concern, and the Dean Witter stockbrokerage. But it knew very little about any of these businesses and had a devil of a time integrating them with existing operations.

So the attempts of Drifters to diversify result only in unclear strategies and confused operations, which are more likely to bleed resources and create disharmony than to contribute to synergy.

The Drift Away from Markets

We now turn to the second kind of decoupling—that of Drifters from their markets. Salesmen had a tendency to pay more attention to image than to product—to marketing rather than to design, R&D, or engineering—and they thrived. Unfortunately, success and the growing gap between marketing and design skills amplify this bias. Firms become convinced that they can sell almost anything to anyone, that their product lines need little renewal or adjustment. Soon, their offerings start to deteriorate, and self-satisfied Drifters begin to dictate to their customers and distribution channels rather than responding to them. Increasingly, the central impetus to action

157

becomes the preferences of managers rather than the needs of customers.

Stale, Unresponsive Offerings

Although Salesmen were rarely the first out with a new product, they did seize upon proven opportunities pioneered by others. Drifters, however, sink deeper into conservatism, allowing lines to become outmoded and permitting competitors to pass them by. From 1978 to 1983, P&G failed to come up with any new product other than Rely tampons, which it soon dropped because of their association with toxic shock syndrome.[73]

In the computer market, small firms such as Sun and Apollo forged ahead with powerful workstations while the giant was caught napping. When IBM entered with products of its own, these were snubbed because they were so underpowered. IBM won only 3.9 percent of this most lucrative and expanding market, whereas Sun and Apollo took 29 and 21 percent, respectively.[74]

At least IBM was attempting, however haltingly, to counter the right threats. That was not true of GM, which continued to view the small car market as an aberration of the oil crisis. According to Chairman Roger Smith, if the price of gas were to drop to "a nickel a gallon," the Japanese penetration of the U.S. market would disappear. He said this in *1982,* after GM had been dragged, kicking and screaming, into competing internationally. Smith, very clearly, had failed to grasp that the deadly inroads made by foreign manufacturers were based as much on quality, performance, and style as on fuel consumption.

GM's inadequate response to this foreign invasion was to cut costs and develop new models such as the J-car, which critics dubbed the Edsel of the eighties—"little more than a modest counterfeit of the machinery the Japanese were already beginning to phase out and replace."[75] Unfortunately, GM refused to make any fundamental changes in its design strategy; it continued to be unresponsive twenty-five years after small cars had begun to devour its market.[76] In fact, GM still took over two years to make a small styling change; twice that to revamp an engine design.[77] With such sluggishness, how could the company possibly compete?

Ten years earlier, Chrysler had also begun to build the wrong kinds of cars for the wrong kinds of buyers. It tinkered with warrantees and advertising as its models grew more and more stodgy. Chrysler's cars came to appeal only to older, conservative buyers who resisted buying high-margin options.[78] The firm remained consistently out of phase with what the market wanted: it was unable to move its big cars during the 1973 oil crisis, and then was caught with too few medium-size and large models when customers turned to these a few years later.[79]

Sears's problem was more one of antiquated retailing strategy than stale product design. It came to be known as an "American institution in decline, an organization that has settled too snuggly into its dwindling market." As Patricia Sellers at *Fortune* magazine put it: "Compared with its fleet-footed competitors, Sears is a 2,000-pound centipede. The antennae work poorly, so the creature is directionless. When some of the 101 legs try to move ahead, others interfere and even move backward."[80]

Core middle-class customers were deserting in droves to specialty stores. Sears's facilities were becoming dowdy, and high costs and prices allowed aggressive discounters like Wal-Mart and "superstores" like Circuit City, Inc., to inflict lots of damage.[81] Twenty years earlier, the story had been very similar at A&P.

Poor Quality

Drifters neglect the design function, and this hurts the quality of their products, which tend to be not only unresponsive to customers' needs but also badly designed, underpowered, or overpriced.

P&G's enduring bias toward marketing became a monomania. Quality plummeted as design and engineering considerations were ignored. In soaps, P&G tried to topple the leading Wisk liquid detergent with two insipid, run-of-the-mill liquids called Era and Solo. It failed to make a dent in this market. In disposable diapers, Kimberly Clark had been stealing market share from P&G since 1979 with its Huggies brand, a premium diaper with non-leaking elasticized legs. This product was far superior to P&G's premium-priced Luvs. At the lower end of the market, generic brands began to eat away at P&G's unexceptional Pampers. P&G's share of the diaper market fell from 69 percent in 1978 to 47 percent in 1985, and profits cascaded from $275 to $25 million. In toothpaste, Colgate-Palmolive erased P&G's 19 percent lead as P&G "snoozed while Colgate and other competitors came up with gels, pump dispensers, and other innovations."[82] Management had fallen asleep behind the wheel.

GM, never an engineering powerhouse, was, according to *Business Week*, "embarrassed over the last few years by poky J-cars, locking X-car brakes, faulty diesel engines, and delays in introducing front-wheel-drive replacements for its bigger cars."[83] From 1978 to 1982, GM recalled a staggering 70 percent of its cars; Chrysler and Ford, less than 50 percent.[84] For every three customers who bought a GM car, two of them had to return it for repairs.

At Chrysler, Townsend's drive to meet sales targets and boost the quarterly numbers put heavy pressure on manufacturing, a problem made more difficult by the wild proliferation of styles. Said the former Dodge controller: "We shipped cars at the end of the quarter we never should have. In the last hour of overtime work on an end-of-quarter shift, we'd ship out hundreds of dogs." Marketing dominance and cost and time pressures drove quality out the window. And the market reacted predictably by abandoning what could have been a long-lived allegiance to one automobile manufacturer.[85]

At retailers such as Sears and A&P, problems became apparent not in quality per se, but in the selection, display, and pricing of goods. Sears, for example, sold products no one wanted—at excessive mark-ups. Like A&P, it kept pushing its private-label Kenmore brands when customers wanted a wider range of choices, and it charged up to 50 percent more than competitors did for the same goods. In fact, Sears's cost structure made it impossible for it to compete on price. Its selling and administrative expenses were by far the highest in the business (30 percent as compared to 17 percent for Wal-Mart).[86] Moreover, high prices conditioned customers to wait for sales before buying—but even then, Sears could be undersold by competitors because its mark-up was so generous.

Presentation and assortment are the cornerstones of retailing. Yet Sears displayed its merchandise poorly. According to *Fortune* reporters who visited some Sears stores:

> Every female mannequin seen—at least ten—has torn stockings. In the maternity department the pillows beneath the mannequins' clothes had slipped—above the belly, below the belly—everywhere a baby is not. The jewelry department had been the cosmetics department "about six months ago," said a salesperson, which accounted for the empty

cosmetic racks and huge photos of heavily made up models that were still on the walls.[87]

At A&P, maintenance standards collapsed as divisions cut back on store painting, shopping carts, supplies, equipment, even lighting fixtures. Stores were "obviously short of help, shelves were poorly stocked . . . what carriages were available were usually in the parking lot . . . only one of six checkstands was operating . . . Cleanliness and courtesy standards, shelf stocking and checkout standards, and store employee morale all deteriorated."[88]

Insensitivity to Marketing Channels

Their past successes and their dominance of the market make Drifters insensitive. Firms believe that retailers, dealers, or distributors should be grateful to sell their products. So they start to dictate to their channels instead of listening to them.

P&G was notorious for its high-handed treatment of wholesalers and retailers. According to Bill Saporito of *Fortune,* "The marketers in Cincinnati . . . viewed . . . the middlemen who sell their products as interlopers standing between them and the consumer. . . . Salesmen routinely insisted that [vendors] load up on all sizes of a product. If a retailer refused he reportedly couldn't get [a brand] when P&G discounted it."[89]

This attitude got P&G into trouble as the industry consolidated and as computerization brought buyers more bargaining power and information. P&G's managers could no longer dictate the terms as they had in the past. And when they tried, they lost market share.

IBM also started to bungle in managing its retailers—namely, its salesforce. It rewarded salesmen for immediate sales but not for investment marketing, that is, working with clients and potential clients to create solutions to their long-term data-processing problems. "We'd go after the quick payoff—the low-hanging fruit," said one sales executive. Many salesmen were "two-year wonders" who seemed just to be flitting through, unable to give proper advice or consistent service to their clients.[90]

A&P, which of course owned its marketing channels (its stores), starved them mercilessly. Headquarters refused to replace deteriorating capital equipment and viewed the stores mainly as repositories for goods made by A&P's plants—goods no one wanted to buy. Said ex-

A&P executive William Walsh: "Stores, in desperate need of help and support, considered themselves as leper colonies of their divisional office as more and more of the wrong medicine was shipped in." It was top-down management all the way.[91]

Competition and Environment

The problems of Drifters are aggravated by environments that are becoming more hostile and competitive. GM and Chrysler both faced fiercer foreign competition and tougher unions. Sears was hit by sharper, more agile rivals such as K mart and Wal-Mart. Even IBM, which remained dominant in the mainframe business, was being pressured by ever cheaper and more powerful mini- and microcomputers and flexible workstations.[92] But these threats were ignored by Drifters year after year.

REMOTE LEADERS

Distant CEOs

The growing scale, complexity, and diversity of Salesmen breeds an impersonal, professional administration. CEOs take over who are usually generalists with accounting backgrounds; men who manage by numbers and are stewards rather than builders.

Starting with Frederic Donner in the 1960s, the style of leadership at GM grew ever more remote from the details of design and manufacture. Little strategic initiative or vision came from the top, only a good deal of annoying interference about budgets and expenditures. Because leaders stressed only abstract, bottom-line goals such as market share and ROI, guiding values came to be ignored and the means to achieve these goals were considered almost incidental. As a result, GM flogged the product lines of yesterday with a few bells and whistles added.

Frederic Donner was an aloof, impatient finance man—"a coldly capable accountant"—who always carried a big black volume of statistics. He had few friends and was said to have perfected the art of winning by intimidation. When asked about his vision for GM's future, Donner replied: "We're just silly enough to think we'll keep on doing the same thing." And that's exactly what they did.[93]

Donner was succeeded as chairman by his protégé James M. Roche (1967–71), who in turn was followed by Richard C. Gerstensberg (1972–74), a cost-control and budget specialist who was fond of reminding people, "I'm no engineer." Then along came Thomas A. Murphy (1974–80), also an accountant, who concentrated on options and pricing. These were all numbers men, not visionary strategists. They thrived on bureaucracy and for decades stood idly by as GM's lines and operations became entirely obsolete.[94]

Arrogant, Complacent Top Management

Much of the reason for strategic complacency derives from past success. Leaders start to think that they and their firms are invincible—that the job is easy. They become conceited and rude. Lynn Townsend, who had effected a brilliant turnaround at Chrysler, is a prime example.

By the mid-1960s, Townsend was obviously losing interest in his job. Inside the company he struck colleagues as distracted and bored. He adopted a cavalier attitude, arriving at the design and styling studios without having bothered to read the briefing books. Before long, he began to drink. Townsend started playing his executives off one another at Officer Council meetings, and often ridiculed and humiliated them. Said former colleague Rockwell Anderson: "He became short-tempered, a little heavy on the martinis from time to time and unfeeling about people and the things he would say to them in front of groups."[95]

Other overconfident executives deny the significance or even the existence of emerging problems. Sears CEO Ed Brennan was asked to name the biggest problem he would face in the coming year—a time when specialty stores K-Mart and Wal-Mart were inflicting much damage and Sears's financial services were bombing. Brennan said confidently: "I don't see any huge problems. I feel very good about how we're positioned strategically."[96] In fact, he had no strategic vision. How could he possibly grapple with the complex task of repositioning the beleaguered Sears when he wouldn't even acknowledge that there was a problem?

A&P took complacency to the level of dormancy. A succession of top executives and A&P boards refused to budge. They failed to gear up for the booming 1960s by relocating stores to the burgeoning suburbs or the thriving Sunbelt. As one former executive commented, they believed it adequate to "build a moat around the castle, guard liquidity, watch and wait."[97] A&P's size and power were partly responsible for this complacency: annual sales of over $5 billion, profits of $50 million, $100 million of cash on the balance sheet, and no corporate debt. Another executive remarked, "If things don't get better we just could go broke in a couple of hundred years." In fact, it took only ten years for A&P to start falling apart.

INSIPID CULTURES

A Loss of Identity

With such complacent, visionless leadership, it is no wonder that the cultural fabric of Drifters begins to shred.

A&P's store managers were allowed to tinker with store hours, hiring, and displays. But they were not allowed to have much say in determining the merchandise that they would carry in their particular stores. Store managers were starved for resources and forced to stock undesirable, company-made products at excessive prices. They received no strategic guidance from headquarters, but had to endure lots of operational constraints. Before long, motivation plummeted, and a sense of helplessness and injustice took hold. Service deteriorated. It got so bad that staff were ashamed to wear their A&P jackets. Said one manager: "It doesn't look right mopping the floor, putting out the rubbish, stocking shelves or operating a checkstand wearing a manger's jacket." Managers also avoided the jackets because customers would make complaints to them for which they had no reasonable reply.[98]

At GM, culture was neutered when the head office took many functions and a good deal of power away from its divisions. Increasingly, division managers found that the identities of their units were compromised and that they had little or no control over their own profitability. The proliferation of the product line was partly responsible for this. When GM began to add models in the sixties, this created an enormous engineering job—so GM spread the tasks across its divisions. Thus Buick specialized in brakes, Pontiac engineered rear suspensions, and assembly operations were taken out of the divisions and grouped under GM Assembly. Executives had so little power over the product lines they were nominally responsible for that they began to feel helpless, and lost their initiative and divisional identity.[99]

Controls That Miss the Point

When cultural controls atrophy, formal controls are needed to replace them to ensure that people are doing their jobs. Drifters therefore turn to numbers and bureaucracy, both of which succeed only in further eroding the company culture. Take numbers first.

Chrysler developed an obsession with short-term sales objectives—with meeting target sales before the end of quarter. This resulted in slipshod, hasty production to meet quotas, inferior quality, and cars rammed down dealers' throats or left to deteriorate on vast "sales bank" lots. The head of manufacturing remembers: "It was drive, drive, drive, during the last quarter. It was 'Here's your quota! Get 'em out the door.' " An obsession with numbers, it seems, overcame the real purpose—to sell cars that people wanted to drive.[100]

A&P's woes also were caused by its obsessional adherence to irrelevant corporate standards, in this case, "pounds per employee hour" and stock losses, both of which assessed stores without regard to their specific type of business or clientele. Many managers responded by cutting back on store labor hours and customer-service levels, which naturally caused sales volume to drop. According to former executive William Walsh, "this magnificent Goliath was being tied down securely by the Lilliputian minds of a small army of statisticians who could not see the beach for the sand."[101]

GM's controls were imposed by finance men who watched cost numbers even to the point of actually killing the product—and some of its customers. The finance staff refused to allow a $15 stabilizer to be used for the notoriously hazardous Corvair. By the time they relented, it was years too late to save the car or the lives that had been lost.[102]

Warring, Political Divisions

The lack of strategic focus and the decline of unifying values encourages fragmentation, which in turn induces political squabbling. Remote, complacent leaders do little to prevent this. Recall that our Salesmen encouraged competition among their smaller units. In Drifters, that competition escalates into war, as suspicion, parochialism, and territorial battles thwart a healthy sense of collaboration. In effect, we have our fourth kind of decoupling—that among departments, divisions, or units.

Heated interdivisional rivalry was common at GM. It usually pitted the finance guys against the car guys against the legal guys. And there was discord among all contenders for the top positions. Accountants were known to sap the resourcefulness of car builders by sniping at their plans and budgets—a GM practice that has gone on for decades and seriously damaged its effectiveness.[103]

Chrysler went to war with its dealers. In the headlong rush to meet quarterly sales targets, executives pushed undesirable models on their vendors. Eventually, the dealers revolted and started playing games of their own, becoming antagonists of the factories. Dealers would wait to order until Chrysler was burdened with excess inventory and they could pull the best terms out of the factory. As one Chrysler executive pointed out, they knew they could "tell us to go to hell and we couldn't get anybody else." It became a dance of mutual destruction.[104]

At Sears, politics took the form of turf battles that tripped up even the tiniest initiatives. Sears experimented with reducing inventories in five men's apparel stores from the usual twenty-two-week supply to eight weeks. Stores packed the goods to ship back the excess fourteen-week supply—but it was never sent. A consultant who worked on the test blamed territorial squabbles: "There was disagreement about who would decide to send what back. It's not a cohesive organization." Buyers purchased goods and sold them to store managers. "The result was a recipe for disagreement and diffused responsibility," said one security analyst.[105]

OPPRESSIVE STRUCTURES

Weak leadership, corporate control, and huge, complex operations spell bureaucracy. And bureaucracy is much of the reason for the strategic stagnation and product-line sluggishness we saw in Drifters. But structures are not just bureaucratic, they are also fragmented—into a confusing array of subunits that have muddled responsibilities and unclear authority.[106]

Cumbersome Bureaucracy

In discussing the organization men of William Whyte, we emphasized their positive aspects—loyalty, perseverance, and probity. The down side of these personalities surfaces later, in the transition from Salesman to Drifter. Organization men are comfortable with rules and regulations; they adopt parochial, internal perspectives, and they are political animals. They also like to conform, and abhor rapid change. It doesn't take much to turn these managers into the perfect bureaucrats—into the fathers of stagnation.

Bureaucrats, according to William Walsh, almost killed A&P. They insisted that everything had to go through head office. "Every new item or new size, every deal or allowance offered, had first to be approved by headquarters. Oftentimes a buyer in Kansas City, for example, would have to justify to a New York purchasing director why his stores should stock an item that was heavily advertised and already selling in volume in competitor's stores in Kansas City. Such policies not only stifled initiative but seriously reduced A&P's effectiveness in the marketplace."[107]

Michael Oneal called Sears "one of the most recalcitrant and lethargic corporate bureaucracies in America." Patricia Sellers deemed it "a century-old, muscle-bound behemoth crushed by its lumbering corporate culture, needing new strategy and probably new management." Sears, with its 526,000 employees, was a mammoth bureaucracy, out of touch with the consumer and too unwieldy to coordinate change.[108] "The good old days are their problem, and they're still there," said Chicago retail consultant Sid Doolittle.[109]

Sears's bureaucracy guaranteed that it would be passed by its competitors. Its centralized buyers controlled the stores, which made it impossible for them to adapt to local conditions. But deficient information systems didn't tell the buyers which lines were doing well or where they were selling. It was a lethal combination.[110]

At GM, the two top policy committees of Alfred Sloan blossomed into a maze of overlapping planning and decision-making bodies. By the early 1970s, GM's middle management had tripled in size from the Sloan years.[111] Committees were not only considering policy matters but operational ones as well. The highly politicized atmosphere ensured that this would cause tremendous delays. Even GM's chairman admitted: "One of the big problems is in our frozen middle management. It is very hard to get those guys to understand. If they don't want the system to work, I promise you they can screw it up. They will stand there and smile at you, but there goes a red seat in a blue car."[112]

Ross Perot was even more critical of GM's bureaucracy and its paralyzing effects:

[The GM system] is like a blanket of fog that keeps people from doing what they know needs to be done. At GM the stress is not on getting results—on winning—but on bureaucracy, on conforming to the GM system. You get to the top of General Motors not by doing something, but by not making a mistake. You form groups, hold meetings, get consensuses, don't make decisions. You just kind of let this big old log keep rolling. . . .

He continues:

I come from an environment where, if you see a snake, you kill it. At GM, if you see a snake, the first thing you do is go hire a consultant on snakes. Then you get a committee on snakes, and then you discuss it for a couple of years. The most likely course of action is—nothing. You figure, the snake hasn't bitten anybody yet, so you just let him crawl around the factory floor.[113]

In 1979, when sales stalled and competition from Japanese manufacturers accelerated, GM's ponderous structure made it almost impossible for the firm to react.

Control Without Strategy

There is a paradox in the structure of Drifters. Head office foists upon them a maze of financial controls and standards, and it interferes in trivial decisions. But at the same time it provides vague, inadequate strategic guidelines. Units are monitored to death by the bureaucracy. Yet they are not guided by a unified strategic vision, a set of clear policies, or a significant ideology.

At GM, headquarters was not providing any strategic leadership; it was only monitoring, controlling, and censoring—not creating purpose. Sloan had wanted "centralization of strategy with decentralization of operations"—but this, strangely, was now reversed. Strategies were ignored, but operational controls were rigidly implemented. According to John DeLorean, former group executive vice-president, "What was happening was a predictable result when the control of a consumer goods company moves into the hands of purely financial managers." The emphasis shifted from people and products to short-term profits.[114]

This was also the case at A&P, which by the 1960s had already lost both its identity and its core policy. As we have seen, in 1968, A&P decided to decentralize into thirty-three autonomous retail divisions, putting authority closer to the point of sale. This seemed like a good idea in light of the previous overcentralization. But the divisions were turned loose without adequate management support or head-office guidance. Anarchy developed. There followed a series of "let's dump this and try that" sales plans. Advertising formats changed, prices fluctuated without reason, store hours expanded and contracted aimlessly, and displays were shuffled.[115] And yet the freedom was more illusory than real. Field managers still had absolutely no choice over their locations or what they could sell—the two most important variables of food retailing.

Muddied Decentralization

One of the most significant problems of Drifters is that responsibility is no longer matched with authority or clearly tied to a product line or market. The accountability of middle management is lost, and with it organizational initiative and responsiveness.

At GM, the decentralization that Sloan had advocated was changing. Divisions were gradually stripped of much of their autonomy. By 1971, a new General Motors Assembly Division had taken complete control of all car making, Fisher Body determined design, and the various component groups decided their spheres of operation. Albert Lee maintained that divisions had become "little more than marketing and public relations operations."[116] Certainly, they were losing the distinctiveness that Sloan had envisioned for them. At GM, "Too many people had a say about the product, but nobody had responsibility," said industry analyst Maryann Keller.[117] Managers closest to the customer could no longer make the key decisions. Once again, we see the decoupling of the firm from its markets.

Insular Decision Making

Past success and bureaucracy have lulled Drifters to sleep. They no longer are motivated to listen to their environments.

Even IBM, the legendary listener, was by 1985 losing some of its former edge. According to Chairman John Akers, IBM had lost touch with its customers. "It persisted in trying to sell them products when what they wanted was solutions—help in getting their thousands of computers to talk to each other, help in wringing both productivity gains and competitive advantage out of their investment in data processing equipment."[118]

The IBM salesforce became more remote from the customer, in part because, according to *Fortune*'s Carol Loomis, "business only a few years ago was so terrific that selling became a breeze." An IBM survey of its sales reps shows just how complacent they had become: amazingly, they had been spending only 30 percent of their time with their customers, whereas in the past they were with the customer almost constantly.[119]

It is perhaps less surprising that GM had the same problems. Ross Perot met with a group of Cadillac dealers, heard their many complaints, and then asked: "Why didn't you put the list [of complaints] down on the annual survey about how to improve Cadillac?" One senior dealer stood up and said: "Ross, I've been a Cadillac dealer for 35 years, and this is the first time anybody has ever given us an opportunity to tell them what is wrong."[120] Perot advised GM execs: "Listen, listen, listen to the customers and the people who are actually doing the work."[121]

MAJOR CHANGES ALONG THE DECOUPLING TRAJECTORY

Many Salesmen become Drifters, with unfocused, proliferating lines and form-over-substance differentiation strategies. These strategies are abetted by—and in turn reinforce—remote leadership, bland cultures, and fragmented, bureaucratic structures.

First, Salesmen capitalize on their reputations and marketing abilities by adding to their lines—offering more models and opening new outlets. This behavior is amplified by overconfident Drifters who expand their lines and outlets too indiscriminately. Offerings begin to overlap and compete; strategic focus and integration are lost.

Second, Salesmen are primarily marketers and image builders, not high-quality producers or innovators. Drifters stress image over substance even more, as engineering and product renewal are increasingly neglected. Offerings begin to deteriorate.

Third, large size, line proliferation, and a lack of strategic focus can weaken corporate cultures and leadership. Conversely, remote leadership allows decentralized subunits to pull in opposite directions and to further blur strategies. And vibrant cultures get replaced by stifling bureaucratic controls—which make strategies ever less responsive to markets.

SOME QUALIFICATIONS   The decoupling trajectory tends to be slower than the others. Salesmen are so powerful, conservative, and well established that their demise is often quite gradual. Losses result not from disastrous megaprojects but from an encroaching staleness and lack of efficiency. So decoupling is very much a lingering affliction.

As a result, some of our Drifters remained strong and were prime candidates for successful turnarounds. Although Drifters are beset by a common ailment, they display a good deal of variation in their rates of deterioration. A&P and Chrysler sank into major life-threatening declines. GM, P&G, and Sears went through periods of stagnating sales and earnings and very significant losses of market share. IBM on the other hand was still strong—but its growth had ceased, and it had begun to stray from the successful strategies of the past.

CHAPTER 6

The Forces Behind the Trajectories

So far, we have looked at the trajectories from the outside—from where it is tempting to think, How incredibly shortsighted were the Disney executives who worshipped the departed Walt and confined themselves to the exegesis of his strategies, or, How insanely reckless of Litton's managers to have moved into areas they knew nothing about. I may have inadvertently given the impression that these managers were unusually dense; but nothing could be further from the truth. The present chapter will, I hope, counter this perception by exposing the deep and insidious roots of our four trajectories. I will try to show just how enormously difficult they are to combat from inside the "closed system" of the once successful firm.

In this chapter, we will try to put ourselves in the position of these leaders and managers to see *why* they went wrong. The one message I hope readers will take away is that many of the problems were terribly hard to avoid for those executives at those times. As outsiders, using hindsight, we can get out our industry and accounting data and show just how inappropriate the old strategies were. As managerial insiders, working within the maze of a closed system, the situation is totally different. All of our models and assumptions about the market, our performance yardsticks, our skills, our information systems, our structures and cultures, and ultimately our understanding of our strengths and weaknesses, would likely have pushed us into precisely the traps that those managers fell into—that is, had we been clever enough to create their initial success in the first place.

The momentum behind the four trajectories stems from many interrelated forces—invisible enemies that used to be powerful allies.

These forces shape the lenses through which managers view the world, and they are embedded in the cohesive cultures, structures, and processes of outstanding companies. They also make successful organizations into circular, self-reproducing systems that keep rolling forward quite independently of what goes on outside their boundaries. The problems this engenders entail:

- not merely a lack of awareness about the environment but a lack of self-awareness;
- not a failure of rationality but a narrow rationality;
- not an inability to solve problems but an inability to recognize or define them;
- not just ignorance of the facts but disregard for them; and,
- not a failure to meet standards but an adherence to the wrong standards.

At the end of this chapter, if I have done my job, the reader should conclude that managers must work harder to become aware of their own lenses on the world—their biases and their deeply buried, often antiquated, assumptions. They can discover these only by reflecting upon themselves; by throwing away their microscopes and buying mirrors.

But before examining why this should be so, let's recap some of the problems common to all four trajectories.

THE MOMENTUM TOWARD EXTREMES

At first glance, the four trajectories appear to be very different from one another. The *focusing* trajectory showed Craftsmen becoming conservative and narrowly obsessive Tinkerers who miss the forest for the trees. The *venturing* trajectory transformed Builders into Imperialists as overconfident, expansionist leaders took on vast, risky projects and moved into businesses that were alien to them. The *inventing* trajectory converted Pioneers into extravagant, unresponsive Escapists. And our image-conscious Salesmen became directionless Drifters by following the *decoupling* trajectory.

For all their outward differences, there are some compelling similarities among all four trajectories. All embody a momentum that extends and amplifies a company's initial strengths and emphases while it extinguishes all secondary characteristics, all nuances. In each case, organizations move from rich character to exaggerated, distended caricature. They become like body builders who develop their biceps while letting their other muscles atrophy.

Figure 1 (p. 11) showed, for example, that momentum drove healthy configurations toward dangerous extremes along the axes of scope and change. Active organizations became hyperactive; focused ones obsessive. But these transformations merely illustrated a general tendency that is worth looking at more closely, especially as it pertains to other changes in a company's strategy, leadership, culture, and structure.

On the *focusing trajectory*, managers turn their concern for quality or cost into a blind pursuit of irrelevant technical standards, and come increasingly to ignore marketing and R&D. Also, their preoccupation with design and technique produces a monolithic engineering culture that is intolerant of other functions and generally devalues the customer. And leaders transform their organization's structure from an orderly, tightly controlled form into a hidebound, overcentralized bureaucracy.

The *venturing trajectory* also exhibits many kinds of momentum. Leaders accelerate expansion, pushing their firms ever further afield and draining resources. They become greedier and more impulsive as they progress from confidence to euphoria. Soon their generalist cultures lose touch with the vital details of products and markets; financial control degenerates into gamesmanship; and decentralization gives way to disorder.

Along the *inventing trajectory*, innovation crescendos into extravagant, futuristic development projects, as managers neglect marketing and financial control. Visionary leaders turn into grandiose missionaries who push vaunted—but frequently unwanted—products and technologies. Cultures are split into R&D insiders, who have all the power, and a much larger contingent of the disenfranchised. And firms loosen their flexible structures so completely that chaos sets in.

Finally, in the *decoupling trajectory*, broad and stable product-market strategies become increasingly diffuse and outmoded. Detached leaders move still further from their operations, rendering their "Organization Man" cultures yet more impersonal and fragmented. And complex, formal structures lapse into paralyzing labyrinthine bureaucracies.[1]

Such momentum in strategy, culture, and structure characterized all our trajectories. It extended successful orientations beyond the point of usefulness, destroyed both subtlety and complexity, and inordinately focused talents and resources. We will try to identify the roots of this process in the remainder of the chapter.

THE GENESIS OF EXTREMES

The reasons for the momentum behind our trajectories are many. They can be found in the way managers think, in corporate politics and rituals, and in insidious programs and systems. Although powerful in and of themselves, these elements reinforce one another to drive the trajectories. And paradoxically, many of the sources of decline were the original causes of success.

Our inquiry into the roots of the trajectories is divided into three major parts:

First, we will look at the roles played by individual factors such as cognitive lenses, monolithic cultures, and entrenched routines. Many of these factors become especially dangerous in the context of the high-performing organization.

Second, we will describe how many of these factors reinforce each other in cohesive organizational configurations. These configurations evolve to extend core themes and to make firms more extreme, more narrow, and more intolerant.

Third, we will address our Icarus paradox: the notion that the very factors that now cause decline were originally responsible for success. This makes them immensely difficult to manage. Strong cultures, clear routines, dominant skills and functions, and focused strategies are all crucial to fine performance. So, indeed, are cohesive, thematic configurations. But ultimately, these very factors, when taken to excess, may cause decline.[2]

LEADERSHIP

Our trajectories are caused, in part, by the evolution of executives' lenses on the world, their rationalizations, their overconfidence, and their defense mechanisms. Some of these factors vary considerably among managers; others are common to all.

The "Lenses" of Experience

Our view of reality is shaped by a series of lenslike cognitive structures—an established set of values, assumptions, and beliefs that has been formed by the experiences of a lifetime. According to Paul Nystrom and Bill Starbuck, "What people can see, predict, understand depends on their cognitive structures—by which we mean logically integrated and mutually reinforcing systems of beliefs and values. Cognitive structures manifest themselves in perceptual frameworks, expectations, world views, plans, goals . . . myths, rituals, symbols . . . and jargon."[3]

These "lenses" dictate what managers will perceive, what they will ignore, and how they will interpret their perceptions. Lenses are also enduring and cause leaders to view the present much as they did the past, even after conditions have changed. The same kinds of stimuli get targeted for attention, and the same mental frameworks are used to try to understand them.[4]

Managers' viewpoints are inevitably colored by their career experiences. Leaders with a marketing background will pay the most attention to marketing; those from manufacturing will give that more emphasis.[5] Indeed, the careers and formative experiences of top executives cause them to perceive their markets and businesses in special ways, and make it natural for them to favor certain goals, strategies, and departments over others—regardless of the issues being faced by their organizations. It is hardly surprising, for example, that scientists such as Dr. Wang would push for an R&D-based strategy, or that accountants such as Hal Geneen would stress financial control—no matter what their environments were trying to tell them.

Success, too, can shape a manager's world view by appearing to reward—and thereby reinforcing—his core beliefs and policies. Thus, success reduces the incentive to learn and thereby antiquates opinions and ideas. Unfortunately, it is usually the failures that challenge the status quo and cause managers to keep looking and questioning. Pain awakens us to the need for action; but comfort fosters complacency.

Unintentional Learning

Most executives, at least initially, concern themselves with finding better ways of doing things. They perform little experiments to determine what works and what doesn't. Much learning, however, takes place unconsciously. There is a memorable example taken from a class of psychology students. The students conspired to "condition" their professor to lecture only from the left half of the classroom. So they simply began to chat among themselves and rustle papers whenever he stood anywhere else. Within a few days they had accomplished their mischievous aim—and completely without the knowledge of their instructor.

In a similar way managers "learn" implicitly to favor particular strategies, processes, and methods, without even knowing *that* they have done so—let alone why.

It's not that managers always decide that "A and B cause success, so forget about C, D, and E." Rather, their attentions, interpretations, and behaviors are subtly molded by their earlier experiences. The end result is the insidious development of a narrower, more deeply embedded and less flexible repertory of concepts and behavior. In the short run, such learning is very useful. But, eventually, it can lead to a rigid, outmoded view of the world, and a narrowness that breeds excess and obscures the need for change.

Single-Loop Learning

Chris Argyris and Don Schon make a useful distinction between single- and double-loop learning.[6] Single-loop learning occurs as organizations compare their performance to a set of preestablished standards and try to make appropriate adjustments. Our firms all accomplished this very well; Craftsmen, for example, adeptly honed the precision of their manufacturing processes. Double-loop learning, on the other hand, requires periodic reassessments of the established standards themselves to ensure that they remain relevant. This is what is missing in our firms—Craftsmen did not question the broader appropriateness of their technical parameters. Because standards are so closely tied to managerial expectations and viewpoints, they are seldom reappraised. And when they are, it is not to challenge their worth

178

but to extend them as a result of past successes—Craftsmen, for instance, go from .001 to .0008 inch tolerances. Standards become antiquated and extreme, and with them basic strategies.

Ambiguity and Rationalization

Psychologists claim that we justify our past behavior through "retrospective rationalizations," an instinct that grows stronger as the behavior is repeated. Managers, for instance, will usually attribute success to their own actions and absolve themselves of responsibility for any failure, especially when what determines performance is ambiguous. Have this year's enormous profits been due to inspired innovation and brilliant marketing, or to an improved economy and a competitor's blunder? It is often hard to tell. So managers interpret weak clues as indicating that their favorite strategies have led to success. Marketers attribute victory to good marketing, engineers credit good design; and both blame failure on "the damn economy" or on the finance guys down the hall.[7] When Chrysler's sales and market share began to increase in the 1960s, Lynn Townsend gave his warrantees and styling policies the credit. But when Chrysler's sales fell, he made the dealers the scapegoats. This, of course, reinforced the company's existing strategies.

Overconfidence

Success not only narrows leaders' perceptions, it also changes their attitudes. It can give them too much confidence, even a sense of infallibility. Successful leaders have triumphed over their competitors and are used to being idolized by their subordinates; they have had many of their opinions enshrined in policies and vindicated by the turn of events. So, many become egotistic and are emboldened to take reckless, impulsive actions. Our Imperialists' early successes encouraged them to initiate ever more ambitious and wide-ranging diversification projects. Escapists blindly accelerated the pace of innovation. Drifters became convinced that they could sell anything with their aggressive marketing.

Success can also make leaders intolerant of opposing points of view. In some cases, bosses become bullies who resent criticism and isolate dissenters. They nurture a corps of sycophants and foster a monolithic band of like-minded decision makers. All capacity for frank discussion and organizational learning is lost. Recall the bullying and binder-throwing at Bucy's TI.

Defense Mechanisms

There comes a point in the lives of many organizations when employees realize that there are serious problems. They may attempt to bring these problems to the leader's attention, but without much success, in part because of the "lenses" and overconfidence we have just described. But there is another reason: leaders, like all of us, have defense mechanisms to protect them against what they don't want to hear.

Leaders usually identify strongly with the strategies they have formulated and the cultures they have nurtured. It is painful for them to have to admit that their policies are obsolete—that their talents might no longer be relevant. So, they might deny that there is a problem, believe that the problem isn't serious, or think that others are trying to steal power by attacking their contributions. Frederic Donner and his followers at GM dismissed the foreign car threat as temporary, and then, using sour grapes reasoning, asserted that GM didn't want that "low margin" part of the market anyway.

Of course, there is a wide variety of defense mechanisms and they depend very much on the personality of the leader in question. Manfred Kets de Vries and I have talked about these in some detail in *The Neurotic Organization*. We found that *depressive* leaders retire into themselves and ignore problems. The more *suspicious* types lash out against their accusers because they believe there is a conspiracy afoot. A few *idealists* cling to utopian scenarios that will solve all problems in their time. And finally, *grandiose* bosses believe that they are infallible and need not take any threats seriously.[8]

CULTURE

All of the leadership factors we have just discussed contribute mightily to momentum. Yet leaders may not only shape their organizations directly, but also via the management teams and corporate cultures they create; and they are themselves often products of such cultures. "Cultures," remember, are constellations of basic views and assumptions—expressed as beliefs and values—that are shared by the key members of an organization. They define an organization's identity, both to its members and to outsiders.[9]

Embedded Values

Leaders who preside over a tremendously successful business are often elevated to the status of guru. Eddie Rickenbacker at Eastern, Ken Olsen at DEC, and An Wang at Wang are good examples. Their goals and strategies came to be regarded as sacred, and their policies were deeply etched into the organizational psyche. Such strong cultures can make work meaningful, galvanize employees to take action, and generate tremendous enthusiasm. But they may also mire managers in a single way of seeing and doing things. In that case, they bring about an oppressive conformity. In fact, the greater the success of a leader and the longer he or she stays in power, the larger the coterie of adherents and boosters, and the more closed and homogeneous the culture. Such narrow cultures, of course, are given to the unrestrained pursuit of one goal and one strategy.

Some leaders have such an impact on their companies that their imprint dominates even after they have left. The Disney example is remarkable in this respect. Walt Disney so imbued his company with his values that his policies were codified into a kind of organizational bible. Ten years after his death, executives were still always wondering "what Walt would have done."

Monolithic Cultures

If particular goals and values can dominate a firm, so can the departments that best embody them. Escapists were taken over by R&D cultures, Tinkerers by production-engineering cabals, and Imperialists by packs of accountants. The way in which this came to pass is interesting. Escapists, because they so greatly valued innovation, gave some initial primacy to their R&D group. Researchers were avidly recruited, handsomely rewarded, and quickly promoted. This increased their ranks, attracted the best candidates, and boosted the resources and impact of the R&D department. The opposite was true for Escapists' manufacturing staff, who were largely disenfranchised, starved for resources, and had little chance of moving up the hierarchy. So the best production people left to work for companies where they would be better appreciated; the worst ones stayed because they had little choice. This further eroded the department's reputation. In short, favored R&D types became more numerous, more talented, and more influential—and manufacturing managers became less so. It was a never-ending spiral.

The same process occurred in our Tinkerers—simply substitute engineers and manufacturing personnel for R&D types, and marketing people for manufacturing types. Imperialists, of course, worshipped managers with financial and accounting backgrounds.

The ascent to dominance of a single function or department creates a monolithic culture in which all managers with any influence revere the same highly constrained values, which they are permitted to pursue unchecked and with increasing fervor. The organization then becomes a victim of what Irving Janis calls "groupthink."[10] The effect is dramatically to narrow the range of viewpoints, abilities, and strategic options. Gareth Morgan refers to such organizations as developing an "egocentric self image"—"they draw boundaries around a definition of themselves, and attempt to advance the self-interest of this narrow domain. In the process, they truncate their understanding of the wider context in which they operate, and surrender their future to the way the context evolves."[11]

Specialized Skills

Just as one function tends to become dominant in an organization, so does the knowledge base and technology that is associated with it. Kim Clark has argued eloquently that an organization's technologies gradually freeze and become more specialized.[12] Its employees and managers develop a very particular knowledge base that resides in knowing *how* to do various tasks, but not in knowing *why* things are done the way they are. The upshot is that most organizations unreflectively absorb a highly constrained set of skills and favor workers whose capacities center on a single technology.

But there is a more general lesson here. Organizations learn only certain skills: those required to implement their current strategies; those corresponding to the knowledge of the managers and departments most valued by the corporate culture. Unfortunately, firms do not retain many other skills since they fail to recruit people with different talents. For example, our Pioneers were great innovators, but usually not nearly so expert at production or financial control.

And our Salesmen were successful marketers, but less adept either at R&D or production. So, strategy is constrained by the existing skill set, one that is very much rooted in the past. Small wonder that GM was so slow to take up the Japanese challenge.

STRUCTURE

An organization's structure consists of its routines, hierarchy, power distribution, and job responsibilities. It profoundly channels managers' perceptions and the way they make decisions. Although leaders and corporate cultures shape the structure of a company, that structure in turn can mold the culture, and channel decision making as well.

Confining Programs and Routines

Nobel laureate Herbert Simon and his colleagues believe that an organization's goals and tasks are organized and translated into routines and programs.[13] These restrict the range of things managers think about and react to.[14] Bill Starbuck and Bo Hedberg argue that an organization's adaptation to its markets becomes stylized and frozen by such routines: "the organization sets up behavior programs that promote habitual responses to expected cues. . . . Because situations appear equivalent as long as they can be handled by the same programs, programs remain in use long after the situations they fit have faded away. . . . Continued success incubates potential failure, by increasing an organization's dependence on its programs."[15]

These routines are costly to change. They also reinforce existing policies and activities by recognizing only anticipated problems, by suggesting only conventional courses of action, and by implementing only traditional solutions. They can promote innovation—but only of a sort that is in line with the organization's current ideologies and strategies.[16]

Political Inertia

Most firms have very stable power structures. These limit change and impart momentum to existing goals, strategies, and structures—which then in turn reinforce the power structures.

"Power is stable in most organizations most of the time," claims Jeffrey Pfeffer.[17] And Henry Mintzberg says that "there is a natural propensity of the power system to seek equilibrium and remain there."[18] But why? First, power is self-perpetuating—it gives power-holders advantages in any political struggle that allow them to get more resources, hire or promote like-minded individuals, and buy off resisters. Powerholders may even set standards of performance that ensure that they will look good. Second, the way in which power is distributed in an organization is a product of many implicit agree-ments, compromises, and even contracts among many different par-ties. To alter these would be cumbersome and expensive. Third, powerful managers tend to surround themselves with the daunting trappings of position and achievement, especially when they have been successful. Any challenge to their lofty authority would take lots of courage and appear to be breaking the rules.

Organizational strategies are closely linked to the distribution of power. First, *power shapes strategy.*[19] If marketers dominate an or-ganization, as was true of our Salesmen, the core strategy will re-volve around marketing. Where engineers rule, the strategy is more likely to center on quality design or efficient production, as in our Craftsmen. Second, *strategy can affect power.* Successful strategies give the parties who developed them considerable power, recogni-tion, and professional satisfaction. Our Escapists, for example, re-vered and empowered their R&D teams. And obviously these powerful groups will resist any changes to strategy that might im-peril their rewards.

In short, because goals, strategies, and power are so tightly inter-woven, an inertial power structure will prevent major reorientations from taking place. It may, however, impart momentum to *existing* orientations: powerful managers have an incentive to extend the strategies that reward them, to reinforce the goals that they believe in, and to refine the structures that consolidate their power.

PROCESSES

The central processes of an organization include learning; making decisions; and managing relationships with the environment. Each of these is influenced by the leadership, cultural, and structural factors we have already discussed. But each can also contribute in its own way to organizational momentum.

Selective Intelligence Systems

With their selective reporting and implicit standards, the intelligence systems of any company mirror the values and viewpoints of the past. And by shaping what managers attend to and concealing change, they help to propagate these very priorities and perspectives. Salesmen's systems favor market-share and sales growth data, while Craftsmen's track indexes of quality or cost. A Salesman might therefore be very slow to become aware of declines in quality or efficiency; a Craftsman may take ages to get wind of customer dissatisfaction.

Also, as Bill Starbuck argues, "Data tend to confirm what the [systems] assume to be true: the gathered data may show mainly good results even when poor results prevail, because people are gathering few data where poor results show up. For instance, people do not monitor events that they believe to be tangential or phenomena that they assume to be stable."[20]

The insistence on quantitative data for most information systems also introduces biases. Tinkerers such as Texas Instruments paid a good deal of attention to their cost figures, but failed to notice that reducing costs had severely eroded both quality and customer satisfaction—qualitative notions that were not tracked by their intelligence systems.

One of our most incisive organizational theorists, Charles Perrow, believes that companies develop special *vocabularies* that also act as information systems: that is, they screen out some parts of reality and emphasize others.[21] For example, "quality" standards may be expressed in terms of strength or hardness coefficients—which, when they become irrelevant to what the customer really needs, give managers the false sense that they are producing superior merchandise. The vocabulary is narrower than the activities or standards it is meant to describe, and so the latter become sterile and out of date.

Even when systems gather the right information, the political agendas of managers may induce them to conceal or deliberately misinterpret that information. At ITT, for example, the divisional chiefs played games with Geneen and his accountants, as they hid facts and told the boss only what he wanted to hear.

Channeled Decision Making

The ever popular "rational models" of decision making view managers as monitors of the environment, who compare a firm's achievements to its goals in order to identify problems. These problems are then resolved by choosing an appropriate solution from a set of sensible alternatives. The fact is, however, that most organizational activities do not take place in response to problems, but rather because policies and programs *automatically* generate particular actions. Bill Starbuck and Bo Hedberg tell us that "An organization ordinarily generates potential actions without the stimulus of specific problems, just because an organization is designed to generate actions. Generated actions become potential solutions on the ground that they appear to be good actions—they are consistent with past behaviors, they resemble what other organizations are doing . . . they are fun."[22]

Routines, job definitions, and information systems create the premises for decision making. They direct managers' expectations, and thereby their perceptions, to produce predictable decisions. In fact, the organization controls both information and the premises for action. And this makes it very hard for managers to recognize fundamental new problems that were never envisioned in designing the systems and routines originally.

For example, Tinkerers such as Caterpillar were quick to focus on quality—an important goal and a central aspect of strategy. There were explicit quality standards, as well as programs, special departments, and information systems for monitoring quality. And, in fact, actions were generated to continue to improve quality, solely on the basis of established policies rather than in response to market needs. However, Cat failed to notice that its product lines were beginning to cater to shrinking markets. There were no explicit programs that were called into play by the declining market, no information systems to tell managers exactly what was going on, no standards against which to measure things, and no departments specifically charged with tackling the problem.

Buffering

Organizations have a tendency to buffer themselves from their markets in order to operate in as smooth and trouble-free a way as possible. Jeffrey Pfeffer and Gerald Salancik claim that to avoid having to adapt, firms may address only those customers who want their products.[23] Craftsmen look for customers who value price or quality and steer clear of those who want state-of-the-art equipment. Pioneers take the opposite tack.

Backward and forward integration—for example, buying distributors or suppliers—can also help firms to buffer themselves from unpredictable environments. Some organizations even try to actively shape their environments. ITT, for instance, lobbied with the government for protective legislation such as tariffs. Other firms form cartels or powerful trade associations in order to regulate competition.

These attempts to avoid having to cope with external uncertainty instill momentum and inertia in an organization in two ways. First, they limit the range of action that is permitted. Trade associations, for example, may dictate certain marketing practices; backward integration constrains manufacturing options. Second, and more important, buffering reduces the occasions for organizational learning and adaptation. So organizations become closed systems that roll forward but rarely change course.

The Environment Within

Managers *choose*—consciously or not—which aspects of their markets to attend to. And their world views, interests, and biases all shape this choice. The "environment," then, is in part an artifact—the set of a manager's psychic theater. And the organization is molded, managed, and changed via this mental construction. According to Karl Weick, "Organizations create and constitute the environment to which they react; the environment is put there by the actors within the organization and by no one else. This reasserts the argument that the environment is a phenomenon tied to processes of attention, and that unless something is attended to, it doesn't exist."[24]

Biologists Humberto Maturana and Francisco Varela believe that all living systems tend not so much to adapt or respond to an objective environment as to *define* that environment via their peculiar interests and capacities.[25] According to Gareth Morgan, such systems are *auto-opoetic*, "self-referential because [they] cannot enter into interactions that are not specified in the pattern of relations that define [their] organization. Thus a system's interaction with its 'environment' is really a reflection to part of its own organization. It interacts with its environment in a way that facilitates its own self-production, and in this sense we can see that the environment is really part of itself." Similarly, formal organizations "are always attempting to achieve a form of self-referential closure in relation to their environment, enacting their environment as projections of their own identity or self image."[26]

Thus, our Salesmen see market demographics as key aspects of the environment; Craftsmen see various technological developments and cost factors as crucial; and Builders view interest rates and the legal climate for mergers and acquisitions as all-important. By fine-tuning their strategies and structures to cope with these "external" forces, organizations are shaping themselves according to their interests and world views, more than they are adapting.

CONFIGURATIONS

So far we have dealt piecemeal with the factors that cause inertia and momentum in core strategies. But we have ignored one of the most important causes of all—the relationships among these factors: their tendency to cohere to produce integrated, thematic configurations such as those seen in Chapters 2 through 5. In order for any organization to succeed, there must be a close alignment among aspects of leadership, culture, strategy, and structure. This alignment amplifies existing orientations and makes them particularly difficult to undo.

The Coherence of Organizational Configurations

Peter Friesen and I have talked about organizations as being "composed of tightly interdependent and mutually supportive elements such that the importance of each element can best be understood by making reference to the whole configuration."[27] The first five chapters of this book described such configurations, with their dominant themes, their complementarities, and their mutually reinforcing ties. Bob Hinings and Royston Greenwood call these configurations "archetypes," "a particular composition of ideas, beliefs and values connected to structures and systems . . . clusters of prescribed and emergent structures and systems given order or coherence by an underpinning set of ideas, values and beliefs, i.e. an interpretive scheme." And they tell us that "organizations operate within the contoured mould" of existing configurations.[28]

Strategies, structures, and cultures embody the goals, and reflect the values, of a dominant group of managers. As a result, many aspects of an organization fit together like a jigsaw puzzle. Strategy, culture, routines, and the power system are all organized by a core theme into a unified whole, a "Gestalt" or configuration, which in turn gives added meaning to the parts.

Our Pioneers, for example, were dominated by the theme of innovation. Their missionary leaders had this as a primary goal and their organizations were designed accordingly. Strategies centered on product novelty and technological sophistication. Cultures rewarded invention and empowered inventors, rendering the skill base of the organization R&D, not marketing or production. And structures were made flexible to facilitate the development and implementation of new product ideas. Collectively, these qualities established the Pioneers' central strengths, weaknesses, and direction of evolution.

Our configurations suggest that organizations have what some call a "holographic" quality. In a classic series of experiments, the psychologist Karl Lashley progressively destroyed up to 90 percent of the brains of his laboratory rats. He expected to find that the rats would lose various functions, one by one, as he destroyed more and more of their brains. This did not happen. Instead, the rats merely experienced a gradual decline in their overall abilities. They maintained much of their capacity to perform quite competently. The undamaged parts of the brain seemed to take over the functions of the excised parts, perhaps, it was reasoned, because each part of the brain "mirrors" or encodes the others, much as is the case with the familiar 3-D hologram.

In the same way, when organizational configurations are broken or damaged, their remaining parts will tend to "reconstruct" the missing pieces. This is because everything seems to be enfolded in everything else. The strategy is mirrored by the culture and structure, and vice versa. Try to reduce the level of innovation in a Pioneer firm, for example, and the culture will regenerate it. Try to bureaucratize, and the R&D strategy will demand the dissolution of confining routines. There is, in effect, so much redundancy in the configuration that the theme of innovation is repeated in culture, structure, strategy, and process. According to a striking metaphor from Gareth Morgan, it is "just as if we were able to throw a pebble into a pond and see the whole pond and all the waves, ripples and drops of water generated by the splash *in each and every one of the drops of water thus produced* [my italics]."[29]

Parenthetically, configurations tell us something about organizational variety. They imply that it is quite restricted. That is, once a firm has adopted a certain set of priorities and a strategy, the range of suitable cultures and structures will be small. Pioneers cannot have bureaucratic structures, for example, as these would suppress innovation, and Craftsmen cannot have very loose or flexible structures, as these would compromise their quality control and efficiency. Although the four trajectories and eight configurations of this book hardly exhaust the range of possibilities, they do describe rather common events and encompass a great many organizations.

Configurations and Change

In essence, organizations are always changing. Configurations must therefore be viewed as dynamic systems. Their initial themes establish a characteristic momentum—a path of development that extends, harmonizes, and projects corporate ideology and infrastructure. This was clearly demonstrated by the trajectories of Chapters 2 through 5. But before discussing the momentum of configurations, let's examine why they so resolutely resist reorientation, that is, avoid radically breaking away from or going backward along the trajectories.

First, configurations are shaped by a consistent theme that very strongly channels strategy, culture, and structure. This theme determines standards of success, what information is attended to, and how it is interpreted. It also underlies an organization's programs and decisions. Thus, organizations remain with their current orientation because it is so deeply engrained in their very being, and because they are blind to the need for significant change.[30]

Second, as we said earlier, configurations resist reorientation because they are tied to the political interests that have generated and benefit from them, and to a limited repertory of strategic skills and resources.

Third, the attributes of a configuration are mutually reinforcing. Try to change one in a manner that is inconsistent with the theme of the configuration and, as we have seen, the others will knock it back into place.

And fourth, complementarities among the elements of a configuration are important to success and costly to dismantle. To quote again from *Organizations: A Quantum View*, "potentially disruptive changes must be delayed until the costs of not [changing] become high enough to justify the widespread . . . modifications that may be required to re-establish harmony among the elements [of a configuration]."[31] Think how expensive it would be, for example, for a Salesman to become a Pioneer or a Craftsman. A whole new strategy, structure, culture, and set of skills would have to be evolved, and in many cases this would require firing the CEO and senior management and starting up from scratch. Few organizations would have the resources to undertake such changes very often.

Although they resist reorientation, configurations are in fact changing all the time. We saw that *configurations have a characteristic direction of evolution, or trajectory, that is largely determined by the themes that created their initial success.* They have a momentum that makes them more internally consistent, extends their strengths, but also, unfortunately, amplifies their weaknesses.[32]

Earlier we said that organizations keep recreating themselves in their own image. They determine their futures according to the world views and programs of their past. We also noted that organizational configurations are driven by a central theme that orchestrates strategy, structure, and culture. Finally, we saw how goals, strategy, structure, and culture reinforce each other. The result: many of our companies amplified their existing practices and propensities over time. They became largely autonomous, closed systems that moved inexorably toward narrowness, conformity, and excess.

For example, Pioneers' goals of technological leadership and their success with early inventions encourage them to undertake more innovation. So, they promote creative scientists and give them significant resources to work with. A growing cadre of "R&D types" then presses for the loose, think-tank structures it finds so liberating and congenial, and it proceeds avidly to pursue new inventions. The new R&D culture increases the likelihood that any successes will be attributed to innovation; it also seeks out customers who most value state-of-the-art products. Interaction with such customers then produces further ideas and incentives for invention. Thus technological leadership becomes an ever more absorbing goal and leaders give even more power, prestige, and resources to R&D departments; other departments come to be viewed as secondary. Before too long, cultures become more monolithic, strategies more focused, skills more uneven and specialized, and blind spots more common. Causal chains such as these "purify" configurations and drive strategy, structure, and culture to extremes.

THE ICARUS PARADOX

Outstanding companies get into trouble when their success engenders excess. And paradoxically, it is precisely those factors which produced success that when pushed too far also cause decline. Too much of a good thing causes failure. And therein lies the twist: *many of the very things we have so harshly criticized in this chapter once produced excellent results.* Icarus' seductive wings did after all permit him to soar to unprecedented heights.

Organizational learning, galvanized cultures, efficient routines, and orchestrated configurations all contribute greatly to success. Learning narrows focus but sharpens skills. Monolithic cultures are parochial but they consolidate efforts around central goals. Routines constrain, but they dramatically improve efficiency and coordination. And configurations reduce flexibility, but they also orchestrate strategy, structure, and culture to promote brilliant achievement. Is it any wonder that organizations get carried away?[33]

Outstanding performance often demands the dedicated, even passionate, pursuit of a single goal at the expense of many others: excellent performers hardly ever observe the Aristotelian mean. To do well, companies need to concentrate—to be "somewhat extreme." Our Pioneers, for example, devoted their brightest employees, the bulk of their resources, and a major proportion of their executives' time to innovation. Since resources were limited, they had to sacrifice manufacturing efficiency and marketing aggressiveness in order to do so. In the same way, the cost-leader Craftsmen employed top-notch production experts, used the most efficient automated capital equipment and the best cost-control systems in the industry. But they, too, had to pay a price for their strategic advantage—they lacked the flexibility to be innovative and responsive to changing markets. To excel requires trade-offs, concentration, and tremendous dedication.

Unfortunately, the difference between the trade-offs and concentration required for success and the imbalances and extremes that lead to failure is often subtle and a question of degree. What appear to be clear excesses to us, as outsiders, seem to star managers operating out of exceptionally successful companies to be attention to the stuff that matters, creative passion, efficient concentration, and other positive things. How we define excess depends on our world views, our standards, and our history. And when we have excelled by concentration, a little more focus and force seems to be just the thing.

CONCLUSION

The momentum that drives our trajectories is associated with orderliness, not chaos. Over time, most organizations become more internally consistent. Their strategies, for example, turn into ever more precise recipes and their cultures narrow to mirror the views and practices of a single group. Meanwhile, routines and systems become more entrenched, specialized, and pervasive. And all of these trends interact to produce tight configurations—but ultimately configurations that are distended, exaggerated, and lacking in richness and subtlety.

Companies come to behave less like organisms and more like machines. Surprise and randomness, the sources of much knowledge, are lost. Before long, there is no more noise left in the system: no devil's advocates, no iconoclasts with any say, no countervailing models of the world. This, of course, decreases flexibility and blocks learning and adaptation.

Paradoxically, however, if the "machine" is beautifully tuned and aligned with its environment, it can soar on Icarus' wings and beat everything in sight. And these stellar successes are impossible to forget; they tempt managers to go just a little bit further.

The next chapter suggests some ways of managing momentum—how to draw on its considerable strengths while avoiding its perils.

CHAPTER 7

Avoidance and Turnaround

IT IS TIME NOW TO TURN FROM PROBLEMS TO CURE—TO SUGGEST WAYS of *avoiding dangerous momentum* and *turning around* those organizations that have gone too far. This chapter discusses general approaches to therapy and presents a Self-Assessment Questionnaire to help managers determine which trajectory best applies to their own firm. The next chapter will present specific tactics that firms have used to combat each of the four trajectories.

In many ways, this was the hardest chapter of the book to write. First of all, I am uncomfortable making blanket prescriptions for an undertaking as complex and idiosyncratic as organizational transition. Also, I had to skate precariously between the Scylla of vacuous generality and the Charybdis of irrelevant detail. I hope, however, that you will find in this chapter and the next some ideas and examples that will be useful within the context of your own organization.

We look first at the practices used by outstanding organizations to avoid dangerous momentum—to fend off the myopia induced by their cohesive configurations. Then we discuss general approaches to turnaround, to reviving firms that have already been damaged by the trajectories.[1]

AVOIDANCE

Managers must confront a poignant paradox: Excellence demands focus, dedication, and cohesive configuration. But these are precisely the factors that give rise to momentum, narrowness, and excess. So what is to be done?

Some successful organizations have adopted a few potentially powerful tacks for avoiding problems. They

- build thematic, cohesive configurations; but also
- encourage their managers to reflect broadly and deeply about the direction of the company.

In addition, they

- scan widely and monitor performance assiduously; and
- where possible, they decouple renewal activities from established operations, at least for a while.

Thematic Configurations

It is tempting to use the sources of momentum described in Chapter 6 to derive the prescriptions for avoidance. Are company world views too confining? Then dismantle them. Are cultures too monolithic? Then open them up. Are configurations too cohesive to allow for meaningful adaptation? Then throw them into question, inject some noise into the system, and make disruptive changes. Unfortunately, such remedies employed too freely might destroy the concentration and synergy that is so necessary for success.

In human beings, greatness demands dedication and focus—a "living-on-the-edge" quality. Prodigies in the arts are not known for their well-rounded lives. Brilliant scientists and entrepreneurs give up much of their family life. And superb college athletes are usually too preoccupied with training to excel at their studies. To do anything really well requires giving something up. Also, there is within us all only so much talent and energy. It must be focused for maximum effect.

As we have seen, the same logic holds for organizations. Concentration and synergy—not middle-of-the-road flexibility—were the hallmarks of greatness. Successful organizations zealously aligned their strategies, structures, and cultures around a central theme to create powerful, cohesive, brilliantly orchestrated configurations.

The Pioneers, for example, were driven through and through by the theme of innovation, embracing a scientist-dominated culture, prodigious R&D, and a free-flowing adhocracy structure. Although such consistency limited Pioneers to a particular market and set of skills (the most innovative firms are not usually the most cost-effective), it also dramatically enhanced their effectiveness.[2]

Conversely, middle-of-the-road strategies may be anathema to competitive advantage; the jack-of-all-trades is too often master of none. The same is true of culture and structure. Parity among marketing, production, and R&D departments might slow down decision making and prevent a coherent strategic theme or competence from emerging. Similarly, organizational cultures that nurture too many dissidents would be stymied by conflict.

Managers, therefore, should reap the benefits of a fine-tuned configuration without regret. They should take care not to kill their competitive edge by prematurely watering things down or permitting too many discordant practices.

I wish to amend Peters and Waterman's thesis: It is not just the pieces of a configuration—closeness to customers, innovation, high quality, differentiated products, loose-tight structures, or skunkworks—that create excellence. Stardom is attained also *through* configuration, the way the pieces fit together—their complementarity, their organization. To create success, *form* or configuration must animate and orchestrate the *substance* of its individual elements.

Liberating Self-Reflection

A major conclusion of this book is that perfect configuration and synergy are usually attained at the cost of myopia. Stellar performers view the world through narrowing lenses. One point of view takes over; one set of assumptions comes to dominate. And complacency and overconfidence result. In the words of my friend Joseph Lampel, such "blind perfection" must be replaced by a "wise perfection."

In order to avoid myopia and the excesses of the trajectories, managers must begin to reflect about their basic assumptions: about their deep-seated views of customers, strategies, and corporate culture. They need also to search for the underlying goals and presumptions that drive their organizations. It is only after they become conscious of such inbred premises for action that they can begin to question and alter them. According to Gareth Morgan, "If one really wants to understand one's environment, one must begin by understanding oneself, for one's understanding of the environment is always a projection of oneself."[3]

Managers, in other words, need to buy mirrors: they have to do more self-reflecting and be less self-centered.[4] They must audit themselves and solicit the views of objective third parties in order to discover their own blind spots. The detailed Self-Assessment Questionnaire presented later will continue this process, but managers can start by asking themselves the following questions:

1. What kinds of customers do we prefer? Why?
2. What assumptions are we making about our customers and competitors? How have our views of them changed in the last few years?
3. Which aspects of strategy have not changed in many years? Why?
4. Whom inside and outside the organization do we pay the most attention to? Whom do we ignore and why?
5. In what ways are our strategy, goals, and culture narrow?
6. Which of our strengths are declining? Which are on the rise?
7. How will we find out if our strategies are wrong? And how fast?
8. Which departments and types of employees do we treasure and reward the most? How come?
9. What biases might filter our views? Who might tell us about these biases?
10. How do others in the industry see us?
11. What are our most cherished goals and values? How have they evolved?
12. Which projects or ventures are we most likely to embrace? Which do we tend to shy away from? Why?

It might be useful for managers first to answer these deliberately general questions individually; then to circulate their written responses to their colleagues; and finally, to come together to discuss the answers very frankly.

Gathering Information

Self-knowledge cannot be attained in a vacuum. Many of the best sources of such knowledge are to be found outside the organization. To discover whether momentum is driving an organization toward dangerous excesses, its managers must test their assumptions against reality—evolving customer needs, new technologies, and competitive threats in particular.[5]

The whole point of gathering information is to create uneasiness;

to combat complacency. Information must serve as the clarion call that awakens a somnolent system; the brake that slows down a runaway trajectory. Combined with self-knowledge, it can prevent many of the excesses that have plagued our firms. What follows are some *general maxims for corporate information gathering,* written in the more lively prescriptive voice.

DEDICATION AND COMMITMENT   Information gathering should not be viewed as a routine accounting function: it is the sentinel that guards the fort. Gather and analyze information as if your firm's life depended on it. It often does. Look at what happened to Sears when it ignored the threats from K mart and Wal-Mart, or to Caterpillar when it missed the shift away from heavy equipment.

Managers at many levels and from a variety of departments must undertake vigilantly to watch and analyze their customers, suppliers, and competitors. Such devotion may take lots of time and money, but it is usually worth it. Xerox trained two hundred of its most astute line managers to look diligently and systematically for any changes in its rivals' pricing, products, and technologies. Milliken & Company, the progressive and highly successful textile giant, is a compulsive information gatherer. At great cost, Milliken regularly sends 150 employees abroad to the international textile machinery show for a full ten days to look for opportunities; its rivals typically send only four or five people. Milliken's staff spend all day at the show and then meet for three or four hours every evening, often until after midnight, to discuss new ideas and their potential application. This massive effort can hardly be considered casual scanning; it is an out-and-out intelligence campaign.[6]

COUNTERINTUITIVE SCANNING   Look for trends in soft data you *don't* normally think are of central importance, then try to interpret them in a manner least favorable to the company. For example, Salesmen should supplement the sales and market reports they are so addicted to with indicators of product quality and manufacturing efficiency. Craftsmen should listen to what the customers are saying about their products as well as looking at cost figures. Pioneers should cost out their innovation projects and try to establish how well their competitors are doing with much less advanced offerings. Finally, Builders should look for which operations to sell, what to cut back on, and how to get more out of their existing divisions.

GETTING THROUGH TO THE TOP Make sure that information goes to the powerful and is gathered by the bold. Don't ever shoot a messenger. Get people at high levels involved in the collection and analysis of information—like the executives at Apple who listen in on customer-complaint lines both to find out what is wrong with their products and to see how those complaints are being addressed.

Members of the board must also play a role in monitoring performance. As they have the power to make a difference, they should become as familiar as possible with their company's products and markets. At United Airlines in the late sixties, the board paid close attention to changes in route structures, computerization problems, and unfavorable CAB decisions. They pushed the CEO to deal more aggressively with these emerging problems. When he didn't respond, they convened a special meeting and decided to replace him and recruit a successor. This paved the way for corporate revitalization.[7]

Keep the game honest and reliable by using multiple sources of information. Leaders such as President Franklin Roosevelt would make themselves very well informed about an issue by using one set of sources before they were formally briefed by another. They would then make their expertise obvious during the briefing, exuding an aura of supercompetence that discouraged any subsequent attempts at concealment.

SOURCES OF GOOD INFORMATION—OPERATIONS If you are a senior manager in particular, make sure you tour your own operations. You could pretend to be a customer or try to buy your own products or services incognito. Talk to lots of employees at all levels—get your teenage nephew hired and listen to his reports; find out what the people in the plants, warehouses, and branches are saying. Sam Walton of the supersuccessful Wal-Mart stores visited every one of his seven hundred stores each year, hitchhiked with Wal-Mart trucks across the country, and frequented distribution centers to chat with the rank and file. Tom Peters and Nancy Austin call this management by wandering around (MBWA). It keeps managers in touch with "the first vibrations of the new."[8]

Peters and Austin talk about one top manager at Bell Labs who made special efforts to be in touch with his operation by roaming around talking to people. He could sometimes be found helping out at the Xerox machine, posing "dumb questions" such as "What's bugging you?" or "What's getting in the way?" He got one complaint about how hard it was to obtain a small personal computer because of all the budgetary red tape. Such annoyances are important in that they shape the way employees view their organizations. By quickly commandeering a PC for his troops, our manager was able to remove a very real source of dissatisfaction. But more important, he gained insight into a major underlying problem; in this case, a control bureaucracy that was stifling initiative.[9]

CUSTOMERS   Visit customers and have them visit you—work on some projects together, benefit from their free advice. Talk to customers—develop relationships of trust and respect with them. Find out what they need, like, and dislike. Allergan, a successful subsidiary of the drug giant SmithKline Beecham, supplied ointments for ophthalmology patients such as contact lens users. In discussions with consumers—whom most drug companies never deal with directly—they heard repeated complaints about dry, itchy eyes, a problem never detailed in the formal prescriptions compiled in their data bank. This qualitative symptom was the source of one of Allergan's most successful new products.[10]

Milliken & Company found that over half of all its new ideas came from its users. Complaints and requests from customers can also be a priceless source of inspiration. Managers should consider having a contest in which the grand prize goes to the employee, manager, or customer who gleans the most evocative and framebreaking gripe.

COMPETITORS   Find out how the firm stacks up against its competitors in the minds of industry financial analysts. Buy and benchmark rivals' products. Determine what customers think of the competition and what new products your rivals are introducing; discover how well your competitors are faring with their new products. Xerox purchased the machines of rivals such as Canon and tore them apart to discover how to economize on or improve their own products.[11] The powerful Komatsu, once an upstart Japanese heavy equipment manufacturer, eventually overtook rival Caterpillar by benchmarking its machines and finding ways to produce equivalent quality at a fraction of the cost.

PERFORMANCE TRENDS   A static statistic tells us so much less than a trend. So, monitor everything over time. Plot graphs of information so that trends will become apparent. For example, try to determine what is happening to the prices, costs, margins, and growth rates of your various products, to their market share and demographics, to your outlets according to geographic region and by store type. Creative aggregation and disaggregation of information is critical. For example, to find out where to expand, monitor the results by region; to find out what kinds of new products to introduce, look at your lines on a product-by-product basis.

GOING BEYOND THE FORMAL INFORMATION SYSTEM   Things change, but formal information systems reflect only the kind of news—mostly quantitative—that was important yesterday. Many acute challenges will not be captured. So, use these systems creatively and then go beyond them. Look for "unobtrusive indicators" of potential problems by finding out things like

- which types of projects are delayed or are always over budget? (where are we being too ambitious or ineffective?);
- which offices take the most photocopies, write the longest and the most memos, and order the most stationery per capita? (is this the locus of too much bureaucracy or overstaffing?);
- how many days are salespeople out of the office; are they traveling more? What percentage of calls goes to new clients? Is this increasing or decreasing? (are we reaching out or closing up?);
- who sits next to whom at lunch and in conferences? at meetings, who are the nay-sayers to which proposals? (are there cliques forming?);
- which departments have the highest absentee rates; the most turnover; the greatest loss of highly rated employees; the smallest loss of poorly rated employees? (where are our weaknesses?);
- how different are the average employee performance ratings of the different departments? (are there serious skill gaps?);
- which departments are all (or none) of the promotions coming from? what is the background and profile of those promoted, those left behind, and those leaving the firm? (what kind of culture do we have? what are its values?).

Almost everything done in an organization leaves traces of information. These potential "watchdogs" should be tapped regularly for information.

PATTERN RECOGNITION   Use your ability to recognize patterns to discover what the mountain of data is saying. Are ominous trends developing that have a common and dangerous cause? Are symptoms intensifying? Is there a vicious cycle that explains this? Ask which configuration is emerging; which trajectory applies. Generate questions that would complete the picture and gather new data accordingly.

Enlist managers from the different functions in these tasks of probing and interpretation. Meet with them regularly, not to plug numbers into a pro forma budget, but for the sole purpose of spotting important threats and opportunities. This is the only way of finding out when it is time to change. No bells will ring when that happens; there are no hard-and-fast rules. It is all a matter of judgment. The only imperative is that every leader must operate with the firm assumption that one day he or she will have to go to war with the past.

Learning and Innovating at the Boundaries

Concentrated, orchestrated configurations produce wonderful results but can slow down both learning and renewal. One way for a large organization to have its cake and eat it too is to establish small, independent units to experiment and do new things outside of (that is, without disturbing) the configuration of existing operations. Firms might, for example, set up small-scale development teams that have the flexibility to get things done quickly and economically. 3M gives such teams much independence but limited resources, killing projects that remain unsuccessful after five years or so. Hewlett Packard's small, agile teams collectively introduced products at the rate of eight a week in the mid-1980s. Some items went from conception to debugged prototype in just seventeen weeks.[12]

Many Japanese companies also use such small development teams to increase the number of new product experiments. These teams always work outside the normal structure. They are populated by young turks with tremendous energy (the average age at Honda was twenty-seven), and are fast tracks for advancement. Some teams even employ subcontractors to produce components, relieving the parent company of burdensome overheads. Although most teams fail, the ones that succeed may go on to become very significant business units.[13]

TURNAROUND

Unfreezing, Changing, and Refreezing

In the words of Kurt Lewin, organizations have to *unfreeze* before they can renew themselves: their managers must try to "unlearn" the past by questioning world views, opening up cultures, and disassembling structures. In research done earlier, Peter Friesen and I found that significant, lasting change required that managers fundamentally challenge their underlying corporate ideologies and basic assumptions. Failing that, the trajectories of their firms just kept pushing inexorably forward.[14]

Of course, the amount of fundamental change needed for a successful turnaround will vary according to the severity of the problem—the extent of a firm's excesses; its residual strengths; and the degree of mismatch between it and its markets. Where there are many strengths and only a modest mismatch, it may well be possible to recover just by adjusting an old strategy, by trimming back the excesses and recapturing the richness of the original configuration (we will see examples of this in Chapter 8). Where weaknesses are more prevalent, however, firms may have to adopt a substantially new strategy and configuration. This is a more complex task that will be our topic here.[15]

Typically, the soundest configurations balance internal harmony with market relevance; they possess a concerted theme and a competitive edge, but also avoid extremes. And once these configurations have been refined and tested, successful organizations *refreeze* around them to exploit their complementarities.

Although successful turnarounds vary, most will progress through three common stages: diagnosis, prescription, and implementation. These stages overlap and firms must often cycle back and forth among them.[16]

What follows must be taken as simply one example of creating change. The purpose is not to hammer out a final blueprint for transformation but to get managers thinking about how difficult it is to bring about significant change, and to make them appreciate just how much there is to do.

Diagnosis

Diagnosing a problem correctly calls for managers to discover and venture beyond invisible boundaries, as they reflect on the basic assumptions, strategic blind spots, and cultural rituals that shield them from painful truths. Diagnosis is not to be confused with the much shallower and more perfunctory investigation of routine difficulties using established standards and systems.

BUILDING A TRANSITION TEAM   Some leaders facilitate change by setting up transition teams. Such teams usually include the directors of most functional areas (division heads in market-based structures) to ensure a broad representation of viewpoints and skills. The most useful team members tend to be those with independence of mind, experience in other firms, the best knowledge of customers, and the social skills necessary for constructive discussion.

Lee Iacocca convened a transition team at Chrysler that was composed of the brightest managers from the most important divisions and departments—marketing manufacturing, engineering, purchasing, R&D, and finance. He also brought into the team several fast-rising executives he had just recruited from Ford, who could bring a new perspective to bear on problems.

The opinions of team members from long-disenfranchised departments may be especially revealing: the marketers of Tinkerers, for instance, the design and quality-control managers of Salesmen, or the accountants and finance executives of Pioneers. The old in-crowd may be jaded and obstinate, but outsiders enter with a fresh and critical viewpoint. The best teams also include—or are in close contact with—representatives from outside groups such as labor, suppliers, and vendors whose cooperation may eventually be useful in implementing change.

COMPILING A LIST OF SYMPTOMS   It may be helpful for team members first to independently create lists of symptoms and then to meet to discuss and aggregate these. Symptoms could include such factors as complaints about quality, declining margins, escalating costs, missed deadlines, and the loss of talented staff. Team members should also elicit symptoms from the external constituents they know best—customers, suppliers, union leaders, and even trade associations.

MAPPING THE PROBLEM   Once a thorough list of symptoms has been generated, the team can jointly begin to map the problem. This is a time for asking questions: *Why* have margins declined; *why* has quality fallen; *why* did that brilliant salesman quit; *how* are competitors keeping costs down; *why* are our distributors so angry?

Clues might be found in:

1. Outmoded assumptions about customers' preferences and competitors' products.
2. Threats caused by technological, economic, and demographic shifts.
3. Goals and standards that are too specialized; for example, narrow, technical definitions of quality that are now irrelevant to customers.
4. Areas of cultural excess or blindness: dominance by one value or group, gamesmanship, turf battles, utopianism, perfectionism, intolerance, or cockiness.
5. Structural extremes: too much or too little centralization, bureaucracy, hierarchy, or control.
6. Gaps in the repertory of skills.
7. Discontent among the rank and file—especially those on the customer firing line.
8. Leadership problems: arrogance, rigidity, grandiosity, remoteness, or management-by-numbers.
9. Problems of communication or coordination.
10. Strategies that are unbalanced, inconsistent, or extreme; too much or too little venturing, innovation, or marketing.
11. Inadequate information gathering or dissemination.

In mapping the problem, it is useful to work back from the symptoms to ask how each came about. Take the following sample sequence:

Why are customers complaining?	Because of bad quality.
Why has quality declined?	Because engineering and research have been ignored.
Why?	Because goals and strategies

	emphasize product image but not good design.
How come the problem has not been corrected?	Because the top executives have marketing backgrounds; also, the engineers have little power or prestige, so engineering departments are weak; and finally, quality control has not been integrated into the routine structure.
What are the basic assumptions contributing to the problem?	That quality is not as important to the customer as image.

The team might go through the same process for every symptom—lagging sales, mounting returns, or whatever. Ultimately, the same underlying factors will be found to explain a multiplicity of symptoms. These should help lay bare the roots of the problem: misguided strategic assumptions and practices, cultural or structural excesses, and even the trajectory that turned a healthy configuration into a sick one.

A variant on this procedure is for team members to construct maps of the problem independently. Then they come together to compare their inferences. Inevitably, there will be much disagreement about what are the problems—and even the symptoms. But an open interchange, perhaps moderated by an outside consultant, can help generate consensus about what went wrong. And such agreement will be invaluable in creating the motivation to undertake the necessary painful changes.

Once the team has generated consensus around the map of the problem, they can test it, or part of it, on other employees, trustworthy customers, industry experts, and dissidents who have not yet been consulted.

Organizational pathologies are much like cancers. Unless misguided assumptions, policies, or systems are eradicated completely, they can regenerate, even after many remedial changes have been made—recall the holographic metaphor of Chapter 6. So our diagnoses must be thorough and run deep. The Self-Assessment Questionnaire at the end of this chapter should help get the diagnostic process under way by enabling managers to compare their organization with the four trajectories of the book.

Prescription

Before discussing prescription per se, it may be useful to say a few words about the conceptual processes involved.

ANALYSIS VS. SYNTHESIS   According to physicists Ilya Prigogine and Isabelle Stengers, "One of the most highly developed skills in contemporary Western civilization is dissection: the split up of problems into their smallest possible components. We are good at it. So good, we often forget to put the pieces back together again."[17] All too often managers value the ability to analyze over the ability to synthesize. Analytical skills are fine for delving into problems, but they are inadequate for generating the insight needed for a workable solution. Analysis requires systematic probing, thoroughness, and logic. Synthesis, on the other hand, calls for artful pattern recognition, receptiveness, and magical insight—traits much neglected in the Western world.

If diagnosis is 80 percent analysis and 20 percent synthetic insight, the opposite is true for prescription, which aims to discover—or recover—a healthy configuration: one that reconciles the values, skills, strategies, and systems of the organization, the needs of its customers, and the challenges of its competitors. To complicate matters, few of these factors are entirely immune from organizational influence, yet few are entirely within managers' control. The trick is to find a focus, a center of gravity, that matches the most outstanding skills and capacities with the most pressing market needs. Managers must identify a theme or a vision for a configuration that is durable, defensible, and economically and politically feasible.

Contrary to most of the literature on strategic planning and decision making, no analytical, step-by-step procedure in which "logical alternatives are systematically generated and the optimal one selected" is likely to identify such a configuration. As in so many aspects of life, insight is required more than calculation; intuition more than lockstep deduction. In mathematics, for example, theorems are proved with logic, but the idea for the proof, as opposed to its distinct steps, comes from inspiration. In painting, technique is important, but quite useless without the aesthetic vision that puts it to good use. Even in composition, it is not a series of grammatical rules but rather an elusive creative capacity that generates good prose. Similarly, there is something mysterious and intangible about the process that discovers a good configuration. But talented managers know one when they see one. It has *quality,* to use the term so wonderfully explored by the thinker Robert M. Pirsig, in his *Zen and the Art of Motorcycle Maintenance.* It's beautiful, it fits; it's much more than the sum of its pieces, it lives.[18]

According to Henry Mintzberg, major strategic change "seems to require a shift in mindset before a new strategy can be conceived. And the thinking is fundamentally conceptual and inductive, probably stimulated . . . by just one or two key insights. Continuous bombardment of facts, opinions, problems, and so on may prepare the mind for the shift, but it is the sudden *insight* that is likely to drive the synthesis—to bring all the disparate elements together in one 'eureka'-type flash."[19]

CONFIGURATION BUILDING   Although there is no simple way to find or rebuild configurations, the map of the problem will suggest what needs repair, which excesses to counter, and which market conditions to address. This map, together with a knowledge of organizational skills and resources, can get the search going. It will put notions into the mental storage bins of managers that may eventually coalesce into a coherent theme—one that could be based on the strengths of an old strategy or configuration, a special market niche, dominant cultural values, or exceptional skills.

Managers might start, for instance, by asking themselves the following questions:

1. What strategy would both appeal to the target markets of the firm and be feasible with its existing (or attainable) skills, talents, and resources? Which orientations can best build on past strengths while undoing former excesses? What neglected functions need to be revitalized?
2. Should new or different markets now be pursued to capitalize on the new strategy?
3. Is this new strategy consistent with the existing aims and preferences of major stakeholders, e.g., managers, labor, customers, and shareholders? If not, what should be changed?
4. What kinds of structures, that is, control systems, positions, hierarchies, and coordinative committees, would be needed to implement the strategy?

5. Is there consistency between market needs, strategy, culture, and structure? If not, what can be most easily changed?

Such questions are easy to ask but incredibly tough to answer. However, posing and discussing them may generate a set of promising, preconscious notions in the minds of managers. If they are lucky, a pattern will begin to form. At this point it is often helpful to resist grabbing for a solution: to wait for insights to emerge, to live with uncertainty, and to avoid premature closure.

To ensure that they are both relevant and feasible, emerging ideas should be discussed with managers from different levels and departments. This is a time for much open consultation within the firm. Such participation not only makes for a better "solution," it also evokes commitment from a constituency of supporters who may be called upon to help in the implementation phase.

The ultimate object, of course, is to discover the basis for a cohesive new configuration. In trying to assess it, the following standards might be useful: does it take advantage of major strengths within the organization; does it counter the excesses of the past; does it satisfy a promising, defensible target market; does it create complementarities among goals, skills, strategies, and systems; and finally, is it politically and economically feasible?

Months of intensive information gathering, discussion, and refinement may be needed before a strong theme and viable design emerges. Eventually, however, the core idea will develop and the collateral changes in strategy, culture, and process that must be made to implement it will become clearer. The crystal will finally have formed.

Much of the preceding discussion assumes the need for far-reaching change. Remember, though, that where diagnosis reveals that firms have not strayed too far from the path of success, incremental changes that recover or develop an initial configuration may be enough to set things right. It is just as bad to perform too many alterations as too few.

Implementation

Implementation is even more of an iterative procedure than design.[20] Good prescriptions must be shaped by the views of many employees, by the reactions of markets, and by emerging political and economic considerations. Such realities change even the best designs. But in accommodating them, wise managers take care not to destroy the theme or core complementarities of a configuration. Furthermore, the wisest prescriptions plot out not only what managers want to achieve, but also what they want to avoid.

Two obvious constituencies must be enlisted to aid effective implementation: insiders and outsiders. Both need to be energetically appealed to, motivated, and solicited for advice.

EMPATHY AND UNDERSTANDING Some of the biggest obstacles to change are political. People resist change because it erodes their authority, challenges their long-held viewpoints, makes them look silly, threatens their pride and security, complicates their jobs, takes away their perks, and generally makes their lives miserable.

Many managers will therefore have to go through a period of mourning their losses before they are ready to accept a new state of affairs. They must "work through" their sorrows and fears before they will even budge, let alone work enthusiastically toward a new orientation.[21] The transition team will thus have to do much handholding and explaining. They must allow objections to be voiced and provide reassurance wherever possible. Just being sympathetic to complaints and ensuring that some "experimentation" errors will be tolerated, even encouraged, during the chaotic transition period may make things easier. Also, an ombudsman may be appointed to handle especially sensitive issues.

CONSULTATION AND PERSUASION Successful transition teams avidly consult managers and workers for their views on design and implementation. Employees are really the "customers" of change; they must accept a new strategy for it to work. It is important therefore that they contribute to—and be sold on—the policies and activities they will be called upon to implement. Regular meetings and coordinative groups can facilitate this meeting of minds.

The National Steel Corporation undertook a major initiative to renew its stale product lines. It set up task forces and coordinative committees to share information about the problems and successes encountered in the change process. Top executives met personally with vast numbers of managers to convince them of the severity of the problems—to establish that this was not "just another cyclical downturn." Meetings also were set up to allow managers from different

211

units to express their concerns, to make them see that they shared a common set of difficulties, and to force them to pull together to find creative solutions. Even barriers to change were identified collectively with the understanding that those who help identify a problem will be that much readier to work toward its resolution.[22]

To obtain the enthusiastic support of the more powerful and skillful managers, variants of the Japanese *ringi* system may sometimes be used, especially where agreement is vital and the solutions proposed are controversial, incomplete, or unclear. This system allows an initial proposal to be amended as it circulates among managers, until the most important parties finally support it. The process is time-consuming, but it does build up a valuable commitment.

SIGNALING DETERMINATION   Once a course of action has been chosen, it can be communicated to all employees by large-scale meetings and conferences. However, because actions speak louder than words, symbolic or frame-breaking decisions may be even more effective in signaling the determination to change. For example, National Steel Corporation announced its decision to sell its West Virginia plant. This was a clear signal to the rest of the organization that the situation was grave and that drastic action was being taken.[23]

Similarly, Tinkerers who want to return to being Craftsmen may broadcast that intent by elevating their marketing and R&D people to executive committees, increasing their advertising and new product development budgets, and convening new design teams. Pioneers trying to become more realistic may cancel some of their most aggressive innovation projects, better define everybody's responsibilities, and install sharper cost-control systems. Such changes tell everyone concerned that the game has changed.

PRESERVING FLEXIBILITY   It is important while shaping and implementing a configuration to accept uncertainty, encourage experiments, and keep policies and operations fluid. Managers should not explain away or pigeonhole the problems that crop up, but must use mistakes as the sources for new ideas. Moreover, a bottom-up approach is usually preferable to imposing rigid strategic plans from above.

ENLISTING OUTSIDE HELP   Since the reactions of outsiders such as customers and distributors will make or break a strategy, these parties must be polled as early as possible. The team should consult with customers about prototypes, ask distributors for marketing advice, and talk to outside experts and suppliers about process design. All of these discussions must elicit specific comments such as "We hate the color and price," "The competition has more stylish stuff," "It looks cheap and is underpowered," "It's a pain to deal with your rude sales staff," or "You're always late." Abstractions such as "It's not quite what we had in mind" demand clarification since they can be molded into whatever managers want to hear. And, of course, information should not be gathered by those with an incentive to suppress bad news. Designers of a new product tend to interpret *all* test-market reactions favorably.

Creeping Convergence

What starts off as a very open, flexible approach will gradually settle down as the new configuration gets installed. Once a strategy has proved promising, once the structure and culture have evolved to implement it, and once power structures, external alliances, and target markets have taken shape to complete the picture, the latitude for change will be reduced. The refreezing so necessary for smooth operation and competitive advantage will have started automatically.

Overcoming Resistance at the Top

I've saved the worst news for last. It is often necessary for the CEO to leave the organization before an adequate turnaround can occur. The biggest barriers to change are leaders with vested interests in the status quo. CEOs often fail to accept responsibility for past mistakes and deny the need for transition. Many find it embarrassing, politically dangerous, and even humiliating to admit that they were wrong. So they rationalize poor performance, blame the environment, and minimize the severity of problems.

In researching change, Peter Friesen and I found that most reorientations occur only after two events: a severe decline in performance *and* a change in leadership.[24] Pain, not good advice, is the doctor most companies listen to. And too many leaders stubbornly cling to disastrous policies of their own making and must be replaced.[25] Could we have foreseen much change at ITT without the departure of the strong-willed Geneen? Could Eastern really have transformed itself

213

with Captain Eddie at the helm? Or Chrysler with Lynn Townsend still in command?

Only the board of directors has the vital duty and the power to dismiss a belligerent or neglectful CEO. Falling performance must trigger the board's prompt assessment of whether a leader and his or her team are able to effect a proper turnaround; if not, a replacement should be sought without delay. Indeed, a talented and independent board is one of the greatest assets an organization can have, and firms, while they are healthy, should strive diligently to develop one.

Where performance has declined precipitously or over a long period, some boards resort to bringing in a new CEO from the outside—one who is free of the old assumptions and vested interests of the ensconced team. Powerful and resistant members of the second tier may also be replaced to good effect. This occurred during the turnarounds of Disney, Gulf & Western, and Chrysler, where a broad infusion of fresh executive talent was imperative to save each company.

AUDITING YOUR FIRM

The following Self-Assessment Questionnaire is designed to help you evaluate your own organization. The questions are very general so that they will apply to many different industries and types of firms. Try when answering to compare your firm to its three or four principal competitors, those selling products that might conceivably appeal to your own customers or potential customers. The questionnaire should be completed by numerous individuals within the firm and be used as a basis for discussing and examining existing assumptions about the business. It may be a good idea for the CEO and the leaders of each of the functional departments to complete the questionnaire independently, and then come together to discuss the differences that crop up.

It takes a good deal of organizational knowledge to answer these questions. So, think carefully before responding. You may also wish to answer the questions based on what the firm was like three years ago, what it is like now, and what it may be like three years from now, to get some feeling for its direction of evolution.

SELF-ASSESSMENT QUESTIONNAIRE

Assign a score of 1 to 5 for each of the following questions or statements where the numbers indicate the following ratings:

1	2	3	4	5
completely false or very rare relative to our competitors		about the same		very true or common relative to our competitors

SET 1:   **RATING**

1. Our style of management is highly authoritarian. ____*
2. Cost leadership is our key competitive strategy. ____
3. Quality leadership is our key competitive strategy. ____
4. Our marketing effort is not one of our major strengths. ____
5. Much emphasis is placed on cost controls and budgets. ____
6. Our quality controls are very sophisticated. ____
7. We pay little attention to advertising and distribution. ____
8. Engineering and manufacturing departments [operations departments for service companies] are far more influential than marketing and R&D departments. ____
9. Managers in engineering and operations departments receive higher salaries, faster promotions, and more status than managers in other departments. ____
10. Goals of cost or quality leadership are very strong. ____
11. Power is centralized at the top of the organization. ____
12. The firm is very bureaucratic, with many rules and programmed routines. ____
13. There is a strong emphasis on formal information systems and formal plans. ____
14. There is much more top-down communication than bottom-up communication. ____*
15. There is little open or intensive communication among the different functional areas. ____
16. Significant new product introductions are very rare. ____
17. The formal hierarchy must be observed in making decisions. ____
18. Important decisions take a long time to make. ____
19. We rarely consult customers about their preferences and reactions. ____*
20. Lower levels of management have very little impact on our policies. ____
21. Our product lines are more highly focused than those of our competitors—that is, our products are more tailored to a narrow and precisely targeted set of customers. ____
22. Engineers are vital to the success of the firm. ____
23. Managers hate taking risks. ____

215

24. Our product lines are becoming obsolete. ____*
25. Our customers stop buying when we increase prices. ____*
26. Sales growth has been leveling off. ____*
27. We have been losing promising managers in marketing and R&D to competitors. ____*
28. Complaints about red tape and bureaucracy are increasing. ____*
29. Managers find customer or competitor behavior puzzling. ____*

Total Items 1 through 29 ____

SET 2:

1. The CEO is an adventurous entrepreneur. ____
2. Sales growth is our dominant goal. ____
3. The firm is highly diversified. ____
4. The CEO owns many shares in the firm. ____
5. We have expanded much more rapidly than our rivals. ____
6. Managers favor risky decisions. ____*
7. The finance and accounting functions dominate those of manufacturing and marketing. ____*
8. Head-office corporate planning staffs are large and powerful. ____
9. Product lines are very broad. ____
10. Acquisitions are favored as a means of expansion. ____
11. Expansion projects absorb or place at risk a large percentage (more than 20%) of capital. ____*
12. Projects are growing in scope and scale. ____
13. The organization is moving into new areas of business. ____
14. The firm is diversifying at an accelerating rate. ____*
15. Specialized staff groups help in our expansion. ____
16. The firm is split into divisions based on type of market or geographic region. ____
17. Heads of divisions are given responsibility for profits and growth. ____
18. Legal and financial staff play an important role in implementing strategies. ____
19. The rate of return on assets is falling. ____*
20. We operate extensively in areas of business that are unrelated to one another. ____
21. Top executives pay relatively little attention to the substance of strategies—e.g., product designs, marketing tactics, manufacturing or service policies. ____*
22. Goals of short-term growth dominate those of long-run profitability. ____*
23. Interest expenses on long-term debt have become onerous. ____*
24. Interdepartmental conflict is increasing. ____*
25. Resources are being depleted. ____*
26. Risk taking is accelerating. ____*

Total Items 1 through 26 ____

SET 3:

1. The firm spends a great deal on R&D compared to its major competitors. ____
2. A high percentage of the product line has been introduced over the last two years. ____
3. The rate of innovation is increasing. ____
4. We are run by scientists and R&D types. ____
5. R&D or new product development departments have much power compared to marketing, finance, and production [operations] departments. ____
6. Goals of innovation and technical accomplishment are more important than those of growth and profitability. ____*
7. Work is accomplished by task forces, teams, and informal work groups. ____
8. Policy and strategy are determined by the managers of engineering, R&D, and product development groups. ____
9. Our structure is very informal. ____
10. Our structure is very loose and flexible. ____
11. The rewards and status accruing to R&D and new product development people are much greater than those going to marketing or production personnel. ____*
12. Leaders have a missionary do-or-die attitude toward new product development. ____
13. Our products are much more advanced technologically than those of our competitors. ____
14. Many very significant risks are incurred in new product development projects. ____*
15. The firm sells to customers who prefer mostly state-of-the-art products. ____
16. Our major losses stem from new product development projects. ____*
17. We make our own products obsolete prematurely. ____*
18. The manufacturing economy of our operations is poor. ____*
19. There are weaknesses in marketing—e.g., excessive prices, poor advertising, inadequate distribution. ____*
20. Cost overruns and long delays in innovation projects are common. ____*
21. There is much discontent among the marketing and production staffs. ____*
22. There is much confusion in lines of authority and job definitions. ____*
    Total Items 1 Through 22 ____

SET 4:

1. Our brand names are a tremendous asset. ____
2. Marketing departments have much more influence on strategy than manufacturing, production, and engineering units. ____*

217

3. Our firm differentiates its products from the competition's via its marketing prowess. _____
4. Excellent advertising is one of our greatest strengths. _____
5. Our distribution system gives us a big competitive advantage. _____
6. Warrantees and good service play a big role in making our products attractive. _____
7. Product lines are so complete that they appeal to a very wide range of customers. _____
8. The firm is organized according to profit centers. _____
9. There are many levels in the hierarchy. _____*
10. Information and budgeting systems are very sophisticated and complex. _____
11. Jobs, reporting relationships, and responsibilities are clearly and formally defined. _____
12. Marketing research is carried out extensively. _____
13. The CEO has a marketing background. _____
14. The firm attracts customers who are mainly interested in image, good service, and reliability. _____
15. The organization is large and well established. _____
16. The number of products and product lines has begun to proliferate aimlessly. _____*
17. Market-share growth is a more important goal than efficiency. _____
18. Leaders are losing touch with their operations. _____*
19. Our product lines are becoming stale vis-à-vis the competition's. _____*
20. Customers are complaining increasingly about bland or poor-quality products. _____*
21. Promising employees increasingly have begun to leave. _____*
22. Employee complaints about bureaucracy and red tape have been mounting. _____*
23. Interdepartmental feuds or difficulties in coordination are becoming all too common. _____*

Total Items 1 Through 23 _____

Scoring

It is time now to find out which of the configurations and trajectories pertain to your own organization. Remember, however, that most firms are not pure types and your company is likely to represent a mixture of several configurations. The fit will by no means be perfect—we are merely trying to find the closest approximation to your firm. The exercise will serve more to generate an interesting discussion than to provide any definitive diagnosis.

Take the sum of the scores on the items for each set. Then divide by the number of items to get the average score.

	Sum of All Scores	Divide by Number of Items		Average Score
SET 1	—	29	=	—
SET 2	—	26	=	—
SET 3	—	22	=	—
SET 4	—	23	=	—

The set with the highest average score is the most relevant to your firm. Where average scores are very similar between two or more sets, this suggests that your firm may be a hybrid of our types. If the average score is below 3 for all sets, this may indicate the lack of a fully developed theme or configuration. Alternatively, it just might mean that your firm does not fit any of our configurations and has a different, and perhaps very successful, orientation of its own.

The sets relate to the configurations and trajectories as follows:

SET 1   From Craftsmen to Tinkerers: The Focusing Trajectory
SET 2   From Builders to Imperialists: The Venturing Trajectory
SET 3   From Pioneers to Escapists: The Inventing Trajectory
SET 4   From Salesmen to Drifters: The Decoupling Trajectory

Now, to determine how close your firm is to the unhealthy end of its trajectory, for each set total only the scores for the questions marked with an asterisk, and then take the average. If that average is more than 3 for the asterisked questions, your company may be on its way to decline. The higher the score on the asterisked questions, the more urgent it is to take action. Scores of 4 and above indicate real danger.

	Sum of * Items	Divide by Number of Items		Average
SET 1	—	9	=	—
SET 2	—	11	=	—
SET 3	—	10	=	—
SET 4	—	9	=	—

Please note that any classification derived from this questionnaire must be extremely rough and approximate. An accurate assessment of your organization would have to take into account its industry, size, and products, and would require far more refined scales for measuring its strategy, structure, culture, and leadership.

So, take the results of this exercise with a grain of salt. Always check back to the detailed accounts of the trajectories in Chapters 2 through 5 to verify the parallels with your own organization. Then continue on to Chapter 8 for some tactics that might help reverse, or even avert, these dangerous trajectories.

CHAPTER 8

Managing the Four Trajectories

Oᴜʀ ꜰᴏᴜʀ ᴛʀᴀᴊᴇᴄᴛᴏʀɪᴇꜱ ᴘᴜꜱʜᴇᴅ ꜱᴛʀᴀᴛᴇɢɪᴇꜱ ᴛᴏ ᴇxᴛʀᴇᴍᴇꜱ, ᴀʟɪᴇɴ-ated firms from their markets, and badly skewed leadership, cultures, and structures. In the last two chapters I tried to explain why, and made general observations about turnarounds and avoiding decline. I also provided an audit instrument to help readers to determine which trajectory most threatens their own firms. The question now is what to do with the diagnosis. How can managers reverse the danger-ous trajectories if their firms are already in trouble? Or, if their organi-zations are still healthy, how can they avoid falling into the traps to which they are most susceptible?

This chapter addresses these issues by examining how sick firms within each of the trajectories managed to turn themselves around. Most pursued some variation of the processes discussed in the last chapter: reviving and broadening their strategic competences and tuning in to their markets. In addition, however, they made changes relevant only to their particular trajectories. And it is to these that we must now turn. We will also look at some examples of Craftsmen, Builders, Pioneers, and Salesmen who have actually *avoided* the trou-blesome trajectories.

One word of caution before we proceed: some of the promising turnarounds I will describe are still under way and may yet fail; and some of my successful "avoider" firms will inevitably lapse into dif-ficulties. In our changing world of organizations, nothing is perma-nent and few things are entirely predictable. So, some of my examples will no doubt come back to haunt me.

AWAKENING THE TINKERER—THE FOCUSING TRAJECTORY

Recall that many malignant transformations took place on the road from Craftsman to Tinkerer. First, managers came to focus only on one or two aspects of cost or quality—to the exclusion of matters that were much more important to their customers. Blindness set in because internal concerns increasingly supplanted external ones. Second, product lines became outdated as tinkering and fine-tuning took the place of significant innovation. Third, the marketing effort became dull and mistargeted. And fourth, these problems were all fueled by Tinkerers' controlling leaders, their technocratic cultures, and their bureaucratic structures.

By addressing each of these defects, some of our Tinkerers were able, ultimately, to restore themselves to good health. And it is instructive to see just how they did so. DEC, TI, Disney, and Caterpillar, for example, were all able to undo some of the damage wrought by the focusing trajectory. Their new (or reawakened) leaders reduced the dominance of production and engineering types and promoted looser, more responsive cultures and structures. This helped to alert managers to the challenges in their environments, and prodded them to renew offerings and broaden their product-market scope. Firms also set up more diligent marketing programs and began to gather more information about their customers and rivals. (These actions are summarized in Table 3.)

Vignettes

In early 1985, a dissatisfied board of directors at Texas Instruments replaced CEO J. Fred Bucy with Jerry Junkins, a far less authoritarian and more visionary leader, who encouraged much broader participation in the decisions being made. Junkins had a big job to do to turn his firm around. TI had lost touch with its customers and markets; its product lines had become dated and unattractive, its diversification efforts were unsuccessful, and its marketing was weak. Junkins revived TI by boosting the efficiency of its manufacturing operations—TI's traditional strength. But he simultaneously speeded up production systems and made them more flexible; flexible enough, in fact, to custom-design chips for TI's largest clients. Junkins then pro-

222

TABLE 3. Managing the Focusing Trajectory

Problems:
   Intolerant leadership and monolithic cultures
   Centralized, overbureaucratic structures
   Blindness to markets
   Narrow focus: destructive parsimony or irrelevant quality
   Outmoded product lines
   Lackluster marketing

Actions Taken:
   Open up cultures to new blood and different values
   Loosen structural strictures
   Scan markets and competition to increase scope
   Diversify out of stale areas
   Boost innovation
   Market more aggressively

ceeded to enhance the sophistication and power of TI's microchips and to broaden its product lines. He also launched a much more strategically targeted and aggressive marketing effort. Performance soon began to improve.

The turnaround at Ken Olsen's Digital Equipment Corporation was remarkably similar. While Olsen remained a strong, directive leader, he began to open up DEC's culture to encourage more participation from marketing managers and even customers. Olsen insisted on preserving his firm's major strength—in this case super-high quality. But it became ever more clear to him that DEC had to cut its costs, to market and price more aggressively, and to become more responsive to customer needs. Olsen also began to realize that DEC needed to innovate more in order to supplement its technical clients with commercial ones. So he moved into the rapidly developing segments of the mainframe and workstation markets and enhanced the networking capabilities of his lines. Before long, DEC's sales and profits began to shoot up again.

LEADERSHIP AND CULTURE

Managers will recognize the need to reorient their strategies only if they are prepared to listen carefully to the suggestions of customers, dissident managers, and disenfranchised staff. This demands a total change of attitude founded in new forms of leadership, cultures, and decision processes. In other words, turnaround will not usually occur unless there is a fundamental transformation in the organization's management philosophy and infrastructure.

Tinkerers, we will recall, were subject to an autocratic leadership; to a culture dominated by engineers and operations managers; and to a surfeit of bureaucratic controls. The only way in which a turn-around can be effected is to change all this. In fact, most turn-arounds were accomplished by newly appointed CEOs who were more open to sharing power, encouraging initiative, and listening to both subordinates and customers. These leaders implemented a culture that allowed equal participation from marketing and engineer-ing types. They also fought bureaucracy by establishing smaller operating units and giving such units the authority to get things done their own way.

For example, at Texas Instruments, Jerry Junkins tried with his low-key management style to move the corporate culture away from the autocratic approach of his predecessors. According to one long-time employee, "Jerry hasn't thrown the reins over the horse's head, but he has relaxed them considerably."[1] Junkins has also stressed a more flexible, service-oriented approach that responds to customers. He pushed managers to look beyond their own fiefdoms and to com-municate and collaborate with other TI managers worldwide. Indeed, TI staffers now made use of a network of over forty thousand termi-nals in fifty countries. This alerted everyone to emerging customer needs and trends, and coordinated TI's manufacturing strategies and service activities to meet those trends.[2]

Similar transformations occurred at Disney where the new CEO, Michael Eisner, waged his continual battle against complacency. Eisner was always open to ideas for improvement and solicited them from customers and employees alike. He summarized his "running-scared" attitude as follows: "As long as you act as if you're coming from behind, you have a shot at staying ahead."[3] Eisner did away with the stifling authoritarian climate and imported fresh management talent. One of his first acts was to raid previous employers such as ABC-TV and Paramount for young, creative managers, whom he turned loose with ample budgets and significant operating discretion. And Eisner's leadership style was encouraging, not oppressive. He saw himself as "the cheerleader of the Walt Disney Company" as he bounded in and out of meetings, prodding his managers for ideas and sparking freewheeling discussions. Said Eisner, "This is a business that succeeds on good ideas. And I find that no matter how long a meeting goes on, the best ideas always come during the final five minutes, when people drop their guard and I ask them what they really think."[4]

In short, Tinkerers need to open themselves up to information from their markets and to new ideas. They have to encourage a culture in which some types of dissent are allowed, even encouraged. Monolithic dominance by any single executive or department must be actively discouraged. And small units should be broadly empowered to keep firms close to their markets.

STRATEGY

Having implemented a more open, interactive leadership and more participative and tolerant cultures, our recovering Tinkerers proceeded to reorient their strategies. They reestablished their central strengths as cost or quality leaders; improved their marketing efforts to better understand and serve customers; and revived their product lines by generally updating their offerings and broadening their scope.

Relevant Quality and Efficiency

Recall that Tinkerers were once Craftsmen who excelled at cost or quality leadership. Although their lines may have fallen out of favor, many former *quality leaders* still have the distinctive product and process design capabilities to come up with superior offerings. But they must also ensure that their products are up-to-date, appealing, and not overly expensive. Quality is desirable only when it is valued by customers and enviable to competitors. *Cost-leader* Tinkerers may similarly use their engineering talents to design efficient production processes. But they need to avoid turning out minimalist goods that nobody wants. In other words, the new strategies may profitably build on the strengths of the past—but they must become more balanced. Firms should never chase low cost or high quality at the expense of everything else.

The TI turnaround was an interesting example of how a cost leader could be efficient while simultaneously increasing the attractiveness

225

of its products. Rushing to the rescue, new CEO Jerry Junkins wanted first of all to augment TI's major strategic asset—its cost leadership in the chips market. To help make TI very cost-effective, Junkins closed down some of the losing home computer and consumer electronics ventures that had been so badly bungled.[5] More importantly, by building state-of-the-art manufacturing plants, one in Japan and one near Dallas, TI became the only U.S. producer of high-volume memory chips that could compete with the Japanese on the basis of cost. In addition, Junkins accelerated the automation of chip design and manufacturing by using robotics extensively.

But TI did more than enhance efficiency. It also changed its manufacturing philosophy, boosting quality by installing acute controls which guaranteed that all chips delivered to customers were free of defects. Moreover, TI's designers ensured that efficiency would not compromise flexibility. They built a pilot plant that delivered special-order chips in just two weeks, compared with the industry average of eighteen weeks. In short, manufacturing improvements allowed TI to lower its costs, increase quality, *and* be more responsive to the needs of its customers. And this is what most cost leaders must do: maintain efficiency while making sure that their products will now appeal to healthy, growing markets.

Caterpillar was a quality leader, not a cost leader. But it began to be trounced by its superefficient Japanese competitor, Komatsu, losing almost $1 billion between 1982 and 1984. Cat's obsession with quality had boosted expenses to the point where it could no longer compete. Its production methods had become too inefficient to enable it to match Komatsu's prices. So CEO George Schaefer initiated a $1.8 billion "Plant with a Future" (PWAF) program. He began to implement a speedy, flexible manufacturing system that is already cutting the costs of some operations by 20 percent. The firm also shut down inefficient plants and slashed payrolls by 30 percent.[6]

Cat has become much more flexible. It can now determine and respond to customer wishes and shifts in demand very rapidly. Computerized machine tools can be adjusted within seconds to meet the specifications of any new order. In fact, order-filling time for machinery parts has been knocked down from twenty to eight days, inventory levels have been cut in half, and manufacturing floor space has been reduced by 21 percent. Cat is also devising a customized software package that links factories with suppliers and dealers, so that it can anticipate demand more quickly and tap suppliers around the world most efficiently.[7] The firm earned record profits of $616 million in 1988.

Clearly the efforts and expenditures required of such firms as Caterpillar and TI were great. But the rewards forthcoming were even greater.

Aggressive Marketing

All of our Tinkerers lacked a competent and energetic marketing strategy. Salesmanship was abandoned entirely; advertising was deemed undignified; and customers were ignored or taken for granted. One of the biggest challenges for Tinkerers is to boost their marketing skills. This is hard because years of neglect have dried up almost all of the marketing talent in the organization. But one thing Tinkerers can do is get closer to the customer and employ their considerable design strengths to adapt products by using what they learn. This is the first important step in marketing—finding out what the market calls for and designing products accordingly.

That is essentially what TI did. TI used to sell standard commodity-like chips; its catalogue was its greatest marketing tool. But it altered its approach when it entered the fast-developing market for microprocessors and semicustom chips—complex components that require close, enduring relationships with large customers and strong engineering support staffs. According to CEO Junkins: "The whole business is becoming oriented towards systems. That's forcing us to deal more directly with the needs of sophisticated users than in the past."[8] To accomplish this, Junkins took control of the semiconductor division away from chip-engineering managers and put it into the hands of Pat Weber, a long-range planner with a strong marketing background in electronic systems. Junkins also charged his top managers with developing significant new customer alliances both at home and in the rapidly growing Far Eastern markets. TI even began to form cooperative ventures with other semiconductor manufacturers to trade its own considerable production expertise for the marketing and R&D skills of its partners. Said Junkins: "The environment has changed. We can't do everything ourselves."[9]

DEC, too, boosted its marketing efforts, which had been notoriously lackluster. It increased its sales, service, and support force, adding 16,000 staff members in 1987 alone, and bringing the total to about 65,000. Ken Olsen poured money into new sales centers to penetrate target industries all over the world. One center occupied an entire floor of a Manhattan office building with mock trading rooms and back offices to demonstrate the value of DEC's VAXes for the financial service industry. DEC even started to soften its hard line on prices. To gain a rapid foothold in the desktop computer market, it cut the price of its basic workstation by 50 percent, to $4,600. And for the first time in years, the company began to advertise on television.[10] DEC's marketing now focused on about one thousand major companies worldwide that set the data-processing trends in their industries. This allowed managers to stay on top of developing client needs and to devise appealing new products.[11]

Disney's newly appointed CEO, Michael Eisner, was especially careful about marketing. He wanted above all to stay in touch with his audience. Movie executives, for example, were told to conduct test screenings of Disney's films to discover the types of audiences that liked the films the most. They then used this information to target distribution, promotion, and timing. Indeed, one of Disney's secrets to success was that it found out what people wanted to see and then advertised where its audience could best be reached. Disney also partitioned its film-making business into adult and family studios—the Touchstone and Walt Disney Studios, respectively. That way it could reach the new adult market with films like *Good Morning Vietnam* and *Down and Out in Beverly Hills*, without alienating its original family clientele.[12]

Eisner then turned his attention to the two Disney theme parks, whose attendance had been waning. He launched a hefty and unprecedented advertising and promotion campaign, and hired such talents as producer George Lucas, director Francis Ford Coppola, and entertainer Michael Jackson to create new attractions. He also relaxed the ban on drinking to lure convention business to the parks. The number of visitors soared. And the increased popularity of the parks allowed Disney to raise its prices, and its profit margins, very significantly. Eisner's acute financial controls extended these margins even further.[13]

Product-Market Renewal

Having reestablished cost or quality leadership and gotten in closer touch with their markets, most of our recovering Tinkerers renewed their product lines by doing more innovation.

Tinkerers sell dated lines whose convenience and attractiveness have been surpassed by rival products. Any turnaround demands that firms renew their offerings in light of changing tastes, new technologies, or the advances of competitors. Needless to say, it is unlikely—given their emphasis on cost or quality—that Craftsmen could out-innovate Pioneers. And certainly, they need not stay ahead of the pack. But they must ensure that their products meet contemporary standards.

TI, for long a manufacturer of low-margin, commodity-type chips, came to realize that it could be more successful with updated, higher-power products. So it began to turn out some of the most advanced chips in the industry by taking advantage of its main distinctive competence—its manufacturing skill. At the Dallas plant, TI started to make sophisticated one-megabit DRAM chips. According to some analysts, this made it the technological leader in the U.S. semiconductor industry. As we saw earlier, TI even introduced powerful microprocessors and semicustom chips tailored to large, individual customers.[14]

Quality-leader DEC scrambled to update its VAX line, creating demand for its larger machines by making them compatible with Apple and IBM personal computers. This facilitated networking for applications such as electronic mail. And unlike IBM, DEC adopted industry standards instead of proprietary ones. It even increased the power of some VAX machines for scientific applications to compete against the mini-supercomputers of its rivals.[15] By introducing significant new products at the rate of one a month, DEC also consolidated its already strong position with technical clients.[16]

Product-line renewal is perhaps best illustrated by the Walt Disney turnaround. Whereas TI and DEC had the engineering talent to devise new offerings, the moribund Disney had to recruit creative talent from the outside. Its stodgy film business was in desperate need of revival when Michael Eisner took over in 1984. Eisner was known as a prodigy in the film industry, "an inexhaustibly idea-filled executive who knew a good story when he saw one and could tell if it would work on the screen."[17] At Paramount, Eisner had been responsible for such hits as *Terms of Endearment* and *Raiders of the Lost Ark*. His daunting task was to resuscitate a mummified Disney by renewing its offerings. He needed to awaken Disney to the values of the eighties and the interests of a more sophisticated, and jaded, audience.

Eisner set about his task by hiring talented writers, directors, and

229

designers from other film companies. He gave them the funds to attract major stars and the mandate to come up with original fare. Unusual and entertaining films such as *Dead Poets Society, Honey, I Shrunk the Kids,* and *Who Framed Roger Rabbit?* were tremendously successful. They were tasteful and of high quality—always a Disney trademark. But they also had some zing and a very broad appeal.[18]

Disney once again began to do well in television by producing conspicuously adult series such as "Golden Girls" and the Sunday Night Movie, as well as some top-rated Saturday morning cartoon shows. And Eisner built up a syndication operation to sell the twenty-nine years of programming that had been languishing in the Disney vaults.[19]

To sum up, Tinkerers must get rid of outmoded products and replace them with new ones, building on their substantial design and production skills. And the only way to do so successfully is to find out what customers want, and then, if necessary, recruit the creative and marketing talent to provide it.

A Broader Focus

Tinkerers have typically focused too narrowly on a very constrained range of dimensions, such as quality or cost alone, and on a rather confined array of products and markets. Now they absolutely have to broaden their horizons. We have seen them do this by balancing cost, quality, and innovation. But many may also benefit from broaching broader markets with a wider array of products.

TI, for example, decided to reduce its dependence on the volatile commodity-chip business. So, it zeroed in on the most promising and rapidly growing segments of the industry, lines such as special-purpose microprocessors for communications signal processing, graphics terminals, and local area networks. TI also became more competitive in defense electronics, having dropped the price of its HARM air-to-surface missile three times. And it purchased Rexnord Automation's industrial systems and control business to strengthen its own industrial automation operations. Notice, however, that TI broadened selectively, always taking advantage of its special engineering and production skills.[20]

DEC, too, expanded its range as it began to broach commercial as well as technical markets. It started to attack IBM's traditional business markets in earnest by offering a broad line of products from desktop workstations to clusters of minicomputers, all of which ran the same software and interfaced beautifully. DEC made its networking facilities uniquely appropriate for automating laboratories, engineering shops, and office departments. More recently, the company entered the market for mainframe computers with its VAX 9000— introduced because of the squeeze put on minicomputer markets by powerful workstations and economical mainframes. The 9000 model was ideal for older VAX customers, who invested heavily in DEC software but had grown to where they need a mainframe.[21] Close to 50 percent of DEC's sales came from commercial accounts in 1988, as against 40 percent in 1984, and its market share in the mid-range computer market has increased from 19 to 25 percent (IBM's fell from 24 to 16 percent during the same period).[22] DEC's 1988 revenues were double those of 1984, and pre-tax income was five times as high.

Caterpillar broadened its lines as well, shifting the emphasis away from heavy equipment, which was in a secular slump. Enormous bulldozers were no longer needed because of the decline in big-ticket energy and highway projects. So Cat redoubled its efforts in small machines such as farm tractors and backhoe loaders, for which there was a growing demand.

Walt Disney Studios had for years been putting out an anemic stream of bland films aimed at the shrinking family market. But, as we saw, Eisner opened things up, offering more red-blooded movies to an adult market. He also started to introduce many more films than in the past. Disney Productions, under Eisner-appointed Chairman Jeffrey Katzenberg, began to bring out about fifteen movies a year, as compared to the three or four introduced before he came on board.[23] The film division became an industry powerhouse as Disney's share of the film business expanded from 4 percent to 14 percent in 1984–87 (total profits quadrupled).[24] Eisner also widened Disney's markets by building more hotels in Florida, enlarging its EPCOT center, and setting up retail stores to sell a whole range of Disney goods.

So, Tinkerers must expand their horizons and tune in to their markets. They need to introduce new products, diversify a little, and recruit new creative and marketing talent. Indeed, the only way to combat the hazards of focusing is by broadening out—by selling a fuller line of more attractive products to a growing set of customers. This is not to say that Tinkerers should become highly diversified. They should probably stay with the markets that most appreciate their cost or quality leadership. But they absolutely must awaken to their surroundings and get away from the products of yesterday, which appeal only to a shrinking market.

CREATIVE CRAFTSMANSHIP

Craftsmen who have managed to avoid the focusing trajectory gather different types of information from a broad variety of sources, disseminate it widely, discuss it vigorously and openly, and then act upon it.

Tinkerers are beset by tunnel vision. They are so intent on boosting efficiency or quality that they ignore everything else. They need, above all, to gain access to information about the environment, and to increase their receptivity to all kinds of data. They also have to become more creative in interpreting what is happening outside the company.

Successful craftsmen use their passion for thoroughness to gather lots of intelligence, rather than to fine-tune themselves into oblivion. Brian Dumaine's anecdote about Mariott Hotels tells the story:

> One Sunday morning in the summer of 1986, six Marriott employees on a secret intelligence mission checked into a cheap hotel outside the Atlanta airport. Once inside their $30-a-night rooms, decorated with red shag rugs and purple velour curtains, the team went into their routine. One called the front desk saying that his shoelace had broken—could someone get him a new one? Another carefully noted the brands of soap, shampoo and towels. A third took off his suit jacket, lay down on the bed, and began moaning and writhing and knocking the headboard against the wall while a colleague in the next room listened for the muffled cries of feigned ecstasy and calmly jotted down that this wall wasn't at all soundproof.[25]

This Marriott team had been traveling the United States for six months, gathering information about potential competition in the low-priced hotel business—a field that Marriott wanted to enter. The intelligence team, which consisted of marketing, operations, finance, and human resources people, got much of its information directly from competitors. Team members visited nearly four hundred hotels, identified themselves as Marriott employees, and asked managers about operations, prices, and morale; and they got a good deal of cooperation. To poll higher-ups at the other economy chains, they hired a headhunting firm to interview their regional managers. As a result of these interviews, they were able to determine compensation and career expectations, as well as what competitors thought about quality and service.[26]

Marriott discovered a host of details on the competition's weaknesses and strengths, and was then able to design its own economy chain of hotels, whose occupancy rate soon exceeded that of the competition by an impressive 10 percent.

Most Tinkerers, however, need not engage in such major campaigns to obtain valuable information about competitors. Hewlett Packard, for decades a consummate Craftsman, kept up with industry events by creatively interpreting information that flowed naturally into the organization. For example, several years back, HP used its in-house travel agency to reserve conference rooms around the country for a new product launch. When the agency called up hotels, it found that a number of the conference rooms had already been booked by one of HP's principal competitors. The intelligence people at HP knew the competitor was planning to announce a similar product—and the travel agency's information gave them a good idea of when. As a result, HP speeded up its product introduction and stole the competitor's thunder.[27]

Benchmarking—buying and taking apart the products of the competition—is another way of getting valuable information. Xerox Corporation had begun to fall behind in its copier business as more agile competitors such as Canon were able to introduce models that retailed for less than Xerox's manufacturing cost. Xerox's market share in copiers shrank from 49 to 22 percent during the early 1980s. In response, it benchmarked Canon's copier and tried to beat each of its competitor's three hundred components on both cost and quality.[28]

Xerox made sure that many people got involved with intelligence gathering by training two hundred of its line managers to look for changes in its rivals' pricing, products, and technologies. Everyone was urged to pass even small details up the line so that the top managers could recognize some overall pattern.[29]

A Proviso: I am not suggesting that Craftsmen respond to every breeze of change. That would be too expensive to preserve cost leadership and too disruptive to maintain high quality. Adaptation to markets should be selective, and where possible it must also capitalize on—not erode—internal strengths.

CONSOLIDATING THE IMPERIALIST—THE VENTURING TRAJECTORY

A panoply of ailments plagued our Imperialists. Their egocentric leaders overexpanded into areas they knew very little about, in the process overtaxing financial and managerial resources and overwhelming the administrative structure.

What must Imperialists do to turn things around? Of course, the answer varies according to the severity of their problems, but some of our firms began to do better after they started paying attention to the substance of business unit strategy and to the complementarities among their divisions. To that end, they recruited and empowered divisional production and marketing managers: a new set of middle-tier heroes, who were rewarded for long-run substantive contributions rather than spurts of growth. They also implemented better coordinative and control procedures to guide these managers.

Recovering Imperialists also pruned away their least promising and least complementary subsidiaries, and built up core businesses by infusing them with new talent and resources. They abandoned grandiose expansion projects and consolidated around a theme—a particular type of business or a strategic advantage that gave them an edge over competitors. And they concentrated as much on the details of product-market strategy for individual businesses as on broader corporate-level matters. (These actions are summarized in Table 4.)

As the cases of Gulf & Western, AM, Litton, and ITT will show, it isn't easy to salvage Imperialists. Because their resources have already been depleted by overexpansion, most companies cannot afford expensive remedies. Also, because top management is populated by financial generalists, managers are frequently too ignorant of specific businesses to reorient their product-market strategies. A further problem is that, unlike Tinkerers, many Imperialists haven't any original distinctive competences to build on. In spite of these difficulties, however, some Imperialists have in fact managed to turn around.

Vignette

Martin Davis became CEO of Gulf & Western Industries upon the sudden death of Charles Bluhdorn in 1983. He was rated one of *For-*

TABLE 4. Managing the Venturing Trajectory

Problems:
　　Few distinctive competences
　　Overwhelmed, fragmented structures
　　Overexpansion
　　Excessive diversification
　　Overtaxing of resources

Actions Taken:
　　Recruit talent in R&D, marketing, and production
　　Establish coordination and control systems
　　Sharpen focus and divest of "dogs"
　　Create strategic competence
　　Revive core businesses

tune's toughest bosses in 1984, and has indeed been ruthless in selling off the subsidiaries acquired by Bluhdorn. Davis was careful to focus G&W more tightly around a few core businesses: publishing, entertainment, and financial services. He realized that it was necessary to concentrate resources where they would do the most good—on major divisions that were dominant forces in their industries and that had major strategic competences in their respective fields. Davis also reduced his own administrative burden by consolidating operations and implementing control systems that were rigorous without being stifling. And he went after the best talent to run his units.[30]

LEADERSHIP AND CULTURE

Imperialists hardly ever succeed in changing without first getting rid of their empire-building CEOs. Our recovering firms appointed consolidators—leaders who are adept at pruning away losing operations and reviving the remaining ones. They work to transform a bottom-line, financially driven culture into one that celebrates good product-market and manufacturing strategies for the individual divisions. Attention shifts from the head office to the field; from staff accountants to functional line managers; and from grand strategies to substantive operating issues. Also, firms hire promising middle managers with extensive industry-related expertise to run the divisions. And they establish effective integrative committees and controls to direct and monitor operations.

At AM there was a total change of emphasis in decision making—managers now tried to improve things gradually rather than launching into major ventures. In other words, AM shifted its focus to the details of operation—to hitting divisional singles rather than corporate home runs. This was demanded by the firm's depleted state of resources. But it also allowed AM to build competences and pursue a number of promising smaller projects simultaneously.

Unlike Roy Ash, the new CEO, Merle Banta, was willing to entrust many of the niggling financial details to his lieutenants. But he held frequent strategy meetings with his four division presidents to discuss substantive product-line, manufacturing, and marketing issues. To economize and concentrate on divisional line operations, a whole layer of corporate staff personnel was eliminated. And in order to quell divisiveness and get everyone to pull together, the top ninety managers had their bonuses tied to how well they achieved their objectives. In addition, ten thousand employees were given over 10 percent of the company's stock.[31]

To ensure that AM was not overdoing things and would be exposed to new ideas, Banta provoked his managers with outside perspectives from such luminaries as MIT technology expert Carl Kaysen and Harvard marketing guru Ted Levitt. Moreover, directors always met at division offices since, as one executive commented, "You make money in the field, not at headquarters." Finally, information systems were constructed to gather additional data on such factors as service response time and the availability of parts, in order to assess the firm's responsiveness and efficiency.[32]

Litton Industries' leaders also started to pay more attention to the substance of divisional strategy. Controls were installed and the structure was revamped to coordinate and monitor operations more closely. The six executives who headed each of Litton's major divisions traveled constantly for personal meetings with their managers. These encounters were designed to tease out information of a type that is never put into written reports and to give leaders a feel for what was really going on in the different divisions.[33]

At G&W, Martin Davis ran a tight ship. He gave his senior executives a good deal of decision-making power while keeping control over substantive strategic issues and closely auditing major projects. He frowned on memos and written reports, favoring actual encounters with divisional personnel. In his office was a little lucite cube on which were printed the words: "Assume nothing." Davis sent replicas to executives who fouled up.[34]

STRATEGY

Imperialists must shed their ailing, alien subsidiaries and divisions, develop a strategy based on a central competence, and revive their core businesses.

Sculpting a Viable Organization

The first task in reversing the venturing trajectory is to stanch the bleeding. Firms stuck with a bunch of weak subsidiaries or operations must often sell off the worst of them until they can raise enough money to revive their most promising units. But selling off unhealthy businesses must be done the way a sculptor works—the idea is not just to get rid of deadwood but to be left with a set of vital, complementary operations.

At Gulf & Western, Martin Davis sold off sixty-five subsidiaries with revenues of over $4 billion within four years of taking over. In 1983, the firm was a mess, with Bluhdorn's hodgepodge of companies generating only $169 million on revenues of $5.3 billion. Return on equity was just 7.7 percent. By pruning the weaker operations and renewing the most promising ones, G&W was able to earn $330 million on revenues of only $2.5 billion in 1987. And indeed, the three remaining core businesses have been doing well. Paramount has led all the major studios in box-office receipts for two years running; publishers Simon & Schuster have expanded beyond their traditional trade books into lucrative educational and information services; and at G&W's commercial and consumer loan company, the Associates, assets have doubled in four years.[35]

But Davis has not entirely given up on acquisitions. He continues in the Builder tradition, searching for opportunities to bolster his publishing and entertainment businesses. According to *Fortune*, however, "Davis is as picky as Goldilocks in the three bears' house." While he bought textbook publisher Prentice-Hall in 1984 for $700 million, he passed on Metromedia's TV stations and Ziff-Davis's flourishing magazines because they were too expensive. It is significant that Davis wanted to build the core of his enterprise around businesses he understands well. He has much experience in the film industry from his days as director of sales and marketing and later as chief operating officer at Paramount.[36]

AM International had gone into Chapter 11 soon after the departure of Roy Ash. Devastated by its losses, the company experienced a series of changes in top management. But it was beginning to turn around. The new CEO embarked on a rigorous fifteen-month cost-cutting project and disposed of four of its businesses, including AM Jacquard Systems, an ailing word-processor maker that had been one of Ash's favorites. In the three remaining businesses, costs were cut by making a 20 percent reduction in payroll expenses and by weeding out the most expensive, inefficient operations. Outdated parts-manufacturing plants were shut down, especially in the multigraphics operation. In fact, AM stopped producing many subcomponents as it was cheaper to buy them from the outside. Clearly, divestment and pruning were helping AM as it began, for the first time in years, to turn a profit.[37]

More significantly, AM consolidated around the businesses that it knew best: offset printing, typesetting, and drafting equipment. There was still a good deal of engineering and managerial talent in these areas that would help AM recover. And the complementarities among these pared-down operations could further help boost economies in operation and management.[38]

Another Imperialist revival took place at Litton Industries. Litton first sold off its weakest businesses and closed down its shakiest plants (e.g., calculators, typewriters, cash registers). It cut back dramatically on its acquisition and expansion program, insisting that any new division would have to dovetail with existing lines and fit into the long-range business plan. Also, Litton now decided only to do business in industries that had high financial and technological barriers to entry. Finally, it would address only markets with long-term growth potential that made use of its managerial and technical expertise in computer technology and data processing.[39]

Unfortunately, Litton's turnaround was not entirely successful—or rather, its successes were short-lived, probably because it still ranged too broadly. In 1985, the firm had to undergo another restructuring as it sold off its business computers and calculators (Monroe), medical products, office furniture, and microwave oven units. The staff complement that had been 120,000 in 1970 was eventually halved.

Litton then refocused on three lines of business: oil services, defense electronics, and industrial automation.[40]

ITT underwent a similar consolidation by selling off myriad units and subsidiaries acquired by Harold Geneen. By 1987, Geneen's replacement, Rand Araskog, had shorn ITT of over a hundred companies, raised over $4 billion in the process, and pared the firm's workforce by 66 percent since 1984 (in fact, the number of employees shrank from 348,000 in 1980 to 123,000 in 1987). He also cut ITT's soaring debt. It took eight years for Araskog to accomplish the radical cutting necessary to restore ITT to health. Finally, it has become a trimmer, more comprehensible, service-dominated collection of nine basic businesses, which include insurance, financial services, telecommunications, automotive products, and hotels.[41]

To recap, Imperialists must shed their least related and least promising operations in order to reduce their administrative and financial burden. They must also shore up their depleted cash positions and establish a complementary, more manageable core of operations. And they must find a common, unified strategy that takes advantage of their existing set of skills and resources. In short, they must pare down the wild profusion of bramble branches into a tightly cropped shrub.

Rebuilding Core Businesses

Of course, it is by no means enough simply to pare away failing operations and find an overarching theme for the remaining ones. Most Imperialists also require a bunch of mini-turnarounds in their salvageable divisions. Subunits devastated by neglect now urgently need remedial attention and infusions of managerial talent.

At G&W, for example, Martin Davis pressed his subsidiaries and divisions to hone their competitive strengths, and he actively recruited the managerial, editorial, and creative talent needed to maintain those strengths. Davis lavished particularly avid attention on Paramount and Simon & Schuster. His oversight was not merely limited to financial control but extended to careful scrutiny of any major project.[42]

AM International, too, put lots of effort into reviving its core businesses. It invested heavily in product development programs to create a new line of duplicators for commercial printers, a new phototypesetter with digital controls, and a multi-terminal system for text composition. It also chose to expand in the rapidly growing market for computer-aided drafting equipment, and began to emphasize services over straight manufacturing. AM's updated products made it once again a vital force in its industry.[43]

Litton performed first aid on its divisions and its faltering product lines. The head office recognized that more innovation was needed to succeed in high-tech markets. So, from 1975 to 1979, Litton invested $750 million in R&D and another $610 million on capital equipment—and these investments were concentrated in divisions that had the most promise. As a result, some of Litton's businesses grew robustly and became leaders in their markets. For example, Western Geophysical, an oil services company, was acquired in 1960 when its sales were only $16 million; by 1979, it had grown to have revenues of $300 million. Litton's missile guidance and control systems division continued to excel and its hardware was chosen for the U.S. cruise missiles.[44]

Unfortunately, some of Litton's businesses ran into trouble. Oil prices were weak and petroleum exploration activity fell off. And although the factory automation market was brisk, Litton fell behind in software support. But the company continues to spend lots of money on R&D to improve its products and to make its plants more efficient. And the new CEO, Orion Hoch, is tightening controls. As with so many former Imperialists, it is taking a long time for Litton to endow its divisions with true distinctive competences.[45]

The importance of reviving core businesses is best illustrated by the case of ITT. For a long time, Rand Araskog favored a corporate-level focus, juggling whole businesses rather than overhauling them. His attempt to crack the U.S. electronics and telecommunications markets met with failure. ITT's XTRA personal computer flopped. And its costly development of the System 12 digital telephone switch for the American market had to be abandoned because the firm was too slow and too bureaucratic.[46] So ITT continued to earn an abysmal return on capital.[47] In fact, Harry Edelson, an analyst with First Boston Corp., said at the time (1984) that Araskog had to do something swiftly. "It's time for the company to be reinvigorated. He's sold the cats and dogs. Let's get into the horses."[48]

Ultimately, Araskog changed his approach. He spun off the telecommunications business into a joint venture. And he got ITT's new president and chief operating officer, Edmund Carpenter, to move into the faltering operations to consolidate them. Carpenter convinced Araskog to get out of the lagging, over-budget telephone-switch venture. Then he effected numerous operating efficiencies while bolstering quality and raising gross margins in the automotive and defense groups. Here was a true manufacturing executive exerting hands-on management, not just another meddlesome head-office accountant.[49]

In short, the only way to turn Imperialists around is to get down to the operational level and trim fat, renew product lines, and replace financial generalists with manufacturing and marketing managers. It is the specifics that need attention—not just the corporate infrastructure.

A Proviso: When paring down operations, managers must try to keep and revive those units with the greatest potential and the most complementarity—even if they are clearly ailing. However, where resources are scarce, such turnaround heroics can be dangerously costly. Managers must therefore take care to match up expenditures, expected benefits, and available resources—a tough balancing act.

GIRDING THE EMPIRE

Some Builders avoid becoming Imperialists because they do two things well: first, they curb the urge—so natural to them—to expand too quickly into areas they know nothing about; and second, they focus broadly without losing sight of details such as product-market match, marketing strategy, and manufacturing policy.

General Mills, for example, was one successful Builder that did not go overboard either in its diversification program or in acquisitions. Or, at least, it recognized the dangers of moving too far afield before they could do too much damage. General Mills sells Cheerios cereal, Yoplait yogurt, and it owns Red Lobster restaurants. It had tried the acquisitions route in the mid-seventies, and experienced relatively little success. In fact, President Mark Willes performed a study of six thousand public companies which revealed that 66 percent of the eighty-eight best performers on return on equity and earnings per-share growth operated in only one or two businesses. His company, as a consequence, has divested nearly $3 billion of businesses over the decade from 1978 to 1988, selling off Kenner Parker Toys, Izod Apparel, Talbots, Eddie Bauer retailers, and a dozen flagging restaurant chains.[50]

General Mills decided to focus on cereals and restaurants—the two areas it understands best. It invests 75 percent of its capital spending—$1.2 billion planned from 1989 to 1991—in these businesses, and it has met with considerable success. Managers agreed that they should be dominant players in their traditional markets. Excessive diversification, they reasoned, would only complicate things and draw attention away from their principal businesses.

According to Willes, "We're very firm in our commitment to internal growth. We tell our managers, 'You are going to get us growth, not acquisitions.' "[51]

Nor was General Mills content to stick to capitalizing on its old brand names. Chairman Bruce Atwater contends that "You have to constantly evolve your product." For example, the forty-eight-year-old Cheerios were now pitched as an oat-packed health food. Adding calcium to Gold Medal flour helped it stay ahead of rival Pillsbury; and bringing out products suitable for microwave cooking increased its lead over P&G's Duncan Hines. The policy of renewal is every bit as aggressive at General Mills's restaurants. Every seven years it extensively remodels its Red Lobster restaurants based on responses from monthly customer surveys. Quite simply, the firm keeps ahead of the competition by staying in tune with its customers. It also started a new and highly successful Italian food venture, the Olive Garden dinner chain, born within its own R&D lab. In 1989, the restaurant business was expanding at the rate of 20 percent per year and Olive Garden had become the fastest growing food chain in the country.[52]

Alcoa, the conservative aluminum giant, wasn't a Builder until its chairman, Charles Parry, began prodding it to broaden its horizons. Parry devised a grand plan for growth and diversification, but his proposed ventures were so ambitious and ill-specified, and his intended acquisitions so out of tune with Alcoa's existing business, that the board of directors became displeased and vetoed the expansion. The story is instructive because it shows a board of directors nipping imperialism in the bud.[53]

Parry tried to break down Alcoa's conservatism by pressing for earnings instead of tonnage and encouraging risk taking. He decentralized authority and shrank the controlling headquarters staff. And he closed down high-cost factories and boosted R&D spending by 36 percent in 1985, with plans to double that by 1990. But managers balked when the boss began to articulate his global strategy: Alcoa was to develop highly engineered products using ceramics, composites, powders, and exotic aluminum hybrids. Parry's goal was to get 50 percent of Alcoa's revenues from non-aluminum business by 1995. Since, at the time, its aluminum sales accounted for 90 percent of revenues, Parry was promising to create a $7 to $9 billion business from scratch within a decade.

The aluminum people were alienated by this wild optimism, especially once Parry announced that most growth was to come from acquisitions, which he intended to bankroll with profits from the aluminum operations. The last straw was Parry's vacillation. According to board member William S. Cook, "There was a new idea every few board meetings. He wanted to buy this and then buy that." Said former Alcoa Chairman W. H. Krome George, "I didn't want Alcoa to buy some blue-jeans factory in Taiwan." The board wanted Parry out—and negotiated his early retirement. Alcoa, it seemed, was to stick to its knitting.

Of course, the aluminum industry is a very mature and competitive one, and the firm still needs to develop some plan for improving its return on capital. However, the board seemed to realize that this could best be done by pursuing higher margin lines, and by doing some related and complementary diversification—while avoiding a wholesale flight from areas of competence.[54] All Builders would do well to subject their plans to the scrutiny of so a resolute and informed a group of directors.

GROUNDING THE ESCAPIST—THE INVENTING TRAJECTORY

Our Pioneers showed a tendency to turn into Escapists—into companies whose R&D elites pursued technical progress almost for its own sake. Excessive innovation eroded production economies and confused clients, while myopic marketing destroyed the potential of even the most promising creations.

What Escapists need is a healthy dose of reality. Our recovering Escapists kept on inventing and innovating, as this was a major strength of theirs. But they also opened themselves up to their surroundings and slowed down their pace. They began to transform their cultures, sharing the glory lavished on scientists with accountants, marketers, and production people. Also, they promoted intensive collaboration between inventors and implementers, and installed better controls to check the profligacy of an overenthusiastic R&D staff.

Firms altered their other strategies as well. First, managers now

243

devised new products only with particular customers and markets in mind—shaping their offerings not just according to technological advances but in light of specific user needs, and avoiding the haste that made for shoddy, bug-ridden products. Second, firms broadened out into markets with greater potential, moving to where the opportunities were rather than simply where science or their personal interests led them. Third, they tried harder to convince customers of the attractiveness of what they were offering—marketing more actively, and paying attention to price, distribution, service, and the utility of their overall designs. And finally, they aborted any grandiose projects and generally husbanded their resources. (These actions are summarized in Table 5.)

Vignettes

With the departure of founder Edwin Land, Polaroid Corporation did three things to revitalize its strategies: it broadened its product-market focus to reduce the dependence on instant photography; it brought out a successful new camera whose superior picture quality revived the interest in instant photography; and it began to do more marketing, paying closer attention to the needs of its customers. In other words, Polaroid reduced its reliance on a shrinking market by expanding its horizons, and it took more care to adapt any innovations to its customers' wishes. It also avoided extravagant expenditure by becoming more selective in its development projects.

TABLE 5. Managing the Inventing Trajectory

Problems:
   Blind, utopian cultures and chaotic structures
   New product proliferation
   Irrelevant technology
   Extravagant megaprojects
   Marketing myopia

Actions Taken:
   Empower and heed marketers, accountants, and production people
   Establish coordinative devices and controls
   Tailor inventions to a well-defined market
   Broaden the market focus
   Market more aggressively
   Scale down megaprojects and economize

Apple Computer, too, reoriented its strategy as it began to cater to the lucrative corporate market, to cut costs, and to tailor products to emerging industry opportunities. CEO John Sculley was recruited from PepsiCo in 1983. By 1985, he had persuaded the board to force missionary co-founder Steve Jobs to end his high-tech-driven steward-ship of the Macintosh operations. Sculley then appointed the former manager of the efficient Apple II division to become chief operating officer. Sculley's primary tasks were to cut costs and extravagance by laying off 20 percent of the workforce, and, more importantly, to reorient the company's single-minded focus away from products and toward markets.

According to *Fortune*'s Stuart Gannes, "with Sculley in charge, Apple is the most marketing-oriented competitor in the desktop busi-ness. And the Macintosh—Steve Jobs's legacy to Apple—comes closer right now to satisfying the requirements of network computing than any other desktop machine."[55] (As this book goes to press, however, Apple is once again in some trouble as it battles the remnants of its Escapist orientation.)

LEADERSHIP AND CULTURE

The goals of Escapists must change from advancing new technology to creating valued goods and services. Their missionary zeal must be refocused on the customer rather than on the design itself. To this end, our recovering Escapists empowered marketing, production, and finance managers—not just scientists and engineers. They paid more attention to product-market match, cost control, and manufac-turing problems—and devoted fewer resources to development, re-search, and technological projects. Indeed, implementation began to be rewarded as much as innovation; selling and manufacturing as much as inventing. And managers installed the coordinative devices needed to ensure broad participation in innovation ventures.

In an interview published in *inc.* magazine in October 1987, John Sculley made clear his plan for reviving and refocusing Apple and changing its culture. He stressed the importance of preserving an entrepreneurial environment and evoking the commitment of a young staff of scientists. The object was now to maintain initiative but also to create a more organized and integrated culture, sensitive to the needs of customers. Corporate controls and creativity, Sculley be-lieved, could co-exist.

Apple was reorganized along functional lines to achieve better control over its escalating costs—the Apple II and Mac divisions, which had been run as independent entities, were now integrated. Cutting expenses and implementing badly needed controls came next. Sculley also reversed some of the old tenets of the Mac culture, such as one person/one machine, and the closed Mac; it was now necessary to link up the Mac to other systems and to make it more flexible and more powerful for new users. But to avoid alienating the prized technical staff, a great deal of consultation and collaboration took place in making these changes. Finally, open communication and a busy informal network were encouraged at Apple to facilitate collaboration between the R&D, production, and marketing departments.[56]

In short, to pave the way for changes in strategy, our recovering Escapists made their cultures more interactive and realistic, and they curbed some of the excesses of their disorganized structures.

STRATEGY

Escapists must increase the relevance of their products by doing the designing only after they have assessed the needs of their target markets. They have also to broaden their horizons to find the most propitious clientele, to market more aggressively, and to limit inventive extravagance.

Tailoring Products to Customers

Both Polaroid and Apple Computer began to try harder to match their products to their markets. At Polaroid, the Spectra camera reignited interest in instant photography precisely because it went beyond Edwin Land's fixation on development time and responded directly to customers' desires for high-quality pictures and automatic focus. The Spectra was customer-driven, not technology-driven.[57]

To shape its Mac computer for the newly targeted business market, Apple beefed up its memory and urged hundreds of outside software firms to write programs for it. Microsoft was persuaded to write a powerful spreadsheet program for the Mac II, called Excel, which was deemed by many experts to be the best spreadsheet package ever developed for any personal computer. Further, an expansion port was installed that allowed peripheral hardware to be plugged into the Mac to perform such tasks as networking and data communications—applications essential for most businessmen. Apple even designed some of its new models to accommodate microprocessor boards made by other vendors, in order to enhance the power and flexibility so much in demand by the lucrative commercial market.[58]

Under Steve Jobs, Apple had had a "we're-too-good-to-touch-IBM" attitude and made no attempt to fit into an IBM-dominated business environment. That impractical arrogance changed dramatically as Macs were made to interface very conveniently with IBM PCs and mainframes alike. In fact, the Mac II can use IBM and Apple software at the same time.[59]

Federal Express also was careful to tailor its offerings to an increasingly competitive market. The availability of products such as FAX and electronic mail, and the entry of rival UPS into the market, caused Federal to work even harder to increase the quality and to lower the costs and prices of its services. FEC couriers are equipped with the most up-to-date computerized tracking equipment, which cuts down on errors and allows drivers to spot delinquent accounts. Computers also plotted out the most efficient delivery routes possible, enabling FEC to lower its costs. Such constant improvements have protected FEC's market share.[60]

In short, Escapists must come down to earth by shaping their offerings for an explicitly conceived and regularly monitored market.

Broader Market Focus

Escapists tended to zero in on a very constrained, unchanging set of clients and to ignore promising new markets. Some competed in increasingly crowded arenas of declining potential. In turning themselves around, such Escapists must broaden out to address more lucrative markets.

Polaroid, for example, set up a nice commercial business to fall back on in case there were problems with instant photography. The commercial division began to account for 40 percent of sales, and included cameras for instant passport and driver's license photos, as well as freeze-frame products for videotape editors in advertising and the media.[61]

Polaroid also developed a high-density floppy disk for personal computers that stored more information than most hard disks. Work was begun on an electronic still camera, the first new variety of instant photography; and the company has done well with its introduction of video cassettes, in part because of its brand recognition. But perhaps the most significant broadening of all is that Polaroid in 1988 introduced conventional film—"Polaroid Super Color."[62]

Apple, too, expanded its scope—reducing its reliance on the supercompetitive home computer market and embracing the more rapidly growing commercial market. The powerful Mac II was designed for the business market, and is practically a small workstation. By 1987, two thirds of Mac sales were to businesses, and sales were growing at 35 percent per year. As Sculley said recently, "We're trying to create the links that will bring the desktop Macintosh into the main stream of corporate computing."[63] Apple does this by linking its powerful microcomputers to the minis and mainframes of its customers.

As Federal Express's traditional market for overnight letters and small packages began to be attacked by FAX, electronic mail, and UPS, the firm started to diversify. It expanded its fleet of airplanes in order to handle bigger packages and boxes, increasing the weight limits on its parcels from 70 to 150 pounds. To complement the famous Memphis hub-and-spokes operation, FEC set up regional sorting centers.[64] It decided to go to where there was more opportunity and less competition. Packages of up to 450 pounds appeared to be FEC's next frontier.[65]

Clearly, Escapists must move to where the opportunities are. They must take advantage of developing markets, bearing in mind that market renewal is just as important as product renewal.

Better Marketing

Missionary Escapists believe so strongly in their products that they refuse to admit that these must actually be *marketed*: that is, shaped, priced, distributed, and pitched to the exigencies of reluctant customers. Many seem to think that high-tech features alone will suffice to sell their wares. But our recovering firms began to pay far more attention to the job of selling, broadly defined.

The new Polaroid president, Mac Booth, shook up the technocrats at Polaroid by declaring that marketing had to become more important—and get more sophisticated. Under Land, the philosophy had been to invent a new camera, and then underwrite a big advertising campaign to sell customers on the merits of its technology. For Spectra, Booth ordered unprecedented amounts of consumer research to *guide* his engineers in designing a camera people really wanted.[66]

Apple crafted one of the most brilliant marketing strategies of all. When Aldus, a small Seattle firm, developed software for desktop publishing, Apple executives soon realized that they had an opportunity to invade the business market so thoroughly dominated by IBM. Because the top computer managers at major corporations were so used to dealing with IBM, Apple devised an ingenious marketing strategy that would allow them to enter by the back door—they touted desktop publishing to individual departments, showing marketing managers, for example, how brochures that used to take weeks to prepare could now be done in days. An Arco executive said that some weighty reports for regulatory agencies that once cost $62,000 each to prepare fell to only $13,000 with the Mac. Once managers began to use the new machine for desktop publishing, its user-friendly features became addictive and sales soared.[67]

Sculley also changed the essential orientation of Apple's marketing strategy. Traditionally, Apple had sold 80 percent of its computers through retail chains, most of which served the home and small business markets. But these dealers lacked the sophistication to cater to the large corporate market that showed the best growth potential for Apple. So Sculley began teaming up Apple's salesmen with those from the retailers, and started to hire more "blue-suited" sales managers from competitors such as DEC and IBM to call upon the largest potential customers. According to Sculley, "In the last 8 months I've changed the lineup of Apple's executive staff so it's biased towards people successful in minicomputers and selling to corporate customers."[68]

Marketing was also becoming much more strategically competitive. For example, Apple's managers reasoned that it would be more productive to go after customers who had bought Digital Equipment machines since they had demonstrated the boldness to experiment with new (non-IBM) vendors. Apple also sold a scheme for attaching Macs to Digital's VAX minicomputers, which store data to be manipulated on the Mac. Chief Operating Officer Del Yocam talks about the ability of Apples to allow "the individual [to] access the power of the mainframe."[69]

Clearly, there is no choice but for Escapists to pay more attention to marketing—targeting growing client groups, and then tailoring their advertising, pricing, and distribution accordingly.

Cutting Extravagances

Escapists are known for their extravagant pursuit of innovation and invention. They introduce too many new products or do things on too grand and risky a scale. This has to stop. Moreover, some Escapists may, for a while at least, have to impose stringent economies if they are to replenish the resources depleted by their former fiduciary excesses.

Polaroid, for example, has been forced to reverse Edwin Land's stringent dictum: "Don't do anything that someone else can do. Don't undertake a project unless it is manifestly important and nearly impossible." This attitude led to some of Polaroid's most sparkling successes; but it also encouraged costly ventures that had little market potential. The Polavision instant movie system, for example, was a technical marvel, but it could not compete against the more economical and more convenient videotape.[70]

To counteract the extravagances of the past, Mac Booth cut the workforce from 20,000 to 9,500 employees and reorganized the company into three profit centers: consumer, industrial, and magnetics, which makes the floppy disks. He also encouraged savings by introducing profit-based bonuses. Polaroid paid back all of its $120 million of onerous long-term debt and began to finance all of its growth out of cash flow. Clearly, it is now a tighter, more controlled operation. In 1986, profits quintupled to $64 million.[71] (It is probably no accident that these major changes in strategy and organization took place after the departure of founder and inventor Edwin Land in 1982.)

When Federal Express's executives realized that their ZapMail project was likely to cost too much, they finally scrapped it. And after that experience they turned over a new leaf. They stuck to ventures that they knew best, and actually became the most efficient overnight small package delivery company in the business.

Some Provisos: Escapists benefit when they implement financial controls, innovate more selectively, pay more attention to marketing, and broaden their horizons. But in the process managers should take care not to extinguish inventiveness or to alienate their talented technical staffs.

ESCAPE TO REALITY

Some Pioneers manage to avoid becoming Escapists, pulling back before their innovations run out of control. They recognize the need to limit risks, to economize, to consider customers, and to find markets that are still fresh.

Cray Research may be one such company, although its future remains uncertain. Recall CEO John Rollwagen's story about founder and supercomputer designer Seymour Cray, who built a new sailboat each spring and burned it at the end of the season so that he wouldn't be bound by that year's mistakes when he set about designing next year's model. That was also the way Cray approached computer design.[72]

Such extravagance in development was beginning to get Cray Research into trouble. It had initiated too many high-risk projects and was having difficulty tailoring products and software to its new, and less computer-experienced, clients. But Rollwagen and Cray recognized these problems early and began to counter them. In May of 1989 they split the company into two entirely independent entities. Seymour Cray's most grandiose, advanced, and risky supercomputer development project was effectively spun off from Cray Research—along with Cray himself and his design team.[73]

The old Cray Research, Inc., with 5,400 employees, is headed by John Rollwagen, an engineer with a predominantly managerial and strategic focus. Its objective is to continue to build the world's fastest supercomputers using silicon-based semiconductors for a broad range of government *and commercial* users. The new company, Cray Computer Corporation, is headed by Seymour Cray himself. It has only two hundred employees, and aims to finish the development of the Cray 3 supercomputer, which is based on an unproven gallium arsenide semiconductor technology, and is aimed at only the most sophisticated computer customers, principally U.S. government labs.[74]

One of the main reasons behind the Cray split was Rollwagen's belief that his firm could not support two major supercomputer projects simultaneously. Rollwagen wanted to avoid the costs of over-aggressive product development and the dangers of competing in too specialized a market. So he pushed his engineers to tailor their products to less sophisticated customers by writing better software. He also began to counter the growing competition from the smaller, dramatically cheaper machines of rivals by initiating the development of slightly less powerful but much more economical computers.[75]

Cray Research's design philosophy changed as well. Rather than relying on the most dramatic technological breakthroughs, the company began focusing on less risky projects that are driven more by the needs of the customers than by raw technology. According to *The New York Times*, "By tying its fate to an evolutionary advance rather than Mr. Cray's riskier approach, Cray Research is finally accepting that it is no longer the kind of free wheeling high-tech garage operation that it was at the beginning. As a company with $750 million in revenue and a large customer base, Cray Research simply can no longer afford to take as many chances as Mr. Cray might have wanted."[76]

A cardinal rule at Cray had been to avoid formal meetings and planning sessions. Cray's insistence on informality was legendary. And his star system conveyed the idea that supercomputers simply spring from the minds of genii. But Rollwagen started replacing that system with a team effort for systematically developing and implementing new products. The shift was reflected by the decision of fifty employees to share equally a salary bonus usually intended as an incentive for special individual achievement.[77] Cray Research, it seems, was fighting escapism on many fronts.

CENTERING THE DRIFTER—THE DECOUPLING TRAJECTORY

Drifters, we will recall, had their share of problems. They were plagued by scattered product lines, lacked market focus, and sold a proliferation of outdated, copycat products. Leaders were remote from and ignorant of their own firm's operations, and fragmented, bureaucratic cultures allowed divisions to work at cross-purposes. Each of these problems was exacerbated by elephantine size and excessive scope. In short, Drifters' executives, departments, products, and markets all appeared to be decoupled from one another.

What these firms need is unity and focus. Our recovering Drifters gave their employees a clearer strategy to pursue and some operational goals to shoot for. They galvanized collective action and conquered parochial politics. And they combated bureaucracy and pushed authority down the hierarchy to make themselves more agile and responsive. In short, Drifters were given the direction and unification they so badly needed.

Our firms also started to improve on quality, updating products and consolidating their efforts around the most promising lines and businesses. They cut costs by discontinuing losing products and closing unproductive plants and outlets. And they revived their marketing impact—their legendary asset—by finding bright new niches and by boosting their sales, promotional, and distribution capabilities. (These actions are summarized in Table 6.)

Luckily, Drifters usually have a good chance of recovering because they are so large, rich, and well known. Typically they are blessed with a good reputation, considerable marketing and financial resources, and an established clientele. Also, unlike Escapists or Imperialists, most haven't yet squandered their resources on megaprojects or doomed acquisitions.

Vignettes

When P&G's CEO John Smale recognized that his company had begun to drift, he undertook to dismantle its notorious hierarchy. He empowered multidisciplinary brand management teams in order to

---

TABLE 6. Managing the Decoupling Trajectory

Problems:
  Remote leadership
  Bland cultures
  Fragmented, politicized structures
  Image replaces substance—poor quality
  Antiquated product lines
  Proliferation of lines and loss of focus

Actions Taken:
  Define overall strategy and set goals
  Push initiative to lower levels
  Improve coordination and control—without bureaucracy
  Improve quality
  Update lines
  Focus lines
  Make marketing more responsive

---

speed up their responses to changing markets. Before long, these units developed a few key superior products that had a real edge over competing brands and carried famous brand names such as Pampers, Crest, and Tide. P&G also began to pay more attention to the needs of distributors and retailers, both of whom it had neglected for years. It even set up teams of marketing, manufacturing, distribution, and engineering experts to serve each of its major customers.[78]

Lee Iacocca's turnaround of Chrysler is the stuff of industry legend. Iacocca began by replacing most of the top managers and importing some of the best marketing and manufacturing talent in the auto business. The new team introduced a set of attractive, sporty new models, such as convertibles and minivans, backed by a five-year, 50,000-mile warranty to restore the customers' confidence. Marketing was bolstered by a revamped, augmented dealer network. And a series of brilliant TV ads featuring Iacocca himself was run to create a bold new image for Chrysler. To boost profits, costs were slashed by rationalizing operations, closing down inefficient plants, and using common parts in different models.[79]

LEADERSHIP AND CULTURE

Drifters need stronger leadership to stop them from drifting. They need a CEO with vision who can motivate the organization around a set of central values. The leaders of our recovering firms tried to reestablish organizational identity, focus strategy, and give everyone something to believe in and to shoot for. They projected a philosophy that motivated everybody to improve the *substance* as well as the form of products and services. Leaders also pushed authority down the line to engender initiative and make their firms more agile and responsive. And they countered bureaucratic red tape and parochial politicking by downsizing multifunctional units and tying them to specific products, markets, or even customers.

IBM is one firm that has undergone a radical transformation in its leadership style and organizational culture. The newly appointed CEO, John Akers, removed much of the bureaucracy to make IBM more responsive to customer needs. According to Bob Djurdjevic, whose Annex Research in Phoenix specializes in keeping customers up to date with developments at IBM, "This is the most radical cultural change in IBM history." Akers's style is to set overall guidelines and hammer away at service values, while forcing managers to act more independently in trying to meet them. He encourages a good deal of participation in decision making. And he has reversed the cumbersome top-down process by which the leaders in Armonk blithely handed down decisions on everything from advertising campaigns to specific R&D limits on individual products. This style suited IBM during its many years of near monopoly, but it was a burden when wrangling with powerful and agile competitors.[80]

Akers reorganized IBM USA into seven autonomous units—personal computers, minicomputers, mainframes, microchip manufacturing, programming, software, and communications—with an eighth unit that handles marketing for all the other divisions. His aim was to send responsibility and initiative right down the ranks, into the hands of the general managers. General managers negotiate their business plans with Akers and the board once a year, and then they go off to run their units. Another important change is that whereas sales used to be the way to the top, most of the current bosses have strong technical backgrounds. Substance, clearly, has become as important as form at IBM.[81]

But Akers was also relentless in prodding his managers to be more daring and creative. He wanted them to display more initiative in renewing lines, tailoring existing products to customers, and developing new technologies. He wished, above all, to force his managers and his salesmen to become problem solvers for the customers. In an unprecedented move, Akers invited several key customers to participate in IBM's strategic planning conference. The corporate culture, in short, was finally opening up.[82]

Similar transformations were taking place at P&G, where John Smale kept tabs on customers' reactions by listening to tapes of the firm's consumer hotlines. To prime P&G's innovative and adaptive abilities, Smale began to compress the infamous hierarchy in quest of speedier collaboration and decision making. He formed business teams to get new products to market as quickly as possible. P&G's new diaper, Luvs Deluxe, for example, took only nine months to get to market—half the usual time—because of the guidance of a multidisciplinary team that cut across departments. And cost-reduction teams were formed that enlisted people directly from the plant floor to help discover new sources of efficiency.[83]

P&G's divisions work together on new product introductions. Take the case of its calcium-enriched Citrus Hill orange juice project: "Researchers in the health care unit . . . had become aware of rapidly worsening calcium deficiencies among U.S. adults. One obvious remedy was to put calcium into the orange juice marketed by P&G's food division. The problem was how to make the mixture palatable. The answer came from a third division, laundry and detergents, which had learned how . . . to suspend calcium particles in liquid soap products."[84]

P&G was truly intent on pushing authority down the line, speeding up decisions, and getting closer to its customers. A newly created position, that of supra-brand manager, embodies the spending power and authority to respond very quickly to changing markets. Another new position, the product-supply manager, coordinates the efforts of engineering, manufacturing, distribution, and purchasing managers to cut the time needed to augment, rationalize, and reposition lines. These have made P&G a fierce and agile competitor.[85]

STRATEGY

Drifters need to improve and update their products, enhance their responsiveness to markets, and streamline operations.

Improved Products

Drifters must start making products that have more quality and more appeal. They have to spruce up their lines if they are to attract more customers and recoup lost market share.

IBM, for example, worked hard to offset the staleness that had begun to plague some of its models. It introduced a starburst of new products and began to invest more heavily in R&D. The AS/400 minicomputer was off to a good start and a new microcomputer PS/2 line was introduced. IBM also pioneered a four-megabit memory chip, the most powerful yet, that propelled it ahead of all its competitors. And it introduced new Office-Vision software, which allowed its disparate mainframes, micros, and minis to communicate with one another. Finally, a powerful new line of workstations that employ the popular UNIX operating system was brought out.[86]

The corporate philosophy has also changed. IBM abandoned its "not-invented-here" arrogance as it initiated joint ventures to develop new technologies with other firms. It invested in twelve software companies, licensed programming technology from Steve Jobs's Next, Inc., and bought a piece of computer whiz Steve Chen's new supercomputer venture. It even began discounting and customizing its products for the Japanese market.[87]

In short, IBM abandoned its strategy of purveying bland, middle-of-the-road products, offering instead superior items that attacked the competition and catered to the hottest segments of the market. Although its future remains cloudy, "Big Blue" has become a less conservative, more hungry, and aggressive company.

Procter & Gamble, too, worked especially hard to revitalize—to give its products a new competitive edge vis-à-vis the competition. It brought out a powerful new laundry detergent, Liquid Tide, that outcleaned and outsold all competing liquids. It then introduced leakproof, superabsorbent Blue Ribbon Pampers and Ultra Pampers disposable diapers; these could hold much more moisture than any other brand, were thinner, and kept the baby dry. P&G also developed tartar-fighting Crest toothpaste with sodium pyrophosphate to reduce tartar buildup. This represented a dental advance comparable to fluoridation. All of these highly attractive products boosted sales dramatically, with Pampers and Crest, respectively, increasing P&G's brand share from 47 to 62 percent, and from 32 to 37 percent between 1985 and 1986.[88] (Recall that Lee Iacocca's product-line changes at Chrysler were of a similar nature—and produced a similar effect.)[89]

Even dowdy A&P was working to improve the potential of its stores. It renovated 75 percent of its remaining outlets, built over one hundred new ones, and bought four hundred more. CEO James Wood increased the company's presence in massive markets such as New York by buying the popular Waldbaum's chain. And to capture different strata of shoppers, he implemented a three-tiered strategy: Futurestores, with the latest service gadgetry and a fully stocked gourmet section for upscale markets; conventional A&Ps for middle-class markets; and warehouse-style, high-volume Sav-A-Centers. Although critics claimed that A&P's stores still did not offer the lowest prices or the best selection, they did, for the first time in years, represent viable shopping alternatives.[90]

More Responsive Marketing

Drifters used to be Salesmen. And most continue to possess considerable marketing resources—from good brand names, to strong distribution channels, to fine salesforces. They need to build on these core skills to help sell their updated and more focused product lines. But they must also use their marketing facilities to get closer to clients and find out how best to please them.

IBM's lackluster sales effort is being revived with a vengeance. The sleeping giant is sleeping no longer. Chairman John Akers has reassigned 21,000 employees from departments such as manufacturing, R&D, and administration into marketing and programming. In order to get closer to the customer, a new division was established to develop applications software to make computers do specific jobs for particular customers. Indeed, the firm now invited users to come and tell them exactly what they need.[91]

IBM also redeployed 11,800 of its people as field sales personnel—marketing reps and systems engineers who are salesmen but who work primarily as technical consultants for customers. This redeployment has increased the size of IBM's salesforce by 20 percent in two years.[92]

The impatience of IBM's aggressive new marketing vice-president, Edward E. Lucente, earned him the nickname "neutron Eddie." Lucente quickly revamped IBM's network of sales offices by having branches in large metropolitan areas specialize in specific businesses. The downtown Philadelphia branch, for instance, handles insurance and finance customers. This specialization allowed IBM's staff to become especially familiar with and responsive to its clients.[93]

IBM's sales training became second to none. It spent over $1 billion a year educating its workforce and customers—a larger budget than that of all of Harvard. All "redeploys" went through an initial thirteen-month period of sales training, after having passed various aptitude tests. Instructors were stand-out performers from the field, who also served as role models. They trained sales recruits to offer business solutions, not raw hardware; and they encouraged salesmen to take the customer's point of view by using role-playing exercises, much of it done with a computer-interactive self-study system.[94]

For its more significant customers, IBM's sales efforts are especially impressive. A team of IBM people spend several *months* interviewing management, touring facilities, analyzing operations, and poring over a potential client's information systems to develop an exhaustive knowledge of the business. Then they construct six-year financial models of that client, with and without assorted new investments in computer software.[95]

Clearly, IBM has put much of the sparkle and attention back into its marketing. "When the customer asks for something, just say yes," is the new philosophy. And it is no longer necessary to call the head office for approval. Indeed, to encourage sales reps to be responsive to clients, they are now paid on the basis of the total *long-run* revenue they generate from a given customer.[96]

Procter & Gamble also became a much more responsive marketer. Because its customers were growing larger and more powerful—one hundred chains accounted for 80 percent of P&G's U.S. sales as compared to 15 percent twenty years ago—the firm could no longer "just bully its way into stores." Now P&G has switched from a product to a customer approach, with teams for finance, distribution, manufacturing, and other functions assigned to cover each of the big retailers. A team of twelve people, for example, attends exclusively to the Wal-Mart chain. This has allowed P&G to stay truly close to its major clients and respond to their special needs.[97]

To make P&G a more agile competitor, John Smale created the "category" management system, breaking down the company into thirty-nine product categories. Brand managers report to their category manager, who has total profit and loss responsibility for an entire product line—all laundry detergents, for example. This system makes sure that brands aren't sabotaging each other. And it allows much faster decision making. In fact, to introduce new products or reposition old ones, the category manager can assemble a small team made up of the brand manager plus managers from sales, finance, and manufacturing. This team quickly makes all the decisions needed to implement the new project. In other words, P&G's response time has decreased dramatically.[98]

At Chrysler, Lee Iacocca recruited Bennett E. Bidwell, a brilliant marketing executive. He also doubled the size of the marketing group, initiated studies that looked for gaps, trends, and opportunities in the market, and launched a catchy advertising campaign, featuring himself as the major Chrysler spokesman.[99]

Streamlining Operations

Drifters are too often stuck with a slew of models or operations that are superfluous, outdated, or uneconomical. Lines have to be pared down; and many operations can benefit from consolidation.

A&P underwent radical surgery to close down its undesirable outlets—stores in dying inner-city neighborhoods, divisions that could no longer hold their own, plants that could not be kept busy. CEO James Wood has closed hundreds of ailing stores. He also reduced expenses by buying merchandise more efficiently and attacking A&P's exorbitant labor costs. By threatening to shut down numerous divisions, Wood got the unions to agree to wage cuts and the abrogation of seniority rights. By 1982, A&P had gotten its wages down to $1.23 per hour less than competing supermarkets in some regions, and had restored many of its losing stores to profitability.[100]

In this way, A&P has, for the first time in many years, been able to boost its gross profit margins to 24 percent, the industry average. The firm has by no means solved all of its problems, but it returned to profitability in 1983 and has remained there.[101]

The situation at Chrysler also called for dramatic cost cutting, and this is precisely what took place. Inefficient plants were shut down, labor costs were slashed by tough bargaining with the UAW, and production costs were lowered by designing different lines of vehicles that used many common parts.[102] Cost cutting also took place at IBM. To eliminate fat and make its prices more competitive, plants were closed, capital expenditures reduced, and discretionary spending cut.

STAYING FRESH AND FOCUSED

Some Salesmen have avoided degenerating into Drifters by selectively coming up with fresh products that strengthen and deepen their lines. For example, Kellogg's, the cereal giant, worked diligently in a mature industry to stay focused and to preserve the quality and novelty of its lines and the efficiency of its plants. And it has done so at a time of increasing threat from a shrinking cereal market and precarious demographics that have forced some of its competitors to flee to other arenas.

In part, Kellogg's reaction may be explained by the fact that it is run by Chairman William E. LaMothe, who is a stickler for quality and whose background includes an eight-year term supervising Kellogg's R&D activities. LaMothe is so taken with the need to maintain quality that the thirty top executives of the firm breakfast together every Monday morning to sample and rate the company's cereal brands from its five U.S. plants and its sixteen factories abroad. "Using terms like 'mouth feel' and 'bowl life,' they discuss flavor, appearance, texture, and if it's Rice Krispies, the sound of the snap, crackle and pop."[103] These demanding judges rate each sample very strictly—and then pass the results to the respective plant managers and quality-control people.

Perhaps an even more important factor in Kellogg's success is that it has tried so hard to tailor its product to the needs and desires of its different target markets. The adult market for cereal had been a dwindling one for over a decade, and Kellogg decided to change the picture. According to LaMothe, "I thought, what are these companies really getting out of diversification? We looked at demographics and saw this big group—80 million baby-boomers. We knew they were health oriented, they were joggers. People said, 'Forget about them. They don't eat breakfast.' We knew they were too big to forget about."[104]

Kellogg did not diversify away from cereal the way General Mills and Quaker did; nor did it follow rivals who introduced dozens of random sugar-coated products for kids. Instead, Kellogg appraised its market carefully, did painstaking market research to find out what its customers and potential customers wanted, and tried its custom-tailored new brands in test markets before launching them. Kellogg also went that extra mile to design different cereals for the tastes of its assorted geographic markets. It had in mind a specific clientele as it opened up and captured the adult market for breakfast cereals after everyone else had dismissed it.[105]

Said one competitor: "We don't see any major areas of weakness in Kellogg that we can attack." Said another: "These guys act like they want it all." And Kellogg's aggressive advertising attests to that fact; it spends about 20 percent of its sales on promotion. LaMothe's formula seems simple: "You have to have enough muscle to bring to the marketplace value-added products that really do offer the consumer something better, and then you've got to be able to tell the consumer about them." And to create that something better, Kellogg spends 1.1 percent of sales on R&D, as compared to only 0.7 percent for rival General Mills. It also introduces technologically innovative cereals such as Crispix and Mueslix to capitalize on changing tastes and on the recent health craze.[106]

Kellogg has paid a great deal of attention to operations, designing the most efficient plants in the industry. Its gross margins are 49 percent, up from 41 percent in 1983 and way above the industry average of 35 percent. A five-year average return on investment of 36 percent and a market share that has risen five points in the last five years to 42 percent bear out the company's stellar performance.[107]

Toys "Я" Us, another brilliant Salesman, has stayed focused on the one thing it knows how to do the best—market toys that are the hottest items around. Its advantage is that it can detect trends in the toy market so accurately and so quickly. The company is "fanatically dedicated to a sophisticated computer system that catches crazes early by keeping track of exactly what is selling in each store at every minute."[108]

Part of Toys' formula for success is having transformed a highly seasonal business into one that enjoys robust sales all year round. The firm has done this with self-service, discount prices, and huge inventories—each of its stores carries over eighteen thousand items. Earnings have been compounding at 29 percent annually for the last ten years and Toys has captured over 25 percent of the U.S. toy market. Seventy-four stores have been opened internationally as well.[109]

Most of our turnarounds addressed a multitude of deficiencies. But some problems and trajectories clearly warrant more drastic solutions than others. Most Imperialists, for instance, required extensive surgery, whereas many Drifters and Tinkerers could be revived with less radical measures.

Indeed, many of our firms were able to move back to their initial healthy configurations. This was possible where skills stayed intact and the target market remained viable. Firms like TI, DEC, and Caterpillar very much preserved their earlier strategic themes. Only they brought these themes more into line with market needs and augmented them with strong secondary strategies: cost and quality leadership, for instance, were supplemented by good marketing, closeness to customers, and new product development. Managers also took care to curb excesses in their strategy, culture, and structure.

Sometimes, however, a devastating period of decline will have eroded a firm's abilities and resources so seriously that it no longer has any really strong theme or distinctive skill. Alternatively, the market may have changed so much that the old strategic competences are no longer of much relevance. In such cases, it may not be useful or even possible to try to recover an old configuration or theme. Instead, a new one will have to be discovered, perhaps by using some of the suggestions in Chapter 7. And those are the toughest turn-arounds of all.

Epilogue

I<small>N HIS MONUMENTAL</small> *STUDY OF HISTORY,* <small>ARNOLD TOYNBEE PAINS-</small>
takingly traced the rise and fall of twenty-one civilizations. All of these
great cultures, except perhaps our own, have collapsed or stagnated.
Toynbee argued that their declines came not from natural disasters
or barbarian invasions but from internal rigidity, complacency, and
oppression. He saw that some of the very institutions and practices
responsible for ascendance ultimately evolved into the perverse idola-
tries that caused decline: "When the road to destruction has perforce
to be trodden on the quest of life, it is perhaps no wonder that the
quest should often end in disaster."[1]

Organizations too are built into greatness and then launched toward decline by very similar factors: focused strategies, galvanized
cultures, specialized skills, efficient programs, and the harmonious
configuration of all these things. Used with intelligence and sensitivity, these factors can make for tremendous success. But when taken
to extremes, they spawn disaster. And, ironically, success itself often
induces the myopia and carelessness that leads to such excesses.

Paradoxically, the power of a tool increases both its potential benefits and its dangers. Icarus could not have flown without the wings so
deftly crafted by his loving father Dedalus. But at the same time the
wings placed a terrible onus upon Icarus' mastery and his discipline.
Similarly, focused cultures and strategies, and orchestrated configurations, contribute mightily to outstanding performance. But they
carry with them daunting risks of rigidity and isolation. To compound
the problem, it is terribly hard to distinguish between the concentration needed for success and the narrowness that guarantees irrele-
vance. Managers of thriving organizations must forever remain alert
to such "perils of excellence."

We should remember that the trajectories outlined here say relatively little about the role played by the environment in causing decline. Yet in so many cases, increasing competition, shrinking markets, and emerging new technologies inflicted significant damage on our firms. Although it seems clear that a combination of internal and external factors contributed to decline, it is also true that the companies described in Chapters 2 through 5 responded less well to the challenges of the marketplace than their competitors, in large part because of their complacency, narrowness, and lack of vision.

Readers should also bear in mind that although our types and trajectories are quite common, they are representative, not exhaustive. There are likely to be additional types quite different from those we have discussed. And, of course, even firms of a given type will not all be identical or follow the same trajectory. Some will remain viable while others will transform themselves into different successful types instead of lapsing into decline; thus Pioneers, as they mature, may become Craftsmen.

Even among the firms that do follow our trajectories, not all will decline at the same rate or descend to the same depths. For example, many Imperialists underwent steep and devastating declines, whereas most Drifters deteriorated much more slowly. There were also differences in the declines of firms within a given trajectory. Imperialists such as IOS, "Automatic" Sprinkler, and Dome were quickly disabled; but Litton, Gulf & Western, and ITT deteriorated more gradually. In short, our trajectories tell us more about what happens during degeneration than when.

Finally, not all organizations become extreme, monolithic, or insular. For reasons given in Chapter 6, this is more likely to happen in firms that have been highly successful, that have a strong and clearly defined culture and strategy, and whose leaders have been in charge for a long time.

In short, we have written about tendencies and threats, not about evolutionary imperatives. Our findings therefore should elicit caution and vigilance in managers, not defeatism.

Research Background
and Methodology

OUR EARLY RESEARCH

The idea that outstanding organizations are seduced by their success emerged only gradually during our research. Over the past fifteen years we have conducted studies involving more than 250 companies. Much of that work is reported in *Organizations: A Quantum View*, and in several academic papers and articles.[1] That research gave rise both to the thesis of this book and our approach to investigating it. Its findings centered on three notions: *configuration, momentum,* and *failure as a variant of success.*

Configuration

FIT AND HARMONY   The parts or elements of effective organizations fit together harmoniously to express a theme. Individual qualities cohere to form a consistent Gestalt or unity. They collectively form configurations, that is, complex clusters of qualities or "elements" that are organized, or better still orchestrated, around a core theme.

Central to configuration is the notion of fit: as soon as a theme becomes prominent—an overriding mission or a core strategy, for example—many other aspects of the organization such as culture and structure begin to reflect and reinforce it. Recall our ITT example of Chapter 1 in which everything seemed to revolve around growth goals and financial control: the entrepreneurial, control-driven leader; a culture dominated by financial staff; the strategy of acquisition and diversification; even the divisional profit centers. All these elements were "shaped and fitted" into a cohesive configuration. They converged around a consistent Builder constellation whose elements were mutually reinforcing.

STABILITY   Their cohesiveness makes configurations hard to change. Core themes are reflected in so many aspects of companies—they are so deeply woven into their fabric—that they aren't easily altered. The whole is reflected in the parts and the parts support the whole. Try to remove or alter one element, and many of the others will regenerate or restore it. For example, at ITT, any attempt to slow down diversification would have been resisted by the growth plans, the incentive system, and the staff culture. Similarly, any campaign to pay more attention to divisional product lines and operations would have faltered because of the bottom-line values of ITT, the vast amount of time divisional managers had to spend at head-office meetings, and the obsession of top management with new acquisitions.

SOURCES OF CONFIGURATION   We wanted to know what generated such configurations. In *The Neurotic Organization*, Manfred Kets de Vries and I found that leaders played a critical role in shaping themes which harmonize strategy, structure, and culture. Indeed, CEO personalities were often reflected in the character of their firms, with obsessional executives stressing efficiency, dramatic leaders favoring entrepreneurial expansion, and so on.

But in many cases, configurations seemed to be shaped as much by strategic commitments, embedded structures, and cultural values as by leaders. Even the forces of competition, customer pressures, and common industry practices could mold an organization by punishing—and thereby discouraging—some of its strategies and methods, and rewarding—and thereby reinforcing—others. In short, configurations can be shaped by forces inside or outside the organization. But once a theme emerges to serve as the critical mass, a configuration can develop quickly into a complementary whole that defies even the most resolute attempts to further shape or redirect it.[2]

EARLY FINDINGS   Our quantitative, statistical studies of many companies found that some configurations were extremely common: these centered on product innovation, efficiency, marketing prowess, and financial entrepreneurship. In fact, we found six configurations that accounted for over 80 percent of the successful firms in our sample, and four configurations that accounted for over 70 percent of our poorly performing organizations. The prevalence of these configurations made them intriguing and important targets for study, and suggested that organizational variety is indeed somewhat limited.[3]

But what is even more important is that the configurations highlight the vast differences among organizations, and the fact that there are numerous ways to be successful—and to fail. They warn us that lumping together organizations for purposes of diagnosis or prescription would be very hazardous indeed.[4]

Configurations also have implications for how we should study our complex world of organizations. First, they suggest that organizations are best understood as complicated, thematically integrated systems, many of whose qualities are closely interdependent. Deep understanding demands that we study many aspects of organizations and search for some unifying theme and underlying dynamic among them. Second, we must pay attention to organizational differences because configurations vary so much. We need to identify the most common types and to make distinctions among them.

Momentum

Our work on configurations made us curious about how organizations changed. We reasoned that if firms' qualities were orchestrated by an enduring central theme, then so might be their evolution. For the reasons given in Chapter 6, we expected that change in organizations would usually be characterized by momentum: a powerful tendency to keep rolling forward in the same direction. So, innovative firms would become more innovative; cost-conscious organizations would strive to become ever more efficient.

And this is exactly what we found. Firms perpetuated their initial thrust until something earth-shaking stopped them. Once ITT began to diversify, for example, it accelerated this policy. Having implemented their initial controls, leaders continued to hone and develop them because that's what ITT was all about; that's what its managers were rewarded for and believed in.

We have already discussed the close ties between the elements of configurations. Momentum in one element will therefore impart momentum to some of the others. Recall how at ITT, as diversification increased, so did the size of the head-office staff and the time spent on divisional meetings. The larger staff then generated additional diversification projects. And the spiral continued. In short, momentum will apply simultaneously to many facets of an initial configuration.[5] Again, this is what we found in our research.

Transition Trajectories: Failure as a Variant of Success

One of the most puzzling of our early findings was that the successful configurations we discovered bore a frightening similarity to the unsuccessful ones. Specifically, many of the successful configurations had an "evil twin" that was very much like it—yet unlike any of its successful counterparts. For example, successful Craftsman-type organizations were quite like stagnant bureaucracies; also thriving innovative companies had a striking resemblance to venturesome failures that squandered their assets by impulsively chasing grandiose dreams.

There were, however, two principal differences between the successful and unsuccessful partners of a pair. First, the unsuccessful configurations exhibited more extremes—they were, for example, either very rigid and bureaucratic or tremendously loose and flexible; either highly innovative or totally stagnant. Successful configurations fell in between. Second, the firms with unsuccessful configurations appeared to devote less effort to organizational intelligence—to scanning the environment, trying to understand competitors, analyzing decisions, or just reflecting about options.[6]

We began to feel that what we were seeing was the outcome of trajectories in which successful firms were propelled into decline by momentum toward extremes in strategy and structure, and by overconfidence or complacency that atrophied intelligence. Unfortunately, these early studies on configurations did not look at organizations over time. Our successful and unsuccessful samples were composed of entirely different firms.

Putting the Pieces Together

These findings on configuration, momentum, and the apparent association between failure and success suggested the thesis for this research—one that puts all of the related notions together. It is that *firms in successful configurations will extend their orientations until they reach dangerous extremes; their momentum will drive them along common trajectories toward related unsuccessful configurations.* Since successful configurations differ from one another, so will their trajectories of decline.

THIS STUDY

We carried out our research in three steps. First, we identified some successful strategic configurations based on our previous research. Then we looked for outstanding organizations that conformed to each of them. And finally, we tracked the histories of all these organizations to see what happened to them.

Choosing the Starting Configurations

We wished our successful configurations to have some basis both in interesting theory and in empirical research. Michael Porter's classic book, *Competitive Strategy*, [7] seemed to be a good place to start. It has been the single most influential work on business strategy of the last ten years and has enjoyed incredibly wide acceptance by business executives and academics alike.[8] Porter identified three generic strategies that would give firms a sustainable competitive advantage over their rivals. He called these strategies cost leadership, differentiation, and focus. *Cost leaders* offer plain, no-frills products; they compete by operating so economically that they can earn generous profits while selling cheap. *Differentiators*, on the other hand, develop offerings that their customers find uniquely attractive, powerful, or otherwise superior, thereby securing brand loyalty and higher margins. *Focusers* apply either of the above strategies to a narrowly targeted group of customers that they understand and serve better than anyone else. It was Porter's thesis that these strategies would create an enduring competitive edge, a defendable advantage, by engendering customer loyalty and preventing imitation by rivals.

Unfortunately, the three generic strategies are too gross for our purposes here. The differentiation category appeared to include some very different strategies. Also, Porter's focus strategy seemed too much based on his other two to really stand on its own. So several years back we tried to build on Porter's work.

Our previous research on a large sample of companies revealed that there were at least three different types of differentiation strategies, each requiring a quite distinct set of organizational skills and activities.[9] The first, *Pioneering*, differentiates products through constant innovation and R&D, that is, by creating state-of-the-art offerings. The second, *Salesmanship*, differentiates offerings through image, using clever marketing, that is, attractive packaging, honest and attentive service, extensive distribution, creative advertising, and aggressive selling. And the third type of differentiation, *Craftsmanship*, is based on product quality, that is, durability and dependability, which requires special skills in operations or production, as does *Cost Leadership*. We also found organizations that followed a fifth strategy, *Building*, whose talents were mainly those of financial entrepreneurship, expansion, and acquisition. Unlike the other strategies, Building is as much a corporate as a business strategy; that is, it may span numerous businesses within a corporation.[10]

Our earlier research demonstrated that it was essential to distinguish between these strategies, in part because they demanded very different skills, structures, and cultures. For example, the Builder strategy at ITT called for divisionalized structures and sophisticated controls. Craftsmen had to have tight quality or cost controls and an elaborate use of routines. Pioneers benefited from flexible structures that gave much power to technical experts. In other words, there was a good deal of evidence for the configuration hypothesis linking strategy to other aspects of the organization.[11]

We were left with five configurations: Salesmen (marketing differentiators), Craftsmen (quality differentiators), Pioneers (innovation differentiators), Cost Leaders, and Builders (financial entrepreneurs, acquirers, expansionists). However, we discovered in the current research project that the configurations and trajectories of Cost Leaders were almost the same as those of Craftsmen. Indeed, cost leadership seemed to be a type of craftsmanship. So these two types were grouped together into the Craftsman category, leaving us with four configurations. They are described in Tables 1 and 2 (pp. 5 and 10). Most of these types, or variants of them, surfaced independently in our own earlier research, and some bear a resemblance to the types identified by Raymond Miles and Charles Snow.[12] Note, however, that these configurations are representative, not exhaustive. There are no doubt numerous other common configurations, and many firms will fail to fit any common configuration.

Drawing the Sample

To research our thesis, we had to obtain rich anecdotal data on what happened to organizations that conformed to the four successful configurations during the years after they had achieved stardom. The only economical sources of such data were published books and articles. We decided to track eight to ten companies per configuration—the maximum permitted by our time and budget constraints. Candidates for our study were found by poring through the business press to find companies that met the following criteria:

- they had grown faster and been more profitable than their major competitors for at least three consecutive years;
- they were well enough known to have been much written about in books, newspapers, and magazine articles (we found many of our cases in *Fortune, Business Week, Forbes, Dun's Business Monthly,* and *The New York Times*).

We tried also to select firms from a variety of industries. Ours, however, was not a random sample even of high-performing organizations, since a firm's probability of selection was related to the number of articles and books appearing on it in the American business press. The bigger, more glamorous, and more overtly successful the organization, the greater its appeal to journalists, and therefore the more likely its inclusion in our study. Moreover, we chose firms such as Eastern Air Lines, Texas Instruments, Dome Petroleum, Chrysler, ITT, IOS, and Montgomery Ward because we were already familiar with their conformity to one of our four types and with their histories of excellent performance followed by decline. In short, this is very much a "convenience" sample.

Note also that our method of sample selection *determined* that many of our excellent firms would deteriorate. Indeed, such declines are extremely common simply because it is hard for stellar performers to stay on top. However, despite the clear bias in the trend of performance, our sample was not constrained to confirm our momentum hypothesis. Performance decline could as easily have been the result of reversing strategies, policies, and cultural values as of extending or amplifying them.

Assignment of Firms to Configurations

Two colleagues (both professors with PhDs in management who were avid readers of the popular business press) read our descriptions of the four successful configurations (see p. 274) and were asked to classify a preliminary list of outstanding firms (with dates specified) into one of the types, or to relegate them to a class of outliers that fit no particular type. The raters were given articles and books for the period in question for the firms they were unfamiliar with. One rater classified 92 percent of the cases the same way I did; the other, 84 percent. The research includes only those cases that were classified the same way by all three of us.

The Successful Configurations Described

- *Craftsmen* succeed by (a) operating very efficiently and thus under-cutting the competition; or (b) producing the highest quality offer-ings. They sell a quite limited range of products to a focused segment of the market. To keep costs down or quality up, they resist changing their products or making too many varieties. Craftsmen are also blessed with talented engineers and superb manufacturing skills. Their cultures most respect and reward design and production peo-ple, and their structures stress control, standard procedures, and formal plans.
- *Builders* parlay their small or stale operations into robust, rapidly growing and diversified ones, often by effecting cost efficiencies or entering promising new businesses. Diversification pulls Builders into a wide array of markets, and the constant quest for growth produces a climate of rapid change. Builders' unique skills are mostly those of entrepreneurship and finance. Cultures prize managers who recognize and pursue growth; and firms structure themselves into semiautonomous divisions. Much emphasis may be placed on head-office strategic planning and control staffs to assess burgeoning oper-ations.
- *Pioneers* innovate more creatively, more quickly, and more effec-tively than their competitors. They cater to dynamic markets that favor state-of-the-art offerings. Although they focus on the few prod-ucts they know best, these products change rapidly because of the many innovations. Pioneers' cultures reward scientists and R&D types. Their structures are loose and flexible, promoting the collabo-ration and freedom so necessary for constant innovation.
- *Salesmen* are image-driven. Their major competitive assets are their famous brand names, dependability, and good service. Their greatest strength is marketing and they have superb advertising, attractive packaging, and unparalleled channels of distribution. Salesmen offer a broad line of products to a very large market, taking advantage of their reach and reputation. But they do not change or innovate exten-sively. Marketers are, of course, the heroes of Salesmen. Because firms are very large, they are sometimes broken down into product- or market-based divisions, each of them a profit center.

Compiling the Histories

Information about the firms was located through the *Business Periodicals Index* and the business history section of the McGill University Management Library. From the many related books and articles we constructed minihistories of each of the companies. Under the major headings of *Strategy, Culture, Leadership,* and *Structure,* and subheadings such as "Marketing," "Quality" (under *Strategy*), and "Bureaucracy" (under *Structure*), we made notes first on the qualities and then on on the changes occurring in each of our firms. Subheadings were suggested by the content of the cases.

Chapters 2 through 5 include only those companies whose performance deteriorated. We tracked firms in each of the four configurations from the time they first became successful until (1) the present; (2) bankruptcy, merger, or Chapter 11; or (3) they addressed their problems in an effort to recover. Some firms that did not decline ("trajectory avoiders") are discussed in Chapter 8, as are attempted turnarounds for many of the troubled firms of Chapters 2 through 5.

This book is a tentative exploration of our thesis, not a rigorous scientific study; it serves not to prove a theory but to put the flesh of anecdote on the bones of hypothesis. It also relies on qualitative historical narrative instead of quantitative measurement; it uses a biased sample; and it leans heavily on the idiosyncratic interpretations of an all-too-enthusiastic author. Still, it does present some potentially fascinating patterns in the troubled evolution of outstanding organizations—patterns that I hope others will now be able to research more systematically.

Introduction

1. William Ouchi, *Theory Z* (Reading, Mass.: Addison-Wesley, 1982); Thomas J. Peters and Robert Waterman, *In Search of Excellence* (New York: Harper & Row, 1982).
2. Our four trajectories push firms toward dangerous extremes, causing a growing mismatch with their environments. Most of the literature on organizations has stressed a different pathology, one of firms stagnating while their environments change. Our firms, however, usually change for the worse whether their environments are stable or not.
3. It is ironic that decline victimized such exceptional organizations; so much so that I was tempted to call the book *The Perils of Excellence, Prisoners to Greatness,* or *From Success to Excess.* Indeed, success did seem to contribute to overconfidence, strategic narrowing, rigidity, conformity, and a whole slew of other traps. But, as we will see, it is not only success that leads to decline but the paradoxical fact that many of the same things that cause initial greatness, when extended, also cause failure.

Chapter 1

1. Much of the earlier research is reported in Danny Miller and Peter H. Friesen's *Organizations: A Quantum View* (Englewood Cliffs, N.J.: Prentice-Hall, 1984). See also Danny Miller, "Configurations of Strategy and Structure," *Strategic Management Journal* (1986), 6, pp. 233–249, and "Relating Porter's Business Strategies to Environment and Structure," *Academy of Management Journal* (June 1988), 31, pp. 280–308. The present study is described in the Appendix.
2. This vignette of ITT was compiled using the many sources on that company

that are referenced in Chapter 3. References for the other case histories in this chapter can be found in Chapters 2 through 5.

3. Configurations are quite enduring. Try to remove or alter one piece, and the remaining parts will kick in to regenerate or restore it. For example, at ITT, any attempt to slow down diversification would have been resisted by the growth plans, the incentive system, and the staff culture. Similarly, any campaign to pay more attention to divisional product lines and operations would have faltered because of the bottom-line values of ITT, the vast amount of time divisional managers had to spend at head-office meetings, and the obsession of top management with new acquisitions.

Chapter 2

1. See the subsequent references on Texas Instruments.
2. Susan Fraker, "How DEC Got Decked," *Fortune,* December 12, 1983, p. 84.
3. Ibid.
4. DEC Annual Report, 1979, p. 3.
5. Ibid., 1981, p. 12.
6. Thomas J. Peters and Robert Waterman, *In Search of Excellence* (New York: Harper & Row, 1982), pp. 213, 217–218.
7. Bro Uttal, "The Gentlemen and the Upstarts Meet in a Great Mini Battle," *Fortune,* April 23, 1979, pp. 98–108.
8. Gilbert Cross, "The Gentle Bulldozers of Peoria," *Fortune*, July 1983, p. 167.
9. "Caterpillar," *Business Week,* May 4, 1981, p. 74.
10. Peters and Waterman, op. cit., pp. 171–172.
11. "The Cat," *Fortune,* May 1938, p. 92.
12. Peters and Waterman, op. cit., pp. 171–172.
13. N. W. Pope, "Mickey Mouse Marketing," *American Banker,* July 25, 1979.
14. Michael E. Porter, *Competitive Strategy* (New York: Free Press, 1980).
15. Bro Uttal, "TI Wrestles with the Consumer Market," *Fortune*, December 1979, p. 51.
16. Ibid.
17. Irwin Ross, "The Private Turbulence of Eastern Air Lines," *Fortune*, July 1964, p. 172.
18. "Sewell Lee Avery," Harvard Business School, Case SPM8, 1969, p. 2.
19. Ibid., p. 4.
20. Peters and Waterman, op. cit., p. 178.
21. *Business Week,* May 4, 1981, p. 77.
22. Uttal, op. cit., December 1979, p. 51.
23. Ibid., pp. 50, 52.

24. Fraker, op. cit., p. 84.
25. Uttal, op. cit., April 1979, p. 100.
26. *Business Week,* November 5, 1984, p. 94.
27. Fraker, op. cit., p. 84.
28. Pope, op. cit., p. 14. See also Peters and Waterman, op. cit., pp. 167–168.
29. Ibid.
30. Ibid.
31. *Business Week,* May 4, 1981, p. 76.
32. Uttal, op. cit., December 1979, p. 51.
33. Peters and Waterman, op. cit., p. 263.
34. Sanford Rose, "The Going May Get Tougher for Caterpillar," *Fortune,* May 1972, p. 162.
35. Ibid.
36. *Business Week,* November 5, 1984, p. 83.
37. Peters and Waterman, op. cit., pp. 129–130.
38. Ibid., pp. 276–277.
39. Ibid., pp. 153, 276–277.
40. Ibid., p. 272.
41. Ibid., p. 313.
42. Fraker, op. cit., p. 44.
43. Ibid.
44. Ibid., p. 88.
45. Ibid.
46. Ibid., p. 84.
47. *Business Week,* November 5, 1984, p. 91.
48. Ibid.
49. Myron Magnet, "No More Mickey Mouse at Disney," *Fortune,* December 10, 1984, p. 58.
50. Ibid.
51. Irwin Ross, "Disney Gambles on Tomorrow," *Fortune,* October 4, 1982, pp. 64, 66.
52. Ibid., p. 66.
53. *Business Week,* March 12, 1984, p. 50.
54. Ross, op. cit., July 1964, p. 174.
55. Ibid.
56. Ibid., p. 172.
57. Ross, op. cit., October 1982, p. 68.
58. Brian O'Reilly, "Texas Instruments: New Boss, Big Job," *Fortune,* July 8, 1985, p. 61.
59. Bro Uttal, "Texas Instruments Regroups," *Fortune,* August 9, 1982, p. 42.
60. O'Reilly, op. cit., p. 60.
61. Magnet, op. cit., pp. 58, 64.
62. "Sewell Lee Avery," Harvard Business School, op. cit., p. 9.

63. *Business Week,* November 5, 1984, p. 91.
64. Ibid., p. 82.
65. Ibid.
66. Uttal, op. cit., December 1979, p. 52.
67. Rose, op. cit., p. 265.
68. Fraker, op. cit., p. 84.
69. Ibid., p. 92.
70. Ibid., p. 88.
71. *Business Week,* November 5, 1984, p. 94.
72. Uttal, op. cit., August 1982, p. 45.
73. Uttal, op. cit., December 1979, p. 52.
74. Uttal, op. cit., August 1982, pp. 41, 44.
75. O'Reilly, op. cit., p. 61.
76. *Business Week,* November 5, 1984, p. 82.
77. "Sewell Lee Avery," Harvard Business School, op. cit., p. 6.
78. Ross, op. cit., July 1964, p. 174.
79. Ibid.
80. Magnet, op. cit., p. 57.
81. Uttal, op. cit., August 1982, p. 41.
82. "Sewell Lee Avery," Harvard Business School, op. cit., p. 7.
83. Ibid.
84. O'Reilly, op. cit., p. 61.
85. Ibid.
86. Uttal, op. cit., August 1982, p. 44.
87. Ibid.
88. Fraker, op. cit., p. 92.
89. Ross, op. cit., October 1982, p. 64.
90. Ibid.
91. *Business Week,* November 5, 1984, p. 82.
92. Uttal, op. cit., August 1982, p. 42.
93. Ibid., p. 44.
94. Fraker, op. cit., pp. 88, 92.

Chapter 3

1. Charles Raw, Bruce Page, and Godfrey Hodgson, *Do You Sincerely Want to Be Rich?* (New York: Viking Press, 1971), pp. 59–60.
2. Ibid.
3. Ibid.
4. Robert Ball, "Bernie Cornfeld: The Salesman Who Believed Himself," *Fortune,* September 1970, p. 136.
5. Raw, et al., op. cit., pp. 3–4.

6. Ibid., p. 94.
7. Jim Lyon, *Dome: The Rise and Fall of the House That Jack Built* (Toronto: Macmillan, 1983), pp. 40–41.
8. Ibid., p. 42.
9. Ibid., p. 46.
10. Ibid., pp. 65–66.
11. Ibid., p. 69.
12. Shawn Tully, "How Dome Petroleum Got Crunched," *Fortune*, January 10, 1983, p. 85.
13. Carl Rieser, "When the Crowd Goes One Way Litton Goes the Other," *Fortune*, May 1963, p. 117.
14. Ibid.
15. Ibid., p. 115.
16. William Simon Rukeyser, "Why Rain Fell on 'Automatic' Sprinkler," *Fortune*, May 1, 1969, p. 89.
17. Ibid.
18. Ibid.
19. Ibid., p. 88.
20. William S. Rukeyser, "Gulf & Western's Rambunctious Conservatism," *Fortune*, March 1968, pp. 122–125.
21. Louis Kraar, "Roy Ash Is Having Fun at Addressogrief-Multigrief," *Fortune*, February 27, 1978, p. 47.
22. Ibid., pp. 47–48.
23. Ibid., p. 49.
24. Ibid., p. 50.
25. "ITT Takes the Profit Path to Europe," *Business Week*, May 9, 1970.
26. "New Master of the Geneen Machine," *New York Times*, April 6, 1980.
27. Lyon, op. cit., p. 77.
28. Rieser, op. cit., p. 117.
29. Rukeyser, op. cit., May 1969, p. 90.
30. "ITT Takes the Profit Path to Europe," *Business Week*, May 9, 1970.
31. Ibid.
32. Ibid.
33. Rukeyser, op. cit., March 1968, pp. 125 and 202.
34. Ibid., pp. 123–124.
35. Raw, et al., op. cit., pp. 226–240.
36. Rukeyser, op. cit., March 1968, p. 202.
37. Raw, et al., op. cit., p. 3.
38. Ibid., p. 24.
39. Harold S. Geneen, *Managing* (Garden City, N.Y.: Doubleday, 1984), p. 112.
40. Lyon, op. cit., p. 84.
41. Ibid., p. 89.

42. Rukeyser, op. cit., May 1969, p. 90.
43. Kraar, op. cit., p. 52.
44. Ball, op. cit., p. 178.
45. Lyon, op. cit., p. 46.
46. "They Call it 'Geneen U,'" *Forbes,* May 1, 1968.
47. Ibid.
48. Raw, et al., op. cit., p. 11; see also pp. 61–62.
49. Ibid., pp. 64–65.
50. Thomas O'Hanlon, "A Rejuvenated Litton Industries Is Again Off to the Races," *Fortune,* October 8, 1979, p. 160.
51. *Forbes,* op. cit., May 1, 1968.
52. Ibid.
53. Lyon, op. cit., p. 78.
54. Ibid., p. 79.
55. See Alfred D. Chandler, *Strategy and Structure* (Cambridge, Mass.: MIT Press, 1962), and Henry Mintzberg, 1979, op. cit., for more detailed discussions of the use of divisionalized and decentralized "market based" structures in diversified organizations.
56. Chandler, op. cit., pp. 1–21.
57. *Forbes,* op. cit., May 1, 1968.
58. Stanley H. Brown, "How One Man Can Move a Corporate Mountain," *Fortune,* July 1, 1966, p. 163.
59. Lyon, op. cit., p. 86.
60. Rieser, op. cit., May 1963, p. 222.
61. Ibid., p. 117.
62. William S. Rukeyser, "Litton Down to Earth," *Fortune,* April 1968, p. 139.
63. Ibid., p. 186.
64. "ITT: Can Profits Be Programmed?" *Dun's Review,* November 1965.
65. Ibid.
66. Ibid.
67. Geoffrey Colvin, "The De-Geneening of ITT," *Fortune,* January 11, 1982, p. 39.
68. Kraar, op. cit., pp. 47–48.
69. Ibid.
70. Lyon, op. cit., p. 75.
71. Douglas Martin, "Dome's Fight to Untangle a Vast Financial Web," *New York Times,* Sunday, August 19, 1984.
72. Ibid.
73. Ibid.
74. Rukeyser, op. cit., May 1969, pp. 88–89.
75. Susie Gharib Nazem, "How Roy Ash Got Burned," *Fortune,* April 6, 1981, p. 72.

76. Ibid.
77. Rukeyser, op. cit., April 1968, p. 140.
78. O'Hanlon, op. cit., p. 155.
79. Ibid., p. 160.
80. Ibid., p. 155.
81. Monica Jo Williams, "Can a Tough Boss Mellow?" *Fortune*, December 21, 1987, p. 105.
82. Ibid.
83. Ball, op. cit., p. 139.
84. Ibid.
85. *Business Week*, op. cit., May 9, 1970.
86. "Tinkering with Geneen's Growth Machine at ITT," *Business Week*, May 15, 1978.
87. Ibid.
88. Rukeyser, op. cit., April 1968, p. 140.
89. Ibid., p. 184.
90. Nazem, op. cit., p. 72.
91. Leslie Wayne, "ITT: The Giant Slumbers," *New York Times*, July 1, 1984, Section 3, p. 1.
92. Ibid.
93. Colvin, op. cit., p. 34.
94. Ultimately, Geneen's unpromising subsidiaries and his mismanagement of others triggered the biggest sell-off of assets in corporate history. Rand Araskog, Geneen's successor, dumped more than sixty-five companies in the baking, natural resources, forest products, consumer products, and services industries, raising $1.2 billion in the process, and cutting ITT's growing debt. "It is unlikely that we would make any acquisitions in a field unrelated to where we are now," said ITT's chief financial officer in 1982. The most famous conglomerate around has plainly made a U-turn.
95. Tully, op. cit., p. 85.
96. Ibid., p. 86.
97. Ibid., p. 89.
98. Colvin, op. cit., p. 38.
99. Michael Brody, "Caught in the Cash Crunch at ITT," *Fortune*, February 18, 1985, p. 64.
100. Ibid.
101. Ball, op. cit., p. 138.
102. Geneen, op. cit.
103. Colvin, op. cit., p. 39.
104. Rukeyser, op. cit., May 1969, p. 90.
105. Ball, op. cit., p. 138.
106. Lyon, op. cit., p. 75.

NOTES

107. Ball, op. cit., p. 138.
108. Wayne, op. cit., p. 1.
109. Colvin, op. cit., p. 36.
110. "New Master of the Geneen Machine," *New York Times*, April 6, 1980.
111. *Forbes*, op. cit., May 1968.
112. Geneen, op. cit.
113. Peters and Waterman, op. cit., p. 322.
114. Ball, op. cit., p. 139.
115. Ibid., p. 141.
116. Rukeyser, op. cit., May 1969, p. 90.
117. Ball, op. cit., p. 138.
118. Ibid.
119. Rukeyser, op. cit., April 1968, p. 186.
120. Ibid.
121. Colvin, op. cit., p. 37.

Chapter 4

1. John M. Mecklin, "Rolls-Royce's $2-Billion Hard-Sell," *Fortune*, March 1969, pp. 123–140.
2. John. C. Camillus, *Federal Express Corporation (A)*, Case Study.
3. Bro Uttal, "Behind the Fall of Steve Jobs," *Fortune*, August 5, 1985, p. 20.
4. Joe G. Thomas, "Apple Computer, Inc.," in *Strategic Management* (New York: Harper & Row, 1988), pp. 672–675.
5. Ibid., p. 673.
6. Ibid., p. 674.
7. Francis Bello, "The Magic That Made Polaroid," *Fortune*, April 1959, p. 125.
8. Michael E. Porter, "Polaroid-Kodak," in *Cases in Competitive Strategy* (New York: Free Press, 1983), pp. 77–79.
9. Jonathan Levine, "Sun Microsystems Turns on the Afterburners," *Business Week*, July 18, 1988, pp. 114–118.
10. Andrew Pollack, "For Sun, a Difficult Adolescence," *New York Times*, July 20, 1989, pp. D1, D7.
11. "Wang Labs Proves Its Mettle," *Dun's Business Month* (December 1984), pp. 48–49.
12. T. A. Wise, "Control Data's Magnificent Fumble," *Fortune*, April 1966, pp. 165, 258.
13. Mecklin, op. cit., p. 126.
14. Ibid., p. 128.

284

15. Thomas, op. cit., pp. 671–686.
16. Porter, op. cit., pp. 76–77.
17. Ibid.
18. Levine, op. cit., p. 115.
19. Mecklin, op. cit., p. 128.
20. Gregory H. Wierzynski, "Control Data's Newest Cliffhanger," *Fortune*, February 1968, p. 128.
21. Camillus, op. cit.
22. Bello, op. cit., p. 125.
23. Ibid., p. 127.
24. Wise, op. cit., p. 260.
25. Uttal, op. cit., pp. 20–24.
26. Dan Cordtz, "Polaroid," *Fortune*, January 1974, pp. 83–87.
27. Porter, op. cit., pp. 77–78.
28. Cordtz, op. cit., p. 83.
29. Levine, op. cit., pp. 115, 118.
30. Bello, op. cit., p. 127.
31. Levine, op. cit., p. 115.
32. "Federal Express," *Detroit Free Press*, July 12, 1976.
33. For an academic discussion of these structures, see Tom Burns and G. Stalker, *The Management of Innovation* (London: Tavistock Press, 1961), and Henry Mintzberg, *The Structuring of Organizations* (Englewood Cliffs, N.J.: Prentice-Hall, 1979).
34. Levine, op. cit., p. 115.
35. Ibid.
36. Wise, op. cit., p. 260.
37. Bello, op. cit. p. 127.
38. Danny Miller, "Relating Porter's Business Strategies to Environment and Structure," *Academy of Management Journal* (June 1988), 31, pp. 280–308.
39. Wierzynski, op. cit., p. 179.
40. *Dun's Business Month* (December 1984), p. 49.
41. Levine, op. cit., p. 115.
42. *Dun's Business Month*, op. cit., p. 48.
43. Mecklin, op. cit., p. 127.
44. Wierzynski, op. cit., p. 126.
45. Thomas, op. cit., p. 684.
46. *inc.* (October 1987), p. 51.
47. *Dun's Business Month* (April 1984), p. 123.
48. *inc.*, op. cit., p. 47.
49. Uttal, op. cit., p. 22.
50. *Boston Globe*, April 28, 1976.

51. Porter, op. cit., p. 80.
52. Cordtz, op. cit., p. 85.
53. Ibid., pp. 83–84.
54. Mecklin, op. cit., pp. 123, 138–140.
55. "Rolls-Royce," *Fortune,* December 1970, p. 31.
56. John Tarpey, "Federal Express Tries to Put More Zap in ZapMail," *Business Week,* December 17, 1984, p. 110.
57. Ibid.
58. "Federal Express," *Business Week,* October 13, 1986, pp. 48–49.
59. *Forbes,* November 4, 1985, pp. 163–164.
60. *Business Week,* October 13, 1986, pp. 48–49.
61. Levine, op. cit., p. 115.
62. Pollack, op. cit., p. D7.
63. Wise, op. cit., pp. 166, 262, 264.
64. Mecklin, op. cit., pp. 123–140.
65. Porter, op. cit., p. 79.
66. Levine, op. cit., p. 118.
67. Pollack, op. cit., p. D1.
68. Porter, op. cit., p. 77.
69. Ibid., pp. 80–82.
70. *Fortune,* July 9, 1984, p. 183.
71. Arthur M. Louis, "Doctor Wang's Toughest Case," *Fortune,* February 3, 1986, p. 106.
72. Uttal, op. cit., p. 22.
73. Pollack, op. cit., p. D1.
74. Wise, op. cit., p. 264.
75. "Polaroid," *New York Times,* April 28, 1976.
76. Terrence E. Deal and Allen A. Kennedy, *Corporate Cultures* (Reading, Mass.: Addison-Wesley, 1982), p. 75.
77. "Cray Research," Harvard Business School, Case 9-385-011.
78. Mecklin, op. cit., p. 136.
79. Uttal, op. cit., p. 23.
80. Ibid., p. 22.
81. Ibid.
82. Ibid.
83. Pollack, op. cit., p. D7.
84. "Cray Research," Harvard Business School, Case 9-385-011.
85. Thomas, op. cit., p. 686.
86. *Fortune,* July 9, 1984, p. 182.
87. *inc.* (October 1987), p. 59.
88. Pollack, op. cit., p. D1.
89. Ibid.
90. Louis, op. cit., p. 106.

Chapter 5

1. See the notes on P&G below.
2. Alfred P. Sloan, *My Years with General Motors* (Garden City, N.Y.: Doubleday, 1963), p. 268.
3. Robert Sheehan, "How General Motors Did It," *Fortune*, June 1963, p. 111.
4. Michael Moritz and B. Seaman, *Going for Broke* (Garden City, N.Y.: Doubleday, 1984), Chapter 5.
5. Peter Vanderwicken, "P&G's Secret Ingredient," *Fortune*, July 1974.
6. Ibid., p. 77.
7. Ibid., p. 78.
8. C. C. Hoge, *The First Hundred Years Are the Toughest* (Berkeley, Calif.: Ten Speed Press, 1988), p. 255.
9. James C. Worthy, *Shaping an American Institution* (Urbana, Ill.: University of Illinois Press, 1984).
10. Thomas J. Watson, Jr., *A Business and Its Beliefs* (New York: McGraw-Hill, 1963), p. 29.
11. Thomas J. Peters and Robert Waterman, *In Search of Excellence* (New York: Harper & Row, 1982), p. 159.
12. Ibid., pp. 160–161.
13. Ibid., p. 159.
14. William I. Walsh, *The Rise and Decline of the Great Atlantic and Pacific Tea Company* (Secaucus, N.J.: Lyle Stuart, 1986).
15. Ibid., pp. 36–37.
16. Ibid., pp. 49, 69.
17. Vanderwicken, op. cit., p. 75.
18. Ibid., p. 78.
19. Robert Sobel, *Car Wars* (New York: E.P. Dutton, 1984), pp. 13–14.
20. Peters and Waterman, op. cit., pp. 161–162.
21. Moritz and Seaman, op. cit., p. 85.
22. Sobel, op. cit., pp. 13–14.
23. *Business Week*, August 11, 1962, p. 63.
24. *Financial World*, May 15, 1981, p. 17.
25. Vanderwicken, op. cit., pp. 75–76.
26. Sheehan, op. cit., p. 107.
27. Sloan, op. cit., p. 65.
28. *Business Week*, October 31, 1964, p. 121.
29. *Business Week*, August 11, 1962, p. 63.
30. Walsh, op. cit., Chapter 2.
31. Ibid.
32. Peter Drucker, *The Practice of Management* (New York: Harper & Row, 1954), p. 32.

33. Peters and Waterman, op. cit., p. 136.
34. Ibid., p. 194.
35. Ibid., p. 160–163.
36. Ibid.
37. Sheehan, op. cit., p. 104.
38. Walsh, op. cit., pp. 49–50, 69.
39. Roy Bullock in Walsh, op. cit., p. 51.
40. Walsh, op. cit., p. 50.
41. Terrence E. Deal and Allen A. Kennedy, *Corporate Cultures* (Reading, Mass.: Addison-Wesley, 1982).
42. Peter Schisgall, *Eyes on Tomorrow: The Evolution of Proctor & Gamble* (Chicago: J. Ferguson, 1981), p. xi.
43. Peters and Waterman, op. cit., p. 238.
44. Walsh, op. cit., pp. 71–72.
45. Ibid., p. 86.
46. William H. Whyte, *The Organization Man* (New York: Simon & Schuster, 1956), p. 3.
47. Michael Maccoby, *The Gamesman* (New York: Bantam Books, 1976), p. 87.
48. Moritz and Seaman, op. cit., p. 83.
49. Ibid.
50. Sloan, op. cit., Chapter 3.
51. Sheehan, op. cit., p. 98.
52. Walsh, op. cit., pp. 35–36.
53. Peters and Waterman, op. cit., p. 213.
54. Ibid., p. 131.
55. Sheehan, op. cit., p. 107.
56. Peters and Waterman, op. cit., pp. 216–217.
57. Ibid., p. 30.
58. Ibid., pp. 151–152.
59. *Business Week,* October 6, 1962, pp. 48, 50.
60. Moritz and Seaman, op. cit., p. 82.
61. Carol J. Loomis, "IBM's Big Blues: A Legend Tries to Remake Itself," *Fortune,* January 19, 1987, p. 48.
62. Moritz and Seaman, op. cit., p. 90.
63. Faye Rice, "The King of Suds Reigns Again," *Fortune,* August 4, 1986, p. 131.
64. Bill Saporito, "Proctor & Gamble's Comeback Plan," *Fortune,* February 4, 1985, p. 30.
65. Walsh, op. cit., Chapters 8 and 9.
66. *Business Week,* January 23, 1984, p. 37.
67. Thomas O'Donnell and Jill Andresky, "Are GM's Troubles Deeper Than They Look?" *Forbes,* September 27, 1982, pp. 133, 135.

68. Albert Lee, *Call Me Roger* (Chicago: Contemporary Books, 1988), pp. 101–103.
69. Thomas Moore, "Make-or-Break Time for General Motors," *Fortune*, February 15, 1988, p. 35.
70. Saporito, op. cit., p. 35.
71. Michael Brody, "Can GM Manage It All?" *Fortune*, July 8, 1985, p. 22.
72. Moore, op. cit., p. 38.
73. Saporito, op. cit., p. 30.
74. Stuart Gannes, "IBM and DEC Take on the Little Guys," *Fortune*, October 10, 1988, p. 109.
75. O'Donnell and Andresky, op. cit., p. 135.
76. Ibid., p. 133.
77. Ibid., p. 131.
78. Peter J. Schuyten, "Chrysler Goes for Broke," *Fortune*, June 19, 1978, p. 55.
79. Sobel, op. cit., p. 286.
80. Patricia Sellers, "Why Bigger Is Badder at Sears," *Fortune*, December 5, 1988, p. 79.
81. Michael Oneal, "Shaking Sears Right Down to Its Work Boots," *Business Week*, October 17, 1988, p. 84.
82. Rice, op. cit., pp. 130–131.
83. *Business Week*, January 23, 1984, p. 36.
84. Charles G. Burck, "Will Success Spoil General Motors?" *Fortune*, August 22, 1983, p. 93.
85. Moritz and Seaman, op. cit., p. 92.
86. Sellers, op. cit., p. 80.
87. Ibid.
88. Walsh, op. cit., p. 132.
89. Saporito, op. cit., p. 30.
90. Loomis, op. cit., p. 52.
91. Walsh, op. cit., p. 132.
92. Loomis, op. cit., p. 36.
93. O'Donnell and Andresky, op. cit., p. 132.
94. Ibid., pp. 132–133.
95. Moritz and Seaman, op. cit., pp. 85–86.
96. Sellers, op. cit., p. 84.
97. Walsh, op. cit., p. 114.
98. Ibid., p. 133.
99. *Business Week*, January 23, 1984, p. 37.
100. Moritz and Seaman, op. cit., p. 91.
101. Walsh, op. cit., p. 91.
102. Lee, op. cit., pp. 46–47.
103. Moore, op. cit., p. 42.

104. Moritz and Seaman, op. cit., p. 95.
105. Oneal, op. cit., p. 84.
106. This is in part due to the lack of strategic focus—which it in turn reinforces. Fragmentation also promotes territorial wars and prevents coordinated action.
107. Walsh, op. cit., p. 81.
108. Oneal, op. cit., p. 84.
109. Sellers, op. cit., p. 79.
110. Oneal, op. cit., p. 87.
111. *Business Week*, January 23, 1984, p. 37.
112. Roger Smith, "Roger Smith Takes on GM's Critics," *Fortune*, August 18, 1986, p. 27.
113. Ross Perot, "How I Would Turn Around GM," *Fortune*, February 15, 1988, p. 48.
114. Lee, op. cit., p. 47.
115. Walsh, op. cit., pp. 124–126.
116. Lee, op. cit., p. 50.
117. *Business Week*, January 23, 1984, p. 36.
118. Loomis, op. cit., pp. 34–35.
119. Ibid., p. 35.
120. Perot, op. cit., p. 49.
121. Ibid., p. 45.

Chapter 6

1. Momentum was not equally strong in all organizations, however. P&G and IBM had just begun to move along the decoupling trajectory, and on only two dimensions—product-line diffusion and bureaucratization. In contrast, A&P and Chrysler, which traveled the same trajectory, had over many years developed severe problems of line diffusion, datedness, warring departments, and remote leadership. Obviously, the more widespread and advanced the momentum, the more difficult it is to correct.
2. We will not be talking about the causes of resistance to change. Our organizations were usually changing—but mainly in a single direction. They continued to evolve according to their managers' viewpoints, strategies, and structures, so that existing orientations were almost always amplified but very rarely reversed. The "causes" we will be discussing have two main effects: First, they impart *momentum,* which pushes firms along the trajectories. Second, they resist *reorientation*—i.e. backtracking on the trajectories.
3. Paul Nystrom and William H. Starbuck, "To Avoid Crises, Unlearn," *Organizational Dynamics* (1984), p. 55.

4. William H. Starbuck and Bo L. T. Hedberg, "Saving an Organization from a Stagnating Environment," in H. B. Thorelli, ed., *Strategy + Structure = Performance* (Bloomington, Ind.: Indiana University Press, 1977), p. 250.

5. D. C. Dearborn, and Herbert A. Simon, "Selective Perception: A Note on the Departmental Identifications of Executives," *Sociometry* (1958), 21, pp. 140–144.

6. See Chris Argyris and Donald Schon, *Organizational Learning: A Theory of Action Perspective* (Reading, Mass.: Addison-Wesley, 1978).

7. Karl E. Weick, *The Social Psychology of Organizing* (Reading, Mass.: Addison-Wesley, 1979).

8. Manfred Kets de Vries and Danny Miller, *The Neurotic Organization* (New York: Harper and Row, 1990).

9. See Terrence E. Deal and Allen A. Kennedy, *Corporate Cultures: The Rites and Rituals of Corporate Life* (Reading, Mass.: Addison-Wesley, 1982).

10. Irving Janis, *Victims of Groupthink* (Boston: Houghton Mifflin, 1972).

11. Gareth Morgan, *Images of Organization* (Beverly Hills, Calif.: Sage, 1986).

12. See Kim Clark in A. M. Spence and H. Hazard, eds., *International Competitiveness* (Cambridge, Mass.: Ballinger, 1988).

13. See Herbert A. Simon, *Administrative Behavior* (New York: Macmillan, 1947); James G. March and Herbert A. Simon, *Organizations* (New York: John Wiley, 1958); and Richard M. Cyert and James G. March, *A Behavioral Theory of the Firm* (Englewood Cliffs, N.J.: Prentice-Hall, 1963).

14. See Richard R. Nelson and Sidney G. Winter, *An Evolutionary Theory of Economic Change* (Cambridge, Mass.: Harvard University Press, 1982), p. 124.

15. Starbuck and Hedberg, op. cit., p. 250.

16. Because routines are costly to change, they lock firms into the status quo. Tinkerers' standardized manufacturing programs and control routines, for example, make change costly, narrowing the range of affordable strategies to those very similar to their current ones. Routines may also be perpetuated by values of efficiency, so that expedient procedures become codified and endure, while the rest die out.

17. Jeffrey Pfeffer, *Power in Organizations* (New York: Pitman, 1981), p. 289.

18. Henry Mintzberg, *Power In and Around Organizations* (Englewood Cliffs, N.J.: Prentice-Hall, 1983), p. 287.

19. See Andrew M. Pettigrew, *The Politics of Organizational Decision Making* (London: Tavistock Press, 1973).

20. William H. Starbuck, "Acting First and Thinking Later: Theory Versus Reality in Strategic Change," in Johannes M. Pennings and Associates, *Organizational Strategy and Change* (San Francisco: Jossey Bass, 1985), pp. 353.

21. Charles Perrow, *Complex Organizations: A Critical Essay* (New York: Random House, 1986), p. 125.
22. Starbuck and Hedberg, op. cit., p. 254.
23. Jeffrey Pfeffer and Gerald Salancik, *The External Control of Organizations* (New York: Harper & Row, 1978).
24. Weick, op. cit., p. 28.
25. Humberto Maturana and Francisco Varela, *Autopoesis and Cognition: The Realization of the Living* (London: Reidl, 1980).
26. Morgan, op. cit., pp. 236 and 240.
27. Danny Miller and Peter H. Friesen, *Organizations: A Quantum View* (Englewood Cliffs, N.J.: Prentice-Hall, 1984), p. 1.
28. C. R. Hinings and Royston Greenwood, *The Dynamics of Strategic Change* (Oxford: Basil Blackwell, 1988), pp. 8, 22, and 301.
29. Morgan, op. cit., p. 80.
30. See Michael Tushman and Elaine Romanelli, "Organizational Evolution: A Metamorphosis Model of Convergence and Reorientation," in L. Cummings and B. Staw, eds., *Research in Organizational Behavior* (Greenwich, Conn.: JAI Press, 1985).
31. Miller and Friesen, op. cit., p. 208.
32. Camille Morin Tutsch in a personal communication suggested a useful metaphor: she proposed that configurations may form a vortex-like force field to which cognitive, cultural, and structural factors all contribute. This vortex "pulls" organizations along their trajectories.
33. The other side of the coin is that moderation too can be taken to excess. For example, although versatile, generalist organizations can do many more things than specialists, they may be unable to do anything well enough to attain a competitive edge. Paying attention to many functions may prevent excellence in any one. And the attempt to please everyone may produce bland offerings. Outstanding companies almost never observe the Aristotelian mean.

Chapter 7

1. Throughout this chapter we will be talking about building or resurrecting a "configuration" rather than a strategy. Change must usually involve reorienting or adapting not only strategy, but basic assumptions, culture, structure, and even leadership, as well as their interrelationships.
2. Notice that in arguing for focus and configuration, we are not advocating that all firms stick to a narrow product line or eschew flexibility in their production processes. This decision will have to be a function of the environment. The conventional wisdom among organizational theorists is that it is fine to be focused and specialized in stable, predictable envi-

ronments, but not in dynamic, uncertain ones. In a sense this is true: firms in changing environments must be prepared to change quickly, and this requires the flexibility to create and produce a wider array of products, at least over time. Specialized, efficient Craftsmen would run into trouble in these settings, whereas the more flexible, innovative Pioneers might thrive. But the Pioneers are also focused and specialized in their own way—they are good at innovation, yet are relatively inefficient. They might do well in changing environments that value novelty, but be beaten by Craftsmen in a stable setting because of their relative inefficiency and superfluous innovation.

In a more general sense, then, *both* configurations are specialized to do certain tasks, and our argument is that that is necessary for success. Even Builders that are strategic generalists and operate in a broad diversity of industries are tightly configured—with matching goals (growth), strategy (expansion, acquisition), structure (divisional, market-based), and culture (finance and control-dominated).

3. Gareth Morgan, *Images of Organization* (Beverly Hills, Calif.: Sage, 1986), p. 243.
4. See Donald Schon, *The Reflective Practitioner: How Professionals Think in Action* (New York: Basic Books, 1983).
5. Lloyd Steier, "Reflections on Learning," *CA Magazine* (1989), pp. 56–58.
6. Tom Peters and Nancy Austin, "A Passion for Excellence," *Fortune,* May 13, 1985, pp. 20, 28.
7. Rush Loving, Jr., "How a Hotelman Got the Best Out of United Airlines," *Fortune,* March 1972, p. 73.
8. Peters and Austin, op. cit., p. 20.
9. Ibid., p. 32.
10. Ibid., p. 16.
11. *Fortune,* November 7, 1988, p. 76.
12. Peters and Austin, op. cit., p. 25.
13. Nick Garnett, *Financial Times* (London), May 9, 1986, p. 13.
14. Danny Miller and Peter H. Friesen, *Organizations: A Quantum View* (Englewood Cliffs, N.J.: Prentice-Hall, 1984). See also C. R. Hinings and Royston Greenwood's *Dynamics of Strategic Change* (Oxford: Basil Blackwell, 1988), and Michael Tushman and Elaine Romanelli's "Organizational Evolution: A Metamorphosis Model of Convergence and Reorientation," in L. Cummings and B. Staw, eds., *Research in Organizational Behavior* (Greenwich, Conn.: JAI Press, 1985).
15. Miller and Friesen, op. cit., Part IV.
16. As Chapter 8 will deal mostly with restoring old configurations, this chapter is concerned mainly with the discovery and creation of new ones.
17. Ilya Prigogine and Isabelle Stengers, *Order Out of Chaos: Man's New Dialogue with Nature* (New York: Bantam Books, 1984).

18. Robert M. Pirsig, *Zen and the Art of Motorcycle Maintenance* (New York: Bantam Books, 1974).
19. Henry Mintzberg, *Mintzberg on Management* (New York: Free Press, 1989), p. 127.
20. Henry Mintzberg, Andre Theoret, and Duru Rainsinghani, "The Structure of Unstructured Decision Making Processes," *Administrative Science Quarterly* (1976), 21, pp. 246–275.
21. See Manfred Kets de Vries and Danny Miller, *The Neurotic Organization* (new edition, New York: Harper & Row, 1990), for a more comprehensive discussion of this problem.
22. A. Lee Barrett and Cortlandt Cammann, "Transitioning to Change: Lessons from NSC," in J. R. Kimberly and R. E. Quinn, eds., *Managing Organizational Transitions* (Homewood, Ill.: Irwin, 1984), pp. 218–239.
23. Ibid.
24. Miller and Friesen, op. cit., 1984.
25. See Danny Miller, "Stale in the Saddle: CEO Tenure and the Match Between Organization and Environment," *Management Science*, in press.

Chapter 8

1. *Forbes,* February 22, 1988, p. 65.
2. Andrew Kupfer, "The Long Arm of Jerry Junkins," *Fortune,* March 14, 1988, p. 48.
3. Myron Magnet, "Putting Magic Back in the Magic Kingdom," *Fortune,* January 5, 1987, p. 65.
4. Thomas J. Murray, *Dun's Business Month* (December 1987), p. 29.
5. Fred V. Guterl, "TI Bets on Chips Again," *Dun's Business Month* (February 1987), p. 37.
6. "Caterpillar," *Business Week,* September 25, 1989, p. 78.
7. Ibid., p. 75.
8. Guterl, op. cit., p. 38.
9. Ibid.
10. *Business Week,* May 16, 1988, p. 92.
11. *Business Week,* July 20, 1987, p. 112.
12. *New York Times,* July 19, 1989, p. C15.
13. Ibid.
14. Guterl, op. cit., p. 38.
15. John Markoff, "Digital Plans to Introduce New Computers," *New York Times,* July 10, 1989, p. D3.
16. *Business Week,* February 1, 1988, p. 83.
17. Magnet, op. cit., p. 65.
18. Ibid.

19. Ibid.
20. Kathleen K. Wiegner, "No More Hubris," *Forbes,* February 22, 1988.
21. *Toronto Globe and Mail,* October 25, 1989, p. B5.
22. *Business Week,* July 20, 1987, p. 112.
23. Magnet, op. cit., p. 65.
24. *Business Week,* February 1, 1988, p. 27.
25. Brian Dumaine, "Corporate Spies Stoop to Conquer," *Fortune,* November 7, 1988, p. 68.
26. Ibid.
27. Ibid.
28. Ibid.
29. Ibid.
30. Monica Jo Williams, "Can A Tough Boss Mellow?" *Fortune,* December 21, 1987, p. 112.
31. *Business Week,* December 3, 1984, p. 168.
32. Ibid.
33. Thomas O'Hanlon, "A Rejuvenated Litton Industries Is Again Off to the Races," *Fortune,* October 8, 1979, p. 164.
34. Williams, op. cit., p. 112.
35. Ibid.
36. Ibid.
37. *Business Week,* June 13, 1983, p. 38.
38. Ibid.
39. O'Hanlon, op. cit., p. 155.
40. Ibid.
41. *Barron's,* August 31, 1987, p. 13.
42. Williams, op. cit.
43. *Business Week,* June 13, 1983, p. 38.
44. O'Hanlon, op. cit., p. 155.
45. *Forbes,* April 27, 1987, p. 54.
46. Michael Brody, "ITT's Wrong Number in the U.S. Market," *Fortune,* March 17, 1986, p. 40.
47. Michael Brody, "Caught in the Cash Crunch at ITT," *Fortune,* February 18, 1985, p. 62.
48. *New York Times,* July 11, 1984, Section 3, p. 1.
49. *Business Week,* March 23, 1987, p. 68.
50. Patricia Sellers, "General Mills A Go-Go," *Fortune,* June 5, 1989, p. 173.
51. Ibid.
52. Ibid.
53. *Business Week,* June 27, 1988, pp. 58–60.
54. Ibid., p. 61.
55. Stuart Gannes, "Tremors from the Computer Quake," *Fortune,* August 1, 1988, p. 48.

56. Brian O'Reilly, "Apple Finally Invades the Office," *Fortune,* November 9, 1987, p. 56.
57. *Business Week,* November 3, 1986, p. 32.
58. O'Reilly, op. cit., p. 56.
59. Ibid.
60. *Business Week,* November 9, 1987, p. 66.
61. *Business Week,* September 5, 1988, p. 36.
62. Ibid.
63. Gannes, op. cit., p. 43.
64. *Barron's,* February 8, 1988, p. 11.
65. *Business Week,* August 15, 1988, p. 140.
66. Brian Dumaine, "Polaroid Flashed Back," *Fortune,* February 16, 1987, p. 72.
67. O'Reilly, op. cit., p. 56.
68. Ibid.
69. Ibid.
70. *Forbes,* May 4, 1987, p. 83.
71. Dumaine, op. cit., 1987, p. 72.
72. "Cray Research," Harvard Business School, Case 9-385-011.
73. Ibid.
74. "Cray Research," *New York Times,* May 21, 1989.
75. Ibid.
76. Ibid.
77. Ibid.
78. Brian Dumaine, "P&G Rewrites the Marketing Rules," *Fortune,* November 6, 1989, pp. 38–46.
79. *Business Week,* November 21, 1983, p. 104.
80. Joel Dreyfus, "Reinventing IBM," *Fortune,* August 14, 1989, pp. 33–38.
81. Ibid.
82. Ibid.
83. Bill Saporito, "Luv that Market," *Fortune,* August 3, 1987, p. 56.
84. Kenneth Labich, "The Innovators," *Fortune,* June 6, 1988, p. 56.
85. Dumaine, op. cit., p. 37.
86. Dreyfus, op. cit., pp. 32–34.
87. Ibid.
88. Faye Rice, "The King of Suds Reigns Again," *Fortune,* August 4, 1986, p. 131.
89. *Business Week,* February 14, 1983.
90. Bill Saporito, "Just How Good Is A&P?" *Fortune,* March 16, 1987.
91. Patricia Sellers, "IBM Teaches Techies to Sell," *Fortune,* June 6, 1988, p. 141.
92. Ibid.
93. Ibid.

94. Ibid.
95. Ibid.
96. Dreyfus, op. cit., pp. 31–39.
97. Dumaine, op. cit., p. 40.
98. Ibid., p. 46.
99. *Business Week*, November 21, 1983, p. 104.
100. Gwen Kinkead, "The Executive Suite Struggle Behind A&P's Profits," *Fortune*, November 1, 1982, p. 101.
101. Saporito, op. cit., p. 92.
102. *Business Week*, February 14, 1983, p. 133.
103. Patricia Sellers, "How King Kellogg Beat the Blahs," *Fortune*, August 29, 1988, p. 54.
104. Ibid.
105. Ibid.
106. Ibid., p. 60.
107. Ibid., pp. 54–55.
108. Faye Rice, "Superelf Plans for Xmas$," *Fortune*, September 11, 1989, p. 151.
109. Ibid.

Epilogue

1. Arnold Toynbee, *A Study of History* (London: Oxford University Press, 1947), p. 246.

Appendix

1. Danny Miller and Peter H. Friesen, *Organizations: A Quantum View* (Englewood Cliffs, N.J.: Prentice-Hall, 1984). See also Danny Miller, "Configurations of Strategy and Structure," *Strategic Management Journal* (1986), 6, pp. 233–249, and "Relating Porter's Business Strategies to Environment and Structure," *Academy of Management Journal* (June 1988), 31, pp. 280–308.
2. For perspectives on how organizational configurations may be shaped by their environments, see Paul DiMaggio and W. W. Powell, "The Iron Cage Revisited: Institutional Isomorphism and Collective Rationality in Organizational Fields," *American Sociological Review* (1983), 48, pp. 147–160.
3. In our research, we described each of the firms in our sample using thirty-one 7-point scales. The number of possible score patterns was therefore almost infinite (7 to the power of 31). Yet we found that approxi-

mately the same patterns kept recurring again and again. See Miller and Friesen, op. cit., pp. 269–276.

4. We have to qualify these observations. First, some organizations are quite unusual and do not fit any common configurations. Second, the emergence of configurations in statistical studies such as ours depended very much on the samples we chose and the dimensions we selected to describe them. Had we selected only a few organizations with dramatically different orientations, we would not have found any common configurations. Finally, all firms are in some senses unique—even the firms that conform to a given configuration do so only approximately.

5. See Miller and Friesen, op. cit., Chapter 10, for the findings on momentum.

6. See ibid., Chapter 4. See also Donald C. Hambrick and Richard A. D'Aveni, "Large Corporate Failures as Downward Spirals," *Administrative Science Quarterly* (March 1988), 33, pp. 1–23.

7. Michael E. Porter, *Competitive Strategy* (New York: Free Press, 1980).

8. Gregory Dess and Peter Davis, "Porter's Generic Strategies as Determinants of Strategic Group Membership and Organizational Performance," *Academy of Management Journal* (1984), 27, pp. 467–488; Danny Miller and Peter H. Friesen, "Porter's Generic Strategies and Performance," *Organization Studies* (1986), 7, pp. 255–263; and Danny Miller, op. cit., 1988.

9. See Miller, op. cit., 1988, and Danny Miller, "The Structural and Environmental Correlates of Business Strategy," *Strategic Management Journal* (1987), 8, pp. 55–76.

10. Danny Miller, op. cit., 1986, 1987, and 1988.

11. Ibid.

12. Most of these configurations surfaced independently in our own earlier research, and in Raymond Miles and Charles Snow's *Organizational Strategy, Structure and Process* (New York: McGraw-Hill, 1978). The Pioneers here are similar to Miller and Friesen's (1984) Innovator configuration and Miles and Snow's Prospectors; the Craftsmen are similar to Miller and Friesen's Dominant firms and Miles and Snow's Defenders; the Builders are similar to Miller and Friesen's Entrepreneurial firms and, to a lesser degree, to Miles and Snow's Analyzers; and the Salesmen are similar to Miller and Friesen's Giants.

INDEX